D1547087

FRANK L. WRIGHT AND THE ARCHITECTS OF STEINWAY HALL

ORO Editions
Publishers of Architecture, Art, and Design
Gordon Goff: Publisher

www.oroeditions.com
info@oroeditions.com

Published by ORO Editions
Copyright © 2021 Stuart Cohen and ORO Editions.

Author: Stuart Cohen
Book Design: Ahankara Art
Managing Editor: Jake Anderson

10 9 8 7 6 5 4 3 2 1 First Edition

ISBN: 978-1-951541-50-7

Color Separations and Printing: ORO Group Ltd.
Printed in China.

ORO Editions makes a continuous effort to minimize the overall carbon footprint of its publications. As part of this goal, ORO Editions, in association with Global ReLeaf, arranges to plant trees to replace those used in the manufacturing of the paper produced for its books. Global ReLeaf is an international campaign run by American Forests, one of the world's oldest nonprofit conservation organizations. Global ReLeaf is American Forests' education and action program that helps individuals, organizations, agencies, and corporations improve the local and global environment by planting and caring for trees.

FRANK L. WRIGHT AND THE ARCHITECTS OF STEINWAY HALL: A STUDY IN COLLABORATION

By Stuart Cohen

EDITIONS
Novato, CA

Table of Contents

PREFACE

To practice and write about architecture in Chicago is to inevitably consider the work of Frank Lloyd Wright. Although he practiced in Chicago and Oak Park for only a little over two decades, his impact on the architecture of that period was enormous.

I was educated at Cornell University's school of architecture in the 1960s by educators known as the "Texas Rangers." They were a group of academic architects, who first taught together in Austin, Texas. The best known of these teachers was Colin Rowe. In the 1960s Cornell was one of the first schools to teach architectural principles through the study of precedents—with a strong dose of LeCorbusier's work circa 1910–29. Although we were taught the intricacies of Frank Lloyd Wright's spatial development, Colin Rowe, my mentor, expressed a dislike for Wright's work. When asked about Wright he would quip, "Well, I rather prefer Mozart to Chopin."[1]

I returned to Chicago somewhat predisposed against the industry that had grown up around Wright's work. As Robert McCarter put it, existing discussions of Wright "fall into one of three categories: biographical, devotional, and scholarly."[2] I believed most of these to be histories lacking insightful architectural analysis. When I finally looked at Wright's Chicago area houses as exemplars of principle, I came to admire the highly original spatial inventions of Wright's early work. These may be first seen in his 1899 house in Oak Park, Illinois. H.H. Richardson's residential interiors had opened spaces to one another through large cased openings. Wright omitted the trim around the openings and folded the wainscoting around the edge of the walls and through the openings, emphasizing connection to the adjacent spaces. At the same time, he maintained the principal definition of each space by the continuity of the wall above these openings. Later, Wright would paraphrase the Chinese philosopher Lao Tzu, inscribing over the fireplace at Taliesin, "The

---

1 LeCorbusier was Rowe's Mozart. Rowe was a student of Henry Russell Hitchcock's and had met Wright on several occasions. In *The Letters of Colin Rowe, Five Decades of Correspondence*, Daniel Naegele, ed., Artifice Books on Architecture, 2016, on p.254, Rowe writes in a letter dated December 10, 1984, "You are aware that I genuinely, but quietly, loathe the architecture of Frank Lloyd Wright, who occupies that Kantian category, the genius with no taste."

2 McCarter, Frank Lloyd Wright A Primer on Architectural Principles, p.5.

1.001. Frank Lloyd Wright. Living Room of his Oak Park Residence. 1889.

reality of the building does not consist in the four walls and the roof but in the space within."[3]

In the mid-1970s, when I began to study the architectural culture of Chicago at the turn of the last century, I started to understand the vibrant intellectual community of architects that existed. This involved the Chicago Architectural Club; the Chicago Arts and Crafts Society; the Chicago School of Architecture classes at the Art Institute; and the luncheon club of architects that Wright dubbed "The Eighteen." Among these groups were many of the architects that had offices in Steinway Hall. Particularly, the building's loft space that was shared by Dwight Perkins, Robert Spencer, Myron Hunt, and Frank Lloyd Wright. I began to wonder if Wright was not the lone genius so often portrayed, but one of a group of architects sharing creative ideas. I was intrigued by Robert Spencer's 1901 cruciform plan published in the *Ladies' Home Journal,* reprinted in H. Allen Brooks's *The Prairie School* in 1972, where I first saw it years ago. It is nearly identical to the plan of Wright's design for the Ward Willits House of 1902. We know that the Willits House, like Spencer's *Ladies' Home Journal,* house was designed in the

---

3 From Okakura's *Book of Tea.*

loft studio of Steinway Hall because Wright tells us, "To this new Steinway Hall office came Ward Willits as client number one."[4] Did the Willits plan result from theft, collaboration, or intellectual cross-fertilization?

Much has been written about Frank Lloyd Wright's early years in Chicago and about the Chicago Architectural Club; but very little about the conclave of architects who occupied Steinway Hall. No one has examined in detail or compared the reciprocal impact of the work that Spencer, Wright, Hunt, and Perkins did in Steinway Hall. This study examines and speculates about the brief period of time when they worked side by side. I have focused on their projects and writings and how these relate to the architectural culture of Chicago at that time. While Wright claims to have contributed to the designs of his colleagues, particularly Myron Hunt's Mrs. Catherine White House in Evanston, the one significant documented collaboration is between Wright and Perkins on the Abraham Lincoln Center. Other possible collaborative interactions considered here are the houses Spencer and Wright designed for the *Ladies' Home Journal*. This collaboration is speculative based on a comparison of their designs. Also included is a discussion of the Luxfer Prism glass-block building competition won by Robert Spencer with Wright acting as one of the jury members. In each case the ideas explored in these works, possible interactions, and the impact of these ideas on each architect's future work is discussed.

When Wright moved into Steinway Hall in 1897, he was still Frank L. Wright. The L. was for his given name, Lincoln. By 1900 he was Frank Lloyd Wright. I have variously referred to him as Frank Wright, Frank L. Wright, and Frank Lloyd Wright depending on the time frame and context.

Mark Hewitt first called my attention to the work of group psychologist Michael Farrell and his book *Collaborative Circles: Friendship Dynamics & Creative Work*. Farrell described the dynamics and life cycle of friendship groups comprised of artists and of writers working together, sharing, and developing ideas. This seemed to perfectly describe the group of architects that occupied the loft in Steinway Hall. Unfortunately, no one who worked on the top floor of Steinway Hall left a written record

---

4 Wright, An Autobiography. p.129.

of this period of time.[5] Wright devotes a page to Steinway Hall in various versions of his *An Autobiography*. Marion Mahony who worked in Steinway Hall and whose memoir *The Magic of America* briefly mentions her time there but does not discuss attribution of work or ideas. A few letters and interviews with members of the Prairie School who worked in Steinway Hall survive. Wright's descriptions of this period changed over time, reflecting his changing perception of his centrality and importance to the group.

From Vasari's *Lives of the Artists* onward, western culture has attributed artistic masterworks to individual artists. While artists often had studios or workshops that assisted in the production of a work, during the 19th and 20th centuries the romantic celebration of the individual dominates art history. Unlike the fine arts, architectural practices are far more collaborative endeavors. Even conceptual designs often reflect the ideas and contributions of more than one architect in a firm. While architectural firms are not collaborative circles, frequently partners and senior employees are true collaborators in the creation of a work.[6]

5 Avery Library has no correspondence between Wright, Spencer, Perkins, and Hunt in the Wright Archives and *Frank Lloyd Wright: an index to Taliesin correspondence*, edited with an introduction by Anthony Alofsin: New York: Garland Pub., 1988, which indexes correspondences belonging to the Frank Lloyd Wright Foundation has no correspondence between Wright and Spencer, Perkins, or Hunt.

6 Part of my fascination with Farrell's work on creative collaborative circles, has been to realize that at various important times in my education and my career I have been privileged to be part of collaborative circles that influenced my views on architecture. I have been a part of two different collaborative circles. The first, at Cornell University, formed around a mentor, Colin Rowe. This group of graduate students developed, along with Rowe, a set of anti-utopian urban design ideas that had an effect on both theories of architectural design and urban planning in the 1970 and '80s. This circle, many of whom became teachers, would later disseminate the teaching methods and ideas of their teachers who came to be known as the "Texas Rangers": they were Colin Rowe, John Hedjuc, Lee Hodgden, Werner Seligmann, and John Shaw, who first taught together the University of Texas, Austin in the 1950s (see Alex Caragonne. The Texas Rangers. Cambridge: MIT Press, 1995). As teachers and deans of prominent schools of architecture, I believe my generation had an impact on architectural education in the second half of the twentieth century. I am particularly indebted to Steven Hurtt and the late Thomas Schumacher in addition to the late Colin Rowe; their influence still shapes my ideas to this day.

The second collaborative circle, in Chicago, set out to change the architectural culture of that city through teaching, writing, and a series of nationally circulated architectural exhibitions about less-known Chicago architecture. This group of would-be radicals called ourselves the Chicago Seven (Architects), after the political radicals of the 1968 Chicago Democratic convention. They were, the late Stanley Tigerman, Tom Beeby, Larry Booth, Jim Nagle, Ben Weese, myself, and the late James Freed, then dean of Architecture at IIT. This group was later expanded with the addition of Cindy Weese, Ken Schroeder, Jerry Horn, and Helmut Jahn. We would resurrect the Chicago Architectural Club, in the hope of recreating an atmosphere of intellectual curiosity and collegiality that had accompanied the original Club and its yearly exhibitions at the beginning of the 20th century. To that end the new club grew to about 100 active members, met monthly at the Graham Foundation in Chicago, held a yearly members exhibition at the Art Institute and at a number of Chicago Art Galleries, and for 10 years published a yearbook of work and essays by members. It was, as Wright wrote of Chicago in the 1890s, "an exciting time." I was also fortunate enough to have Stanley Tigerman and Thomas Beeby as teaching colleagues at the University of Illinois Chicago. To both I will always be grateful.

ACKNOWLEDGMENTS

In 1978, Robert Sweeney's annotated bibliography of books and articles by and about Wright listed over 2,000 entries. This number has continued to grow raising the impossibility of knowing everything that has been written. That said, I would like to acknowledge Lehland Roth's article about the history of the *Ladies' Home Journal* houses; Joseph Siry's article about Wright and Perkins's collaboration on the Abraham Lincoln Center in Chicago and his subsequent book on Unity Temple; Dietrich Neumann's article about the Luxfer Prism Company; Wilbert Hasbrouck's definitive history of the Chicago Architectural Club; Donald Leslie Johnson's book that helps correct the chronology of Wright's early years; and Paul Kruty's articles on both Wright and Spencer. I am indebted to all these sources. In addition, I wish to acknowledge the work of Wright scholars, H. Allen Brooks, Robert Twombly, Donald Hoffman, Norris Kelly Smith, and Neil Levine. Both Smith and Levine have provided keen insights into the meaning of Wright's work. All of these authors have influenced the way I look at the work of Frank Lloyd Wright as has Meryle Secrest's fine biography of Wright with her useful insights into Wright's personal psychology.

I would like to thank David Van Zanten for his encouragement and enthusiasm for this project. Also, for his insights into Chicago's architectural zeitgeist circa 1900 and the importance not just of Sullivan, but of Louis Millet, Emil Lorch, Claude Bragdon, and the Pure Design movement. His insights into Sullivan's ornament as a key to understanding an entire design process including the spatial development of Sullivan's residential plans was an important influence on my understanding of Wright's early work and Chicago's first generation of 20th-century architects.

I want to thank Jacob McCarthy who worked as a research assistant on parts of this book and Kris Hartzell who generously shared her knowledge of Myron Hunt and Steinway Hall. Thanks also to Christopher Payne for sharing information on the work of J.L. Silsbee. My thanks to the staff of the Art Institute of Chicago's Ryerson and Burnham Libraries particularly Nathaniel Parks (archivist) and Autumn Lorraine Mather for generously allowing me to reproduce numerous images from their library's digital archives. I want to thank Pamela Casey (architecture archivist) and Katherine Prater of the Avery Library at Columbia University. For Frank Lloyd Wright's material still under copyright I would like to thank Margo Stipe (director and curator of collections for the Frank Lloyd Wright

Foundation) for generously allowing me to reproduce images from their archive at the Avery Library. Thanks to the Chicago History Museum: Nancy Hadley (director of archives and records); Katie Levi (rights and reproduction coordinator), and to Leslie Martin in their research library for permission to reproduce illustrations from their Perkins Papers collection. Thanks also to Lyndy Jensen at the Lake Bluff History Museum and to William Tyre of the Glessner House Museum who generously supplied illustrations. Thanks to John Leeker (director of the library and archives of the Meadville Lombard Theological School for permission to reproduce material from their Jenkin Lloyd Jones collection. Thanks also to Richard Linten of the Luxfer Gas Cylinder Company. Special thanks to Paul Lane of PhotoSource who helped manage as well as enhance and sharpen many of the digital copies of archival images reproduced in this book. At a time when the worldwide COVID-19 pandemic has closed institutional libraries and archives, I want to thank those institutions that, unable to supply specific images from their collections, have given me permission to reproduce materials they own from published sources and from the Internet.

I am in debt to Mark Hewitt, Susan Benjamin, Michelangelo Sabatino, Christian Bjone, Steven Hurtt, Julie Hacker, David Van Zanten, and all those who have read drafts of this work or parts of it and provided comments and criticism. Finally, I would like to thank my partner Julie Hacker, FAIA. She has been a design collaborator and, as partner in our architectural practice, she has made it possible for me to teach and to write.

Chapter 1

SPENCER, WRIGHT, PERKINS, AND HUNT, "FIRST ASSOCIATES IN THE PROFESSION OF ARCHITECTURE."

" *Wright had much to gain from close contact
with his peers... As newcomers to the profession,
the members of Steinway Hall as a group were
concerned with making an architecture that was
in tune with the times yet characterized by a
regional sensitivity.*

Neil Levine

This is a book about collaboration. The creation and
working out of shared ideas as well as collaboration
on architectural projects. It is about the time during
which Robert Closson Spencer Jr., Frank Lincoln Wright, Dwight
Heald Perkins, and Myron Hubbard Hunt shared office and studio
space in Chicago's Steinway Hall building. The idea of considering Spencer, Wright, Perkins, and Hunt as a collaborative circle
was suggested by Michael P. Farrell's book, *Collaborative Circles:
Friendship Dynamics & Creative Work*. In it Farrell writes, "I saw
the possibility of using group theory to understand the dynamic
of circles of artist and writers."[1] Among the groups Farrell discusses are: the French impressionist painters, the Bloomsbury
group in London, the writers who lived outside of London in
the area around Rye known as the Inklings, the group in Vienna
around Freud who developed psychoanalytic theory; and Susan
B. Anthony and women's rights advocates in New York. While
Farrell doesn't discuss collaborations in science, these working
relationships are abundant.

According to Farrell the defining characteristic of creative
collaborative circles are usually people in their twenties or thir-
ties who see their work in opposition to the status quo, challenging the established traditions in their field. Although they may
not yet know what they will come to profess, they know what
they dislike about current work in their discipline or profession.
These circles are formed by friends who come together to work

---

1 Farrell. Collaborative Circles, p.ix.

through the parameters of a new shared vision. These groups are usually three to five people all in the early stages of their career. They often work together on collaborative projects and will later undertake projects aimed at winning public support for their ideas, such as exhibitions and publications. As members increase in skill and intellectual maturity, they will leave the collaborative circle, and therefore the life span of such associations is rarely more than 10 years. The group will often have a charismatic leader, "a relatively narcissistic member whose self-assurance and charm draw the members into discipline related activities."[2] Members of the group often share a common teacher or mentor, but this person is rarely a member of their collaborative circle.

For the architects of Steinway Hall, the shared mentor and initial source for their ideas was Louis Sullivan, Wright's former employer. Wright says that, "At this time these young architects were all getting the gospel modified through me, never having known Sullivan themselves,"[3] However, Walter Burley Griffin claims that he met Sullivan around 1900 at Steinway Hall[4] and tells us, "He [Sullivan] lectured to the younger members of Chicago's architectural profession sometimes formally at the Chicago Architectural Club more often on an informal basis in the lofts of the Steinway Building where he was a frequent visitor."[5]

Sullivan was an influential and well-known presence in the architectural community. Starting in the mid-1880s he lectured extensively and frequently published his architectural ideas and theories, culminating in the "Kindergarten Chats," which appeared in serial form from 1901 to 1902. Even though none of the other Steinway Hall architects may have known Sullivan very well, as Wright claimed, he was their philosophical mentor. He was speaking directly to them when he wrote "The Young Man in Architecture," an address to the Architectural League of America in June of 1900 in Chicago (published that same month in the *Brickbuilder* magazine). Sullivan wrote, "It is my premise that the Architectural League of America has its being in a sense of discontent with conditions now prevailing in the American

---

2 Farrell, op.cit., p.85.

3 Wright. *An Autobiography*, p.129.

4 Peisch, *The Chicago School of Architecture*, 1964. Interview with Ralph Griffin, St. Louis, Mo., May 20, 1955.

5 Peisch, op. cit., p.26.

malpractice of the architectural art; in a deep and wide sense of conviction that no aid is to be expected from the generation now representing that malpractice; and in the instinctive feeling that, through banding together, force, discretion and coherence may be given to the output of these feelings which are, in themselves, for the time being, vague and miscellaneous, however intensely they may be felt."

So it was with a sense of discontent with the architecture of the day and with Sullivan as both mentor and role model; with professional and personal friendships; mutual respect for each other's architectural work; and a desire to distinguish themselves as architects; that Robert Spencer, Frank Wright, and Myron Hunt joined Dwight Perkins in the loft studio in the attic of Steinway Hall. Wright remembered, "I had met Robert Spencer, Myron Hunt, and Dwight Perkins. Dwight had a loft in his new Steinway Hall building—too large for him. So, we formed a group—outer office in common—workrooms screened apart in the loft of Steinway Hall. These young men, newcomers in architectural practice like myself, were my first associates in the so-called profession of architecture."[6]

This book will consider the relationship between these men and the development of many of the architectural ideas that Wright subsequently claimed for himself. Parts of Perkins's career have been documented. Very little has been published on Myron Hunt. While Robert Spencer wrote extensively about architecture for many national publications, little has been written about his life and work.[7] Included as appendices are brief biographies of Spencer, Perkins, and Hunt, and a description of Wright's time in Chicago just before he moved into Steinway Hall. These have been included because it is important to understand who these men were both before and after they worked side by side.

---

6 Wright, An Autobiography, 1932, p.131.

7 Studies are forthcoming on Wright's friend Robert Spencer Jr. by Paul Kruty and the late Wilbert Hasbrouck was working on a book on Dwight Perkins at the time of his death. There are currently no major treatments of Myron Hunt excepting the essays in David Gebhard's exhibition catalog for the Baxter Art Gallery, 1984.

Chapter 2

CHICAGO 1900: MILIEU AND INFLUENCES

" *How great is the privilege granted as in being*
part of not a Renaissance, but of a naissance
in architecture. For there is surely being born into
our world a new style, the style of America.

Dankmar Adler[1]

What was the architectural culture of Chicago in the decade leading up to and immediately after 1900? What were the ideas and aspirations of Spencer, Wright, Perkins, and Hunt as young Chicago architects? Where did these men come from and how did they find each other? These are some of the questions we need to answer before we consider their participation in the loft studio in Steinway Hall.

The progressive work young architects admired most came from just a few Chicago offices. Like William Le Baron Jenney's and Adler and Sullivan's, the office of J.L. Silsbee was considered one of the best Chicago offices in which to work and learn about architecture—particularly, for anyone interested in residential architecture. Frank Wright, George Maher, and George Grant Elmslie all worked there at the same time. Silsbee's residential work was done in a manner that would become known as the Shingle style, an American style that combined the formal classical elements of the Queen Ann with picturesque massing, rooflines, and porches, all sheathed in wall hung wood shingles. The use of roofing shingles on sidewalls was H.H. Richardson's response to the English architect Richard Norman Shaw's use of wall-hung clay tiles which were unavailable in the United States. The interiors of these houses shared a new sense of spatial openness and connection that paralleled similar experiments in the architecture of the English Arts and Crafts movement. What the picturesque massing of Arts and Crafts architecture offered was a new freedom in the composition and arrangement of floor plans. This new openness and the creation of interconnected spaces

---

1 Quoted in Smith, Wright on Exhibit.

was a response to the growing relaxation of social formalities accompanying the growth of a middle class of mercantile and professional people who were building houses. For author Henry James it signaled nothing less than the coming breakdown of manners and civil society; he wrote in *The American Scene,* "This diffused vagueness of separation between apartments, between hall and room, between one room and another, between the one you are in and the one you are not in, between place of passage and place of privacy, is a provocation to despair."[2]

Henry Hobson Richardson was among the most admired and influential architects in the United States at the time. Richardson was the towering figure of American architecture at the end of the nineteenth century. He was revered not only for his innovations in residential design but also for his adaptation of the forms of Romanesque architecture to the United States' civic and institutional buildings. It is easy to understand the appeal of the Romanesque style to both architects and the general public, but hard to understand why architectural critics of the day considered it to be appropriate for the US. Perhaps the Romanesque became an American style by default, rather than Gothic or Classical, because of their close association with the great monuments of Europe. What is equally of interest is the consensus that existed, particularly among younger architects, that there should be a uniquely American style of architecture. The appeal of the Romanesque lay in a number of factors that critics of the day noted, chiefly its imposing solidity and strength. With highly textured variegated stone surfaces the buildings had an immediacy not associated with classical stone buildings. The massing was picturesque with varying roof profiles. Most importantly the loose arrangement of articulated elements in plan meant that the Romanesque could accommodate the growing internal complexity of civic and institutional buildings. It could do this within a schema that allowed the most important internal spaces to be given identity and exterior expression. Rather than the rigidity of classical symmetry, buildings done in the American Romanesque style could accommodate the various internal functions

---

2 James, Henry, *The American Scene,* lits@iappublishing.com, 2010 reprint, p.72. Quoted more fully later in this text. James laments the loss of privacy and civility and seems to perfectly describe the latest spatial and planning developments in the American house. Versions of this passage are quoted in David P. Handlin, *The American Home* and Clive Aslet, *The American Country House.*

required of modern buildings. By the end of Richardson's career, the Romanesque was almost ubiquitously used for civic and institutional buildings, yet Richardson did it better than any of his contemporaries and the style became known as Richardsonian Romanesque. His genius was to be able to compose building masses and the disposition of openings in wall surfaces with equal brilliance. Chicago architect John Wellborn Root who was admired by young architects and built in the Romanesque style wrote, "Richardson's influence has always tended to make architecture more simple and direct, and it has led architects more generally to avoid the hideous mass of shams which in America preceded him."[3] The ornate stylistic confusion that characterized residential architecture at this time was noted beyond the architectural press. Describing the excesses of residential architecture in her 1905 book *House of Mirth,* Edith Wharton wrote, commenting on a new house, "The man who built it came from a *milieu* where all the dishes are put on the table at once. His facade is a complete architectural meal, if he had omitted a style his friends might have thought the money had given out."[4]

The historian James O'Gorman grouped Richardson, Sullivan, and Wright together in the title of a book, suggesting a continuity of thought as well as influence. It is important to note that Richardson never espoused a theory of architecture, nor did he argue for the appropriateness of Romanesque architecture as an expression of Americanness. His impact rested solely on his built work. In Chicago his influence affected the work of Burnham and Root and more importantly the work of Louis Sullivan. Of the younger generation of Chicago architects, Dwight Perkins had worked briefly for H.H. Richardson. Robert Spencer had worked in Boston for Richardson's successor firm, Shepley, Rutan & Coolidge during the year following Richardson's death (1886), and he then worked in their Chicago office. Like Spencer, Myron Hunt also worked in both the Boston and Chicago offices of Shepley, Rutan & Coolidge. At this time the firm's work was in transition from Romanesque to classical. This can be seen in

3 Root, "The City House in the West," *Scribner's Magazine,* vol. VIII, no.4 October 1890, p.416–34.
4 Wharton, Edith. *House of Mirth,* "Chapter 14," p.130. Dover, 2002.

their Chicago projects for the Chicago Public Library and the Art Institute.

Where Richardson had created an architecture expressive of the permanence of American institutions, Sullivan set out to make an architecture that was poetically expressive of American democracy, the common person, and the importance of nature to a society whose roots were still agrarian. For Sullivan, nature and its forms, offered examples of first principles. These were the idea of organic growth, both literally and as a metaphor, and the suitability of a form to its purpose, again as exemplified in nature. Sullivan wanted buildings to also be poetically expressive of their use. Nature was both a model for his individualized reimagining of Romanesque ornament and as a metaphor for a growth process that interrelated all the parts of a building, including its decorative details. Thus, Sullivan's idea of an architecture that was "organic" extended beyond the use of motifs based on plant forms. The uniform extension of modules and planning grids in the design of buildings (and cities) was thought of in terms of expressing democratic equality. In the skyscraper, the uniform repetition of window openings, expressed the equality of the individuals who inhabited them. Perhaps the best interpretation of Sullivan's tall office buildings came from his supporter and apologist Claude Bragdon. In his 1918 book *Architecture and Democracy*, Bragdon described Sullivan's Guaranty Building in Buffalo, "This rude, rectangular bulk is uncompromisingly practical and utilitarian; these rows on rows of windows, regularly spaced and all of the same size, suggest the equality and monotony of obscure, laborious lives; the upspringing shafts of the vertical piers stand for their hopes and aspirations ... the building is able to speak thus powerfully to the imagination because its creator is a poet and prophet of democracy. In his own chosen language he declares, as Whitman did in verse ... 'A Nation announcing itself.'"[5] Bragdon wrote the introduction to Sullivan's *Autobiography of an Idea* when it was published in 1924 ten years after Sullivan's death and edited Sullivan's collection of essays, *Kindergarten Chats*, for publication in book form in 1934.[6]

---

5 Bragdon, *Architecture and Democracy*, p.18–19.
6 Bragdon was a practicing architect in Rochester and then a theatrical set designer in New York City.

Sullivan's *Kindergarten Chats* was originally published in *The Interstate Architect and Builder* (Cleveland, Ohio) in 52 serial installments between February 16, 1901 and February 8, 1902. It was addressed to the next generation of architects. In these short essays Sullivan set forth and codified his views on architecture for a younger generation, personified by the "student" being addressed in each of the *Kindergarten Chats* essays. These essays would serve as a rallying call to set aside eclecticism and create an indigenous American architecture. The *Kindergarten Chats* were a rambling poetic summation of what Sullivan had been writing and lecturing about for years. In 1918 Sullivan wrote by way of introduction to the reprinting of his essays, "The plot if such it may be called, is very simple, namely a graduate of one of our architectural schools comes to the author for a post-graduate course ... The central purpose of the work is to liberate the mind from serfdom to tradition and to exhibit man's natural powers in their creative capabilities when expanding in the open-air-of-the-spirit-of-responsible freedom: in other words, in the true spirit of democracy ... The ideas underlying the work are simple and elementary; hence the title 'Kindergarten Chats.'"[7]

As early as 1885 in an address to the Western Association of Architects, Sullivan noted, "Many who have commented upon the practice of architecture in this country have regarded the absence of a style, distinctively American, as both strange and deplorable," noting that in America, "Our literature is the only phase of our national art that has been accorded serious recognition, at home and abroad." And, "The first step toward a new order of things is accomplished where there appear minds receiving and assimilating fresh impressions, reaching new conclusions, and acting upon them ... We surely have in us the germ of artistic greatness ... but architects as a professional class have held it more expedient to maintain the traditions of their culture than to promulgate vitalizing thought."[8]

Bragdon was the designer of the Rochester Station of the New York Central Railroad, the Rochester First Universalist Church, and the Oswego Yacht Club along with private houses. He was a proponent of geometrical and musical proportioning systems in architecture and in the design of geometric ornament. This he referred to as Projective Ornament based on mathematical patterns abstracted from nature. He was a prolific author and among his books are: *Architecture and Democracy, Projective Ornament, Four Dimensional Vistas,* and *A Primer of Higher Space.* Bragdon also believed in and wrote about reincarnation, occultism, philosophy, and yoga.

7 Reprinted in *Kindergarten Chats and other Writings.* NY: Wittenborn, 1947.

8 Ibid., p.177–80.

Sullivan's essay "The Young Man in Architecture," read before the annual convention of the Architectural League of America held in Chicago in June of 1900, was his call to arms. Acknowledging the youth of his audience, suggesting that the formation of the Architectural League was in response to, "a sense of discontent with conditions now prevailing in the American malpractice [*of architecture*]," Sullivan rails against eclecticism, and in conclusion asks, "Do you intend, or do you not intend, do you wish or do you not wish, to become architects in whose care an unfolding Democracy may entrust the interpretation of its material wants, its psychic aspirations?"[9]

It would be hard to overestimate Sullivan's impact in Chicago. In his book *Sullivan's City* David Van Zanten wrote, "Around 1900, at the height of the Progressive Era, there came a new twist in Chicago architecture: Sullivan's work was taken up as a cause ... Sullivan's architecture was seen as encapsulating and illuminating a general system of design ... The young draftsmen of Chicago—including Frank Lloyd Wright—tried to shape this system into an alternative course of architectural design and design education."[10]

Sullivan and Root were the intellectual mentors and inspiration for a younger generation of Chicago architects. Both were frequent speakers reading papers before the Chicago Architectural Club. Sullivan participated in the Architectural League of America, which held yearly conferences. The League was a national association made up of representatives from Architectural Clubs in Chicago, New York, Boston Pittsburgh, St. Louis, Cleveland, Philadelphia, and Toronto, Canada. It also included local chapters of the AIA from Pittsburgh and Cleveland, as well as the New York Society of *Beaux-Arts* Architects. They met yearly beginning in 1899 to discuss issues of concern to the profession. According to their constitution their purpose was," The encouragement of an indigenous and American architecture in agreement with modern methods and conditions." The tenor of the League's meetings was often anti-establishment, given that members of architectural clubs across the country tended to be draftsmen and younger architects. The League was founded in

9 Ibid., p.214–23.
10 David Van Zanten. *Sullivan's City*, p.73.

Chicago, with its first meeting in Cincinnati, and the second in Chicago. Dwight Perkins, Robert Spencer, and other members of the Chicago Architectural Club played key organizational and leadership roles. Even Frank Wright attended the yearly conferences as a Chicago delegate.

At the League's Chicago Convention Dwight Perkins read a paper prepared by New York Architect Ernest Flagg entitled, "American Architecture as Opposed to Architecture in America." Flagg wrote, echoing a growing discussion nationwide, "At no time has there been anything which might properly be called an American style of architecture. There have been American ways of building, as, for instance our high buildings with skeleton construction ... but the decorative features have been used in accordance with passing fashions, supposedly modeled on European usage." Flagg suggested that an American style would evolve, "Owing to the peculiar situation of America and to the natural independence and lack of reverence of the American mind the course of architecture here has presented an anomaly in the development of style, and rules which apply elsewhere do not seem to apply here." Also at the 1900 Convention Elmer Grey of Milwaukee, who would later become Myron Hunt's partner, spoke about an "Indigenous and Inventive Architecture for America," suggesting that an American architectural style would arise out the conditions of building, noting that "Style is not the external adornment of a building: it is the vital quality of it which has resulted from conditions inherent in its making."[11]

Among the topics addressed at the early annual meetings were not just the question of an indigenous American architecture, but ethics, architectural licensing, and, importantly, the basis of architectural education and its reform through the teaching of Pure Design. The philosophical issues important to the younger generation of architects were the question of eclecticism and designing from precedent as taught in architecture schools of the day. This was articulated by George Dean in his paper *Progress before Precedent*, which was published in the *Brickbuilder* in May of 1900. It was a topic of discussion at the Architectural League of America's second meeting held in Chicago in 1900. "Progress before Precedent" was adopted as the Leagues' motto by Albert

---

11 Both Flagg and Grey's papers were reprinted in *Scientific American Building Edition*, August 1900.

Kelsey, the League's first president and the editor of the League's annual publication. The motto appeared in a seal designed by Kelsey on the covers of the League's annual yearbooks beginning in 1900.

The *Brickbuilder* magazine had asked Dean about his title, *Progress before Precedent.* "Is the maxim of the Architectural League of America finding favor with the coming men of the Middle West?" In his article Dean expressed a growing new sentiment about the use and importance of architectural precedent rather than its banishment from architectural studies. He wrote, "Precedent in architecture has two very distinct and entirely different meanings. If that of slavishly copying the forms of ancient architecture is meant, let us say 'Progress without Precedent.' If, however, the meaning is the following of the principles which led the great architects to produce monuments of art which we revere and fondly worship, let us say 'Precedence and Progress.'"[12] This is similar to the position on education held by the Pure Design movement, proponents of which believed that the study of composition would enable architects to understand the underlying principles behind the great architecture of the past. Reflecting Sullivan's position, Dean wrote, "What the young men of the League desire is an architecture free from vulgar importations. The American people are no more in sympathy with the modern French architecture than they are with life on the French boulevards."[13]

George Dean was a friend of Robert Spencer's and like Spencer had worked for Shepley, Rutan & Coolidge in Boston before joining their Chicago office. Dean traveled with Spencer in Europe in 1892–1893 and was president of the Chicago Architectural Club in 1894 and again in 1895. The *Brickbuilder* solicited responses to Dean's short paper which were published along with it in the *Brickbuilder.* Wright, commented, "George Dean is right ... His feeling against the present hidebound condition of architecture as a fine art, and his hope for its future, are characteristic of a growing group of young men in the Middle West."[14]

---

12 *Brickbuilder 9*, no.3, p.91–97.
13 Ibid.
14 *Brickbuilder. Op.cit.* See also Hasbrouck, *The Chicago Architectural Club*, p.266.

It is important to note that many saw Pure Design, as Dean suggests, as a way to understand principles first, not necessarily as an argument against the use of historical precedents. Howard Van Doren Shaw, usually dismissed as an eclectic architect, was a member of the dining club Wright labeled the Eighteen and an active member of the Chicago Architectural Club. Shaw put it succinctly in an address, which he planned to deliver at the National AIA convention in 1926, "Most architects know too much architecture and too little composition."[15]

Pure Design as an ideology would come to be an influence on the younger members of the profession. This was championed in the teaching and publications of Denman Waldo Ross (1853–1935), Arthur Wesley Dow (1857–1922), Emil Lorch (1870–1963), and Claude Bragdon (1866–1946). Historian Marie Frank wrote that, "Pure Design, a formalist pedagogical method, relied on exercises with abstract design elements—the dot, the line, shape, and color—to encourage the creative ability of students … By the 1890s, American aesthetic thought had shifted from a Ruskinian emphasis on the moral and historical value of art, dominant at mid-century, to a focus on form as the primary source of assessing aesthetic merit."[16]

Arthur Wesley Dow was one of the principal proponents of Pure Design and a teacher at Pratt Institute and Columbia University Teachers College. He was also a painter and referred to the fine arts and architecture as "space-arts." His textbook *Composition: A Series of Exercises Selected from a New System of Art Education* (1899) argued that the formal (compositional) criteria for judging (and teaching) good design were independent of questions of style or technique and that they applied to both contemporary and historic architecture. He wrote, "Historical styles will now serve as examples of harmony, not as mere models."[17] Denman Waldo Ross was also a painter. He was a professor of art at Harvard University and had been a student of Charles Eliot Norton and Henry Adams. Ross wanted to bring the scientific method into the evaluation of aesthetic properties.

---

15 Shaw who was awarded the AIA's Gold Metal in 1926 died a few months before receiving this award. His speech to the AIA was never delivered. It is in manuscript form in the Shaw Archives in the Ryerson and Burnham Library at the Art Institute of Chicago.

16 Frank, JSAH vol. 67, no.2 June 2008, p.248.

17 Arthur Wesley Dow, Composition. Quoted in Frank, "The Theory of Pure Design," JSAH, p.255.

He believed that art, like science, had underlying general and universal principles—laws that could be taught. In *A Theory of Pure Design: Harmony, Balance, Rhythm With Illustrations and Diagrams* (1907) Ross wrote, "By design I mean order in human feeling and thought and in the many and varied activities by which that thought or feeling is expressed."[18]

Emil Lorch had studied architecture at MIT and then worked in Boston for the architectural firm of Peabody & Stearns. While traveling in Europe he met N. H. Carpenter, secretary of the Art Institute of Chicago, and was invited to come to Chicago. In 1899 he began teaching at the Art Institute. A member of the Chicago Architectural Club, he was also a founding member of the Architectural League of America. He taught at the Art Institute advocating for Pure Design until 1901 when Daniel Burnham and other Art Institute Board members ousted him in favor of a *Beaux-Arts* curriculum. Lorch, who was from Michigan, would go on to be appointed the first director of the school of architecture at the University of Michigan.

At the annual meeting of the Architectural League in 1901, the question of architectural education was addressed with a session devoted to Pure Design. This was the same year that Robert Spencer was elected president of the League with Emil Lorch serving as second vice president. Spencer and Lorch organized a session on Pure Design at the 1901 meeting, and both presented papers. Spencer's addressed the question, "Should the Study of Architectural Design and The Historic Styles Follow and be Based Upon a Knowledge of Pure Design?" It was published in the *Inland Architect* and put forward the idea that composition should be the basis of all art and architecture and that the value of studying architectural precedents was in the identification of useful principles of design.[19] Spencer espoused the importance of Pure Design and the teaching of composition independent of architectural precedents. Pure Design proponents Arthur Dow and Denman Ross were not in attendance at the convention but sent papers for Emil Lorch to read. Claude Bragdon, another important proponent of Pure Design, was also there.

---

18 Ross, *A Theory of Pure Design*. Quoted in Frank, "The Theory of Pure Design," *JSAH*, p.255.

19 *Inland Architect*, vol XXXVII, no.5, June 1901, p.34–35, also H. Allen Brooks wrote, "The fundamental idea behind pure design was that all architecture is based upon abstract, geometric order." Brooks, *Prairie School*, p.39.

The *Inland Architect* reported on the conference that "it does not seem improper to say under the leadership of Mr. Emil Lorch, for the past two years, the League has devoted much attention to the discussion of the necessity for the study of Pure Design in architectural education in place of the time-honored practice of training the student along classical and historical lines. The clubs of the League have endorsed the movement for which the Chicago Club gave initiative, and it has already grown so strong and developed such practical and feasible characteristics as to compel the attention of architectural educators everywhere."[20] H. Allen Brooks wrote, "The concept of pure design, like so many theories for architectural design in the nineteenth century, might well have come to naught but for one listener at the League convention. Upon Wright they made a deep impression and through his subsequent work the essence of pure design was transmitted to the world. These discussions helped Wright apply his early Froebel kindergarten experiences to the practical requirements of building."[21] Wright refers to Pure Design in *An Autobiography* in relation to his design of Unity Temple. In the loft at Steinway Hall, Wright would have discussed this idea with his friends Robert Spencer, Dwight Perkins, and Emil Lorch. This was the intellectual milieu in which the architects of Steinway Hall were to develop their work. Ideas about Pure Design and the development of an American architecture would have been a continuing discussion for many of the architects of Steinway Hall. These ideas would drive the work they built and the articles and projects they prepared for publication.

---

20 *Inland Architect and News Record*, 17, 1901, p.33. Quoted in Brooks, *Prairie School*.
21 Brooks, *Prairie School*, p.40.

Chapter 3

THE CHICAGO ARCHITECTURAL CLUB, THE CHICAGO ARTS AND CRAFTS SOCIETY, AND THE EIGHTEEN

❝ *Most collaborative circles consist of a core group who interact frequently and a peripheral 'extended' group who vary in their degree of involvement. The core comprise those members who meet together on a regular basis, discuss their work, and through their interaction develop a new vision.*[1]

Michael P. Farrell

❝ *From its earliest period the Club has been a social center, a breeder of friendshps. From its earliest period today the Club has been an educational factor in the lives of its members and also in the life of the community.*[2]

Irving K. Pond

In Paris in the fall of 1862, Auguste Renoir, Frederic Bazille, Alfred Sisley, and Claude Monet met as young art students in the studio of Charles Gleyre. All were in their early 20s and they soon were friends going out for drinks after class. By the late 1860s they were meeting weekly at the Café Guebois along with Camille Pissarro, Edward Manet, and Edgar Degas. They would rebel against the Paris art establishment: rejecting classical subject matter, choosing to paint together out of doors rather than in the studio, and ultimately developing a new color palette and new techniques for applying paint to canvas. Their friend and art historian Theodore Duret wrote in *Manet and the French Impressionists* (1910), "A constant feature of the history of Impressionists was their influence on each other and their mutual borrowing ... they developed side by side."[3]

---

1 Michael P. Farrell, *Collaborative Circles*, p.29.

2 Chicago Architectural Club Catalog, 1910.

3 Duret, Theodore, Manet and the *French Impressionists*. Philadelphia: J. B. Lippincott, 1972, p.129. quoted in Ferrell p.27.

Monet was the group's charismatic leader. Pissarro was described as the group's theoretician with Manet often acting as the provocateur in their discussions. It was Bazille who was responsible for creating recognition for their art through exhibitions and the sale of their work. Like the Impressionists, the architects who practiced on the top floor of Steinway Hall would form a collaborative circle. Wright and Spencer were the group's theoreticians. Spencer and Perkins arranged for the inclusion of work by members of the group in exhibitions. Spencer and Wright lectured and published their writings. All were socially adept and charismatic based on both early descriptions of them and the degree to which they all enjoyed professional success. Collectively they impacted Chicago architecture, helped to transform the American house, and ultimately changed the architecture of the 20th century. In turn, the Steinway Hall architects would influence their Chicago colleagues primarily through their active participation in the Chicago Architectural Club and the Chicago Arts and Crafts Society.

For Perkins, Spencer, Wright, and Hunt their participation in the meetings and social activities of the Chicago Architectural Club was not where they initially formed their friendships. In Chicago in the late 1890s Perkins, Spencer, and Wright were all members of Wright's uncle's All Souls Church. All four were about the same age when they moved into shared office space in Chicago's Steinway Hall. Along with Myron Hunt they had known one another socially, and except for Wright had all studied architecture at MIT. They had worked together as employees in the same architectural firms. They would also become members of a group of eighteen young architects who would meet together to dine on a regular basis and to discuss architecture. They all shared a similar dissatisfaction with the current architectural establishment and wished to create a new uniquely American architecture.

The Chicago Architectural Club was founded as the Chicago Architectural Sketch Club in 1885 by James H. Carpenter an English-born draftsman working in Chicago. Its purpose was to teach the history of architectural styles and other subjects related to building to men with no formal training who were working in architect's offices. At the time, the American Institute of Architects and the Western Association of Architects, which later merged with the AIA, were only open to trained architects.

The Chicago Architectural Sketch Club was founded to fill this gap. The club was exclusively for the education of draftsmen. They met twice a month, invited prominent Chicago architects to speak to them, sponsored competitions for members, and held sketch nights with prizes for the best drawings. The Sketch Club was also able to sponsor scholarships and traveling competitions. These funded a year of study and travel in Europe. The club would become important to the development of the architects of Steinway Hall, including Frank Wright, who never officially joined but attend meetings.

The *Inland Architect and Building News* from December 1897 carried an article on the Sketch Club by Robert McLean, its editor. McLean, who had helped facilitate the formation of the Sketch Club, wrote of its founding by "a few draftsmen who have since become prominent among the best designers in the country, they teach and are taught and work together for the common purpose of advancement in their chosen art." The *Inland Architect and Building News* would report on each of the club's meetings recording who spoke and what was discussed, publishing papers that had been presented to the members, and recording who was in attendance. This detailed record allows us to understand how deeply involved the architects from the loft in Steinway Hall were in the Club and its activities.

Writing for the *American Architect and Building News* in 1888, Clarence Howard Blackall, their Chicago correspondent, described an, "'esprit de corps' among the younger members of the profession. There is an architectural sketch-club which does very creditable work, and there is a very friendly feeling manifested among the members of the profession, who help each other and work together ... One of the most hopeful signs of Western architecture is the desire and willingness of the architects to mingle together, to show each other their work, and exchange criticism. Only in such ways, can growth come about. There is everything to be gained by intercourse, and we fancy that Eastern architects are sometimes inclined to disregard this means of progress."[4]

In 1885 the Sketch Club adapted bylaws and a constitution based on those of the slightly older Architectural League of New York and the Boston Society of Architects. It set forth the club's

---

4 *American Architect and Building News*, vol. XXIII, March 24, 1888, p.142.

educational and social purpose. These were to be accomplished by "regular meetings; by increasing the facilities for study; by readings or lectures on professional subjects; by the friendly discussion of practical matters; by competition in designs for exhibition; and by visiting and studying selected buildings." The original bylaws also established an Executive Committee to organize the club's activities, appoint subcommittees, and manage the club's funds.

By 1892 the construction of the World's Fair involved most of the Sketch Club's membership. When the fair opened, the Fair's Fine Arts Building included exhibits of architectural drawings and models many from Sketch Club members. The exhibit was selected by a national jury, chaired by Louis Sullivan's partner Dankmar Adler.

In 1892 Robert Spencer Jr. arrived in Chicago to work in the Chicago office of Shepley, Rutan & Coolidge. Myron Hunt would begin working there in 1895. Also, In the office at the time was George Dean.[5] Spencer would assist on the development of the interiors of the Chicago Public Library and begin attending meetings of the Chicago Architectural Sketch Club shortly after his arrival. In September of 1893 the club held an exhibit of Spencer's watercolors done while he was traveling in Europe on a Rotch Scholarship during 1891 and 1892. This would have been held in the Sketch Club's new rooms on the 9th floor of the Burnham and Root designed Masonic Temple Building. The Inland Architect reported, "about sixty of Mr. Spencer's superb collection of watercolor sketches ... were studied with a marked degree of interest by about fifty of the club members who were present."[6] Spencer was also working on the Chicago Art Institute's new building where the Chicago Architectural Club would later hold their exhibits.

In 1894 the Sketch Club established a relationship with the Chicago Society of Artists. The Club's desire for larger and more suitable space to hold the drawing, watercolor, and sculpting classes that were taught for members led to the Club taking a lease on the Lyman Blair Mansion, along with the Chicago Society of Artists. The Blair Mansion was one of the great houses

---

5 The number of architects who were to be members of the Eighteen and who also worked in this office may have been due to the recession which caused layoffs in many other Chicago offices.
6 The Inland Architect, vol. 22, no.3, October 1893, p.30.

4.001. Frank L. Wright. Frederick Bagley House, Hinsdale, Il. 1894.

that used to stand on Chicago's South Michigan Avenue. That year the new Art Institute Building opened and the Club, wishing to reach a larger audience with their annual exhibitions, worked out an agreement to hold their exhibits in the Art Institute's galleries. The requirements for the first exhibit there were that all materials had to be original drawings or renderings. Photographs were not allowed, although, a few years later, after professional architects were included in the club membership, annual exhibits would include photographs of built work. Robert McLean wrote in the *Inland Architect* for May of 1894, "the club secured the Art Institute in which to hold the exhibitions and put themselves into closer touch with the art appreciative public."[7] A review of the first annual exhibit at the Art Institute in the *American Architect and Building News* singled out Robert Spencer's watercolors and a perspective drawing by Spencer for the main stairway and stair hall of the Art Institute done for Shepley, Rutan & Coolidge.[8] Also mentioned were watercolors done by Ernest Albert, who exhibited renderings for Frank L. Wright, which included the Frederick Bagley House in Hinsdale, Illinois.

Ernest Albert was a painter who was part of a group of artists that included the painter Charles Corwin,[9] the brother of

7 The *Inland Architect*, vol. 23, no.4, May 1894, p.38. Also see Hasbrouck, *The Chicago Architectural Club*, p.168.

8 See Spencer biographical Appendix 3 for an illustration of his drawing for the Chicago Public Library, which should be compared with his design for the main hall of the Art Institute of Chicago.

9 Charles Corwin, also practiced as an architect and in 1889–90 was briefly in partnership with George W. Maher. George Maher who worked in Silsbee's office at the same time as Wright and George Elmslie was a club members. In 1887 Maher presented a paper to the Sketch Club

Wright's friend Cecil Corwin. At the time, the work exhibited was only work by Sketch Club members, many of whom were employed as "delineators" by other architects. They prepared the drawings they exhibited for their employers or as freelance work for other architects, as the club did not yet include professionals.

Although Wright would never officially join the club, his work would be included in many of the club's exhibitions. The 1894 exhibit included Wright's classical design entry for the Milwaukee Public Library Competition. At this time, his office was still in the Schiller Building and was adjacent to that of his friend Robert Spencer. Spencer may have had an impact on Wright's entry. The Chicago Public Library commission had been the result of a judged competition, and Spencer may have convinced Wright to design his entry in a classical manner hoping to win or at least receive recognition in the Milwaukee competition. Spencer had recently worked on the classical Chicago Public Library as well as the classical Art Institute building. Wright's elevation was clearly based on the Palace of Fine Arts, the most praised building at the 1893 World's Fair.[10]

Some years later, hoping to win the Luxfer competition, Wright would again design for a presumed jury. For this competition he designed two different buildings: one to appeal to William Le Baron Jenney and one to appeal to Louis Sullivan, both of whom he thought would be on the jury. However, the classical library design may have simply been a reaction to the uniform praise for the classical buildings of World's Fair's "Court of Honor." Sullivan would write, almost 24 years later, that the World's Fair would set the development of American Architecture back fifty years. Wright's assessment of the fair's influence was a bit different. Delivered in a 1939 lecture given in London, he suggested that the, "World's-fair's wave of pseudo 'classic,' now an 'ism, swept over and swept us all under."[11]

---

on "Originality in American Architecture." He had a distinguished practice, and while he is often considered one of the "Prairie School" because of the originality of his work, it is very different from his contemporaries. Maher was not friendly with the group in Steinway Hall and was not particularly active in the Chicago Architectural Club.

10 Meryle Secrest, a Wright biographer, compared Wright's Milwaukee Library design to Charles Rennie Mackintosh's (1890) classical design for a Science and Art Museum published in the *British Architect*. Seacrest, *Frank Lloyd Wright. A Biography*, p.116.

11 Wright, *The Future of Architecture*, p.223.

Apparently, it did. Hitchcock and his student Colin Rowe both suggested that Wright had turned down Daniel Burnham's job offer, which was accompanied by an offer to send Wright to study at the *Ecole des Beaux-Arts* in Paris, because, "Wright already knew himself to be the best *Beaux-Arts* architect in Chicago."[12] Wright's skill at manipulating geometry, classically shaped rooms, and the axial arrangement of spaces can be seen in his butterfly plan for the Cooper House project of 1890 for La Grange, Illinois and his Blossom House project of 1892, both of which predate the Fair, as well as in his earlier George Furbeck House of 1897 in Oak Park. The Blossom and Furbeck houses take classical plans and substitute the homes central hearth for the main stair as a terminus of the entry axis. In the Cooper House the dominant cross axis extending from the garden terrace also terminates in a central hearth. These houses should be considered along with his later symmetrical plans for Unity Temple, the Larkin Building, Midway Gardens, and the Imperial Hotel in assessing the influence of *Beaux-Art* classicism on Wright's development.

Wright would have learned the planning principles of the *Ecole des Beaux-Arts* when he worked for Sullivan who applied them primarily to the design of his ornament. Sullivan's use of planning grids, symmetries, axial arrangement, and the repetition and pairing of elements were also ideas about organizing floor plans that Wright shared with his MIT educated colleagues.

---

12 Colin Rowe in conversation with Chicago historian Kevin Harrington.

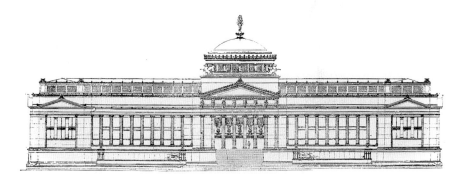

4.002. Frank L. Wright. Milwaukee Public Library Competition.
Exhibited Chicago Architectural Club. 1894

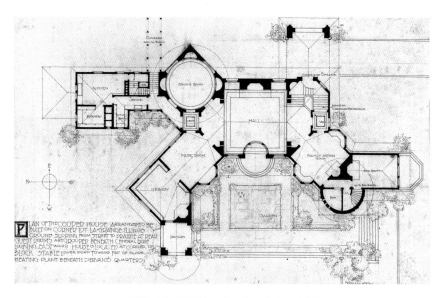

4.003. Frank Lloyd Wright. Cooper House Project. La Grange, Il. 1900

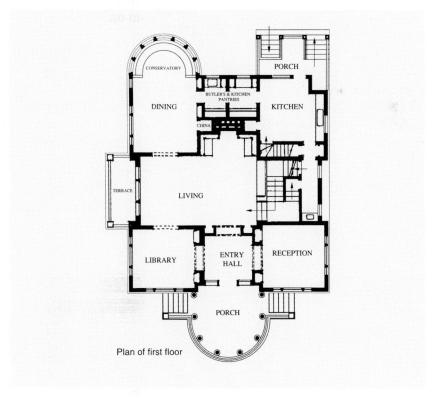

Plan of first floor

4.004. Frank L. Wright. Blossom House. Hyde Park, Chicago, Il. 1892

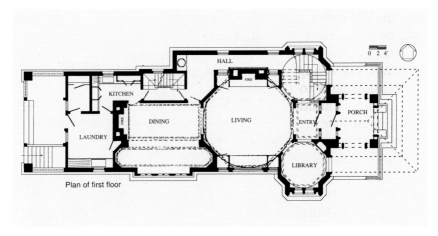

4.005. Frank Lloyd Wright. Furbeck House. Oak Park, Il. 1897

In spite of the World's Fair, classicism does not seem to have been a predominant influence on the work exhibited by club members.

The 1894 exhibit was the first annual member's exhibit for the Sketch Club. An event that would continue for many years with the Architectural Club's last annual exhibit in 1932.[13] In the same 1894 club show, Dwight Perkins exhibited drawings of his first independent commission, the Stevens Point Normal School with its Richardsonian influences.

---

13 The original club disbanded in 1967 and was reconstituted in the 1979 with the new club's annual exhibits held at the Chicago Art Institute and their meetings at the Graham Foundation.

4.006. Perkins and Selby. Stevens Point Normal School. Steven Point, Wi. 1893-94

In 1895 the Chicago Architectural Sketch Club officially became the Chicago Architectural Club. It was incorporated and no longer restricted its membership to draftsmen deciding to admit practicing architects as professional members. This restriction seems to have been relaxed with respect to the previous year's exhibition. Even though the name and membership requirements were changed the structure established in the original 1885 bylaws and the Sketch Club's objectives were retained. That year George Dean was elected president of the Club with Richard Schmidt as first vice president and Myron Hunt as the second vice president. The 1895 catalog's cover was a photograph of a bas relief by the sculptor Richard Bock. Bock would be an important collaborator, first with Perkins and then with Wright, creating sculpture for their buildings. Bock was listed as a Chicago Architectural Club member and taught a modeling class for other members. The Club's yearly catalogs, beginning in 1895, along with the issues of the *Inland Architect,* give us a complete record of the club's activities.

In 1895 *The Brochure Series,* an East Coast publication, reported on various architectural clubs in a column called "Club Notes." They covered the renamed Chicago Club along with the activities of other art and architecture associations writing, "an illustrated catalogue has become one of the important features of exhibitions of architectural drawings, and these catalogues are now exceedingly valuable records of recent progress in architecture,"[14] further noting that now "nearly every city of importance in the United States has an active and flourishing society of draughtsmen and young architects."[15]

In 1896 Richard Schmidt was the Club's president with Dwight Perkins as the first vice president. The jury selecting the work to be exhibited was made up of Irving Pond, Robert Spencer, and Theodore O. Frankel. That year, travel sketches done by Robert Spencer, Myron Hunt, and Elmer Grey were included in the show. Hunt, who was still working in the office of Shepley, Rutan & Coolidge, had returned from a trip abroad and gave an illustrated lecture to the Club, "An Impecunious Draughtsman Abroad." He showed his sketches and work by other Chicagoans

---

14 *Brochure Series* 1, no.3, March 1895, p.41.
15 Ibid., p.45.

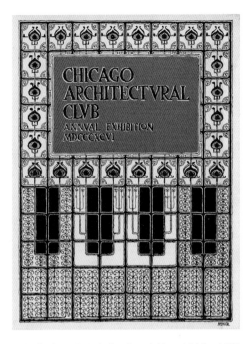

4.007. Robert Spencer. Design for Cover Chicago Architectural Club Annual. 1896

while discussing the methods of "working in the field."[16] The member's exhibit included work from other architectural clubs as well as work from schools of architecture. The catalog's cover was designed by Robert Spencer.

Included in the 1896 show was a rendering by Spencer, of the First Congregational Church of Wilmette designed along with Dwight Perkins. The collaboration on the design is interesting since Perkins was working in Steinway Hall and in 1896, Spencer's office would have still been in the Schiller Building. We know little about the collaboration as no written records of their project survive. It was done in an Arts and Crafts style and the entry porch and massing are reminiscent of Spencer's residential work. The Congregational Church was founded in 1875 and in 1905 an Arts and Crafts-style church was built at

---

16 Hunt's talk was reviewed in *Architecture and Building*, vol. 23. No.17., October 26, 1895, p.206.

4.008. Perkins and Spencer. First Congregational Church. Wilmette, Il. 1896

1125 Wilmette Avenue, although not from Perkins and Spencer's design.

The Club's biggest event continued to be the Robert Clark Testimonial Design Competition, which allowed members to compete for recognition and a gold medal. The Club's design competitions and the discussions they engendered along with lectures and social events continued to bind together the Club's membership. The Club continued to teach younger draftsmen who did studio design problems under the supervision of senior members. Perkins, Spencer, Dean, and Garden acted as tutors for members work that was exhibited, critiqued, and discussed at club meetings.

The year 1897 was significant for the Club. The president, Edward Garden, resigned and moved to St. Louis and the first vice president, Francis Kirkpatrick, became the club's new president. Kirkpatrick had worked for Burnham and Root. In 1896 he was listed at room 1107 Steinway Hall. This suggests that he was there working for Perkins before Spencer, Wright, and Hunt arrived. Kirkpatrick probably worked for Perkins and on his own commissions as well. Hasbrouck writes, "Following Kirkpatrick's assumption of the office of president ... the annual exhibition, became heavily dominated by the men who were to become known first as the Chicago School and later as the Prairie School of practitioners. That situation would continue for the next five years."[17]

The Chicago Arts and Crafts Society was also founded in 1897; an organization in which members of the Chicago Architectural Club and architects from Steinway Hall played an important role. Chicago's young architects had a growing interest in the English Arts and Crafts movement. *The House Beautiful* magazine, which began publication in Chicago in 1896, *The Studio*, an English publication available in the United States, and the *Studio Yearbook,* published in America, played major roles in introducing the English Arts and Crafts movement to the country. *House Beautiful* frequently published the work of English Arts and Crafts architects such as Voysey and Bailee Scott. With an emphasis on hand crafts, woodworking, and decorative metal work, the tenets of the Arts and Crafts movement meshed perfectly with

---

17 Hasbrouck, *The Chicago Architectural Club,* p.228–29.

the Settlement movement in America. In Chicago Jane Addams and Ellen Gates Star founded the Hull House in 1889 on Chicago's near-west side. They taught social and vocational skills to immigrants and to the socially and economically disadvantaged. On October 22, 1897, the Chicago Arts and Crafts Society was founded at Hull House "To cultivate in its members, and through them in others, a just sense of beauty," and "To call the attention of those engaged in the production of articles of everyday use to the possibility of developing in these articles the highest beauty through a vital harmony with the conditions of production."[18] Among the original members were Steinway Hall architects Robert Spencer, Mr. and Mrs. Myron Hunt, Mr. and Mrs. Dwight Perkins, Marion Mahony, Frank Wright and his clients Mr. and Mrs. Herman Winslow, as well as Irving and Allen Pond who were the architects for Hull House's various buildings. For Spencer, Wright, Hunt, Perkins, and the Pond brothers, an interest in the design of furniture and household objects was part of their growing belief that a house and its furnishings should be a totally consistent work of art.

The connection between the Steinway Hall architects, Hull House, and the formation of the Chicago Arts and Crafts Society was undoubtedly through the Pond Brothers who had moved into Steinway Hall earlier the previous year as well as through Dwight Perkins's mother and his family who were active at Hull House. Pond & Pond would be the architects for the Hull House building complex. Allen Pond, who was trained as an engineer, was a social activist. He had been secretary of Hull House since its founding in 1889, when it occupied the former residence of Charles Jerald Hull. By 1911 the Hull House Settlement occupied 13 buildings designed by Pond & Pond adjacent to and surrounding the original residence. The regular meetings of the Chicago Arts and Crafts Society were held in the Hull House's lecture hall twice a month. At this time, papers on some aspect of a craft were read and discussed. The initial programs were on stained glass, terra cotta, and metal work, with the talk on metal work given by Herman Winslow. Winslow spoke about the decorative

---

18 The Chicago Arts and Crafts Society Constitution was adopted October 31, 1897 and is published in their first exhibition catalog in conjunction with the Art Institute of Chicago. The catalog also lists the original members.

wrought iron, which his company, the Winslow Brothers, manufactured. The society arranged to exhibit along with the Chicago Architectural Club as part of its eleventh annual members show at the Art Institute. The overlap between the memberships of the two organizations with the Chicago Architectural Club holding weekly meetings must have provided a stimulating forum for the exchange of ideas as well as a locus for social interaction outside professional architectural offices.

The cover of the eleventh annual Chicago Architectural Club exhibition catalog was designed by Birch Burdette Long. The catalog listed the members and exhibits of both the Club and the Chicago Arts and Crafts Society. A review published in *Brush and Pencil*[19] commented that while there was a lot of work sent to the exhibit from other cities, the "most notable exhibits in the Chicago group are those sent over by Messrs. Shepley, Rutan & Coolidge, Pond & Pond, H. M. G. Garden, Handy & Cady, Robert C. Spencer Jr. D. H. Perkins, Frank Wright, Arthur Heun, Richard E. Schmidt, Waid & Cranford, Joseph C. Llewellyn, George R. Dean, Howard Shaw and Henry L. Ottenheimer." Of the group that were singled out, many were residents of Steinway Hall. Along with the Club's exhibit was the work of the Chicago Arts and Crafts Society, which included work sent to Chicago for the exhibition by C. R. Ashbee from London. This was the first of several Chicago exhibits Ashbee would participate in.

Shortly after the 1898 exhibit closed at the Art Institute, Chicago hosted the Fourth Annual Congress of the Central Art Association. The meeting was chaired by William Le Baron Jenney and the club provided five speakers at the meeting: Dean, Handy, Spencer, Perkins, and Louis Millet, a club member who headed the architectural education classes at the Art Institute. George Dean spoke about, "Some Modern Ideas in Architecture" and Robert Spencer addressed the question, "Is there an American Style of Domestic Architecture?" Wright, who was a member of the Central Art Association, also spoke on "Art in the Home." At the Congress, the Association committed to erect and furnish a model house costing $10,000 at the Trans-Mississippi Exposition in St. Louis. A committee to design the house was announced in the *Brickbuilder* in the May 1898 issue. The committee was

---

19 *Brush and Pencil*, 2. no.4, April 1898, p.20–29.

comprised of George Dean, Frank Wright, and Robert Spencer Jr. Plans were never completed, and no house was built. The project, had it been designed, would have given the collaborators the opportunity to address the same issues Spencer and Wright would address in the model houses they were to design a few year later for the *Ladies' Home Journal.*

It was probably during the summer of 1898, after the Club's weekly meetings ended for the year, that the group of architects Wright referred to as "the Eighteen" began dining socially to discuss architecture. Writing in 1957 in *A Testament,* Wright recalled, "before long a little luncheon club formed, comprised of myself, Bob Spencer, Gamble Rogers, Handy and Cady, Dick Schmidt, Hugh Garden, Dean, Perkins, and Shaw, several others; eighteen in all. We called the group the 'Eighteen.'... the little luncheon roundtable broke up after a year or two."[20] In 1939 Robert Spencer, addressing the Illinois Society of Architects on the subject of the "Chicago School of Architecture," remembered that "[we] used to meet for some years once a month at the old Bismarck Restaurant for a steak dinner in one of the private rooms... At these little informal dinners we could discuss our architectural problems and theories." As to the name of the group, Spencer noted, "by some we were the 'Ten Percent Club' because we believed in adequate fees."[21] Perkins remembered a luncheon club of both architects and civic leaders, that according to Irving Pond's autobiography met at the "Tip Top Inn" on the ninth floor of the Pullman Building. Both Perkins and Pond referred to the group as "The Committee on the Universe," but from Pond's description, this was clearly not the same group as the Eighteen although some historians have assumed that they were the same. Wright named only nine architects and various Wright scholars have speculated on the unmentioned members of this group. A discussion of the Eighteen and its members is included in Appendix 2.

By 1898 the Club's annual exhibit and catalog had work by most of the Steinway Hall group with only a single entry from Wright, his glass-tile decorative patterns for the Luxfer Prism Company. The catalog carried an essay by George Dean

---

20 Wright, A Testament, p.34.
21 Quoted in Brooks, The Prairie School, p.31 and Hasbrouck, op. cit., p.235.

called "Modern Architecture," which had been presented at one of the Club's meetings. In it Dean criticizes the way architecture was taught in schools, asks for the development of an American Architecture, and emphasizes the importance of nature as a source for architectural design. These were all ideas championed by Sullivan, written about by Spencer, and later echoed in Wright's first important article, "In the Cause of Architecture" from 1908.

The Jury of Admission and the Hanging Committee for 1899, the 12th annual members exhibition at the Art Institute, was made up of Dwight Perkins, Frank Handy, Alfred Granger, George Dean, Robert Spencer, Irving Pond, and Howard Van Doren Shaw. The result, as Wilbert Hasbrouck pointed out, was that "The avant-garde of Chicago architecture would have virtual dictatorial control over the club's annual exhibitions for the next four years."[22] The annual exhibition for 1899 listed 151 exhibitors, 39 from Chicago. Among those represented from Steinway Hall were Birch Burdette Long, Pond & Pond, Adamo Boari, and Robert Spencer. Boari, who had won second place in the Luxfer Prism Company competition for the design of a building using their glass tiles, exhibited an alternate proposal to his original competition entry. The street view showed his new design in the center of a wide boulevard with the building he designed as his winning entry on the opposite side of the street. Spencer's winning entry in the competition was also exhibited but, unlike Boari's drawing, was not included in the catalog. Also illustrated was Spencer's rendering for a library he designed for Geneva, Ohio. Myron Hunt had 12 items in the exhibition, these included drawings of the Catherine White double house in Evanston, Illinois and a house for J. E. Nolan also in Evanston. The rendering of the Nolan House was signed by Frances Kirkpatrick.

The year 1900 was an important year for the Chicago Architectural Club's young architects. Spencer was the first vice president as well as serving on the executive committee, and the hanging and publicity committees. Dwight Perkins served as editor of the exhibition catalog. Members of the Eighteen were well represented, as was Wright who had 11 items selected for the exhibition. Wright's projects would also be included as

---

22 Hasbrouck, op. cit., p.238.

illustrations in Spencer's article on him for the *Architectural Review,* which came out just three and a half months after the exhibition. In the catalog, Wright's work was grouped together into a special 10-page section. Neither the Club's exhibitions nor its previous catalogs had featured the work of a single exhibitor in this way. In spite of the economic recession in the 1890s Wright's residential practice was flourishing and as Kathryn Smith wrote in *Wright on Exhibit,* the Club's show "announced that he was open for business as a residential architect of exquisite sensibility while the *Architectural Review* presented an important new American architect of great originality."[23] Both Wright's exhibition at the Art Institute and the article on his work had been arranged by Robert Spencer to serve as the announcement of a new direction in American residential architecture. This was a new direction that not only represented the ideas of the Steinway Hall collaborative circle but exemplified them.

In reaction to the exhibition of the previous year, which some Club members felt had been hijacked by the Steinway Hall architects, many of the group were intentionally excluded from the 1901 catalog. Photographs of Sullivan's Guaranty Building in Buffalo were featured but the catalog still had projects by Hugh Garden, Pond & Pond, and Howard Van Doren Shaw, who were members of the Eighteen. A further exception were two farmhouse renderings by Robert Spencer that were included in the exhibit. The most space was devoted to six drawings by Elmer Grey, who practiced in Milwaukee and would become Myron Hunt's partner after they both moved to California.

The Clubs 1902 annual exhibition opened in March of that year, with Robert Spencer serving as the Club's president, George Dean as the editor of the exhibition catalog, and Dean, Spencer and Richard Schmidt on the jury of admission. By 1902 the Club exhibition and catalog again featured projects by the Steinway Hall architects and the Eighteen. These all shared similar design features with the work Wright exhibited, low hipped roofs, large roof overhangs, second-floor string courses, and horizontal groupings of casement windows: particularly in George Dean's project for a dining hall for Strawberry Island,

---

23 Smith, *Wright on Exhibit,* p.8.

his Alpha Delta Phi fraternity house for Cornell University,[24] and Spencer's "Gardner's Cottage at Lake Delevan." The Club's exhibition catalog also had an article by Spencer on farmhouse design. It followed his farmhouse projects exhibited the previous year and his work for the *Ladies' Home Journal,* which published a series of Spencer's model farmhouses. Myron Hunt's Catherine White House in Evanston visually related to the work as well. Elmer Grey exhibited a house he had designed for the *Ladies' Home Journal* model house program.[25] Dwight Perkins exhibited a Settlement house and gymnasium building. Pond & Pond, Hugh Garden, and Richard Schmidt also had work selected for inclusion in that year's catalog.

The 1902 exhibit provided Wright with what was essentially a one man show, again in his own gallery space at the Art Institute. Kathryn Smith writes that Spencer, Schmidt, and Dean, "breaking with club precedent, accorded him [*Wright*] privileges never given to others. First, he was allocated a separate gallery at the Art Institute and the freedom to design the installation. Second, he was allowed more items than anyone else, sixty-four in total: Wright expanded his exhibition technique beyond simulacra-drawings and photographs to include furniture and decorative arts such as lamps, bowls, vases and lighting, which made up at least half of his display. In addition, the catalogue, which was monopolized by progressives, contained a fourteen-page section devoted to the Oak Park architect titled in his own graphic style 'The Work of Frank Lloyd Wright,' certainly selected and designed by Wright, which amounted to a small monograph in and of itself."[26] The installation was designed and furnished in the manner of his Oak Park Studio. The walls were covered with brown burlap with strips of brown oak and wood framed drawings hung from picture rails. Desks and tables, designed by Wright for various residential commissions displayed decorative objects, bowls, and tall, copper vases filled with dried branches. Included among Wright's projects were Sullivanesque works

---

24 Both illustrated in the George Dean entry in Appendix 2. The plans for the Alpha Delta Phi men's fraternity are illustrated in the Architectural Club Annual for 1902 and should be compared to the phallus shaped plan for a brothel designed by C. N. Ledoux.

25 Grey, *The Ladies' Home Journal,* September 1901. This suggests that Grey was friendly with Spencer and the Steinway Hall group.

26 Smith, *Wright on Exhibit,* p.9.

such as the Isidore Heller House and a number of breakthrough projects with low-pitched hipped roofs, wide overhangs, and horizontal runs of casement windows ganged together, resembling his *Ladies' Home Journal* house designs.

By having his own gallery space, Wright was able to go beyond the display of draftsmanship, the original purpose of the club's exhibitions. Art and Crafts architects such as, Voysey, Mackintosh, and Bailee Scott, admired by Chicago's younger architects along with their continental counterparts, Berlage, Behrens, and Olbrich, all designed entire environments. These were comprised of furniture, lamps, rugs, and fabrics. By exhibiting furnishings, Wright sought to position himself in relation to these architects as well as putting forward a complete vision for a new type of American house.

Not all the reviews of the 1902 exhibit were positive and some questioned the prominence of Wright's work. The review in *The American Architect* read, "Collected under the banner of Mr. Frank L. Wright ... one of the smaller galleries is given up entirely to his exhibit. From the standpoint of professional ethics it seems questionable whether such a pronounced personal exhibit should have its place in a general architectural exhibition, as it certainly smacks of advertising more than anything else ... why in an architectural exhibit, the chief one in Chicago for the year, why should Mr. Wright's tables and chairs, and his teazles and milkweeds and pine-branches cover so much space ... If indeed the Club's exhibitions at the Art Institute were intended to promote the work of club members to the public, the question is, why would the Exhibition Committee choose to prominently promote Wright's work, even recognizing his genius, over the work of its other members?"[27] While much has been written about this event by Wright scholars, only Hasbrouck suggested that, "Clearly the goal was to present the work of the young disciples of Sullivan who were developing a new architecture."[28]

Once again, there was a reaction to the 1902 exhibit among the conservative members of the Club. A rule was adopted to prohibit special exhibits of the work of an individual. Writing in retrospect about the Chicago Architectural Club's exhibitions,

---

27 *American Architect and Building News*, 76, April 25, 1902, p.29--30.
28 Hasbrouck, the Chicago Architectural Club, p.298.

Robert Craik McLean, who had moved to Minneapolis to edit the *Western Architect*, observed, "One year almost the entire exhibit was monopolized by a member for his private showing; and whose work had undoubted merit and interest, but who took an unfair and unwarranted advantage of this to the general obscuring of other exhibitions. It was probably for this reason that the special exhibit, otherwise a most attractive and logical method, was abolished. But the members who take exception were wrong, for it is the club, and the advancement of their art that counts and not the individual."[29] In featuring Wright's work, Spencer, Dean, and Schmidt were promoting a shared vision of architecture. They must have agreed that Wright's work was both the most developed and articulate example of what they jointly believed represented a new direction in American architecture. It is important to remember that in 1900 Spencer had written that Wright's work, "embodied new thought and new ideas" and that "Mr. Wright has been doing for the typical residence and apartment house what Sullivan has done for the theater and office building."[30]

---

29 McLean, *Western Architect*. April 1909, p.43.
30 Spencer, "The Work of Frank Lloyd Wright," *The Architectural Review*, June 1900, p.66.

4.009 Chicago Architectural Club Exhibit, 1907, at the Art Institute of Chicago. Wright's gallery.
Models are from l-r, the Larkin Building, the Abraham Lincoln Center, and Unity Temple.

In 1907 Irving Pond, Alfred Granger, and Howard Van Doren Shaw were on the jury of admission and decided that Wright would again be given his own separate gallery. Wright was allowed to design and furnish the gallery with his furniture, stained-glass windows, and his drawings, also exhibiting plaster models of the Larkin Building, Unity Temple, and the third version of his and Dwight Perkins's design for the Abraham Lincoln Center. Why Pond, Shaw, and Granger allowed Wright to have his own exhibit after the criticisms of the 1902 show, is unknown. While Pond was one of the Eighteen, was a considered a progressive architect, and worked in Steinway Hall, he was certainly not one of Wright's supporters. Pond's autobiography suggests that he considered Wright a narcissistic egomaniac. Likewise, Shaw, while he was also one of the Eighteen, is generally thought of as an Arts and Crafts practitioner and an eclectic architect. Wright had publicly criticized Shaw for his continuing use of historic forms. Clearly these men had no personal reasons to promote Wright's career. The only explanation is that, in spite of any personal animosity, they must have recognized Wright's genius and felt that his work best represented the new directions in architecture coming out of Chicago.

Chapter 4

IN STEINWAY HALL

5.001. Perkins and Selby. Steinway Hall. Chicago, Il. 1895. Main Entrance.

❝ *The best things come ... from the talents that*
are members of a group: every man works
better when he has companions working in
the same line, and yielding to the stimulus of
suggestion, comparison and emulation.

Henry James, 1901

Steinway Hall would figure prominently in the history of early 20th-century Chicago Architecture. The August 1894 issue of the *Inland Architect* carried the following notice: "Architects Perkins & Selby: Have completed drawings for the ten-story "Temple of Music" to be erected on Van Buren Street between Wabash Avenue and Michigan Avenue. It will be of pressed brick and terra cotta front, of fireproof construction, have hardwood finish, marble mosaic and tile work, steam heating, electric light, elevators and all the necessary conveniences; ... It will be used for musical purposes exclusively, excepting a recital hall occupying most of the first and second stories, which will be used Sunday morning as a church by the Swedenborgian Society. This society will also occupy offices in the building ... The old Swedenborgian church now on the ground is being torn down and building will be commenced as soon as the ground is clear."[1] The church building which stood on the site had been dedicated in 1882 and was built to be The Church of the New Jerusalem, the Swedenborgian Society's main location after two of their five New Jerusalem churches burned down in the Chicago fire of 1871.

---

1 *Inland Architect*, August 1894, p.10.

LYON, POTTER & CO.
(STEINWAY PIANOS)

5.002. Perkins and Selby. Steinway Hall.
Chicago, Il 1895. Drawing by Henry Holt.

5.003. Perkins and Selby. Steinway Hall.
Chicago, Il 1895. Looking East.

Founded in 1817, the Swedenborgian Society's headquarters were in Bryn Athyn, Pennsylvania. Its teachings were based on both the New and the Old Testament and the theological works of Emanuel Swendenborg. The Swedenborgian Church did not see itself as a denomination of traditional Christianity, they believed in one God, that Christ was simply his manifestation, and that the afterlife was open to all persons who rejected sin, regardless of religion. The Chicago Swedenborgian society was founded in 1835 and by the 1890s included many prominent Chicagoans, including Daniel Burnham and Joseph Sears who built the suburb of Kenilworth. The church's pastor, the Reverend Lewis Pyle Mercer, took over the newly formed Union Swedenborgian Church of Chicago in 1877. In 1881 the Chicago Church was united with the Chicago Society of the New Jerusalem. Mercer was, along with Wright's uncle Jenkins Lloyd Jones, an organizing member of the World Congress of Religions that met in Chicago during the 1893 World's Columbian Exposition.

By 1894 the Society decided, for financial reasons, to lease its centrally located land to the New Temple Music Company. They joined with the Music Company in a mortgage which covered the land, leasehold rights and the cost of the proposed building amounting to $140,000. The final cost of the building being about $320,000—not including the land. The church had rented its facilities out for meetings of local women's clubs and other associations and it was intended that the new building, which would be called Steinway Hall, after its main tenant, would function in the same manner.

The announcement in the *Inland Architect* listed W.H. and F.A. Winslow[2] as the owners and developers of the building, along with the New Temple Music Company. The Winslow Brothers Company were makers of decorative and ornamental iron and bronze work for buildings throughout the country. They made ornamental work for Adler and Sullivan as well as Daniel Burnham. Winslow Brothers had produced all the decorative iron work for Sullivan's Schlessinger & Meyer building (later Carson Pirie Scott and Company) and it was at Sullivan's office that William Winslow met Frank Wright. Winslow would

2 For a brief biography of William Winslow see Eaton, *Two Chicago Architects and Their Clients: Frank Lloyd Wright and Howard Van Doren Shaw*.

hire Wright as the architect for his River Forest House—soon after Wright started his own practice. The Winslow Brothers also would produce the decorative iron entry canopy for the new Steinway Hall. William Winslow was a member of the Society of Ethical Culture, one of the religious groups that would hold their meetings at Steinway Hall.

The commission for Steinway Hall probably came through Daniel Burnham. By 1893, Dwight Perkins wanted to start his own practice. He was persuaded by Burnham to run Burnham's Chicago practice while he ran the south-side office established to produce the construction drawings for the Chicago World's Fair. In exchange, Burnham promised to help Perkins launch his own practice. As a prominent architect and a member of the Sweden-borgian Society in Chicago, it is understandable how the commission for Steinway Hall would have come to Daniel Burnham. However, it is unclear how he convinced the Society and the Church to employ Perkins. In the year following the opening of the Fair, Chicago was experiencing a major economic depression. Burnham's office was slow, and he was encouraging his employees to take independent work. Perkins probably left Burnham's office mid-1893 around the time Burnham resigned as the Fair's chief of construction. Dwight Perkins's daughter Eleanor wrote in her unpublished memoir *Perkins of Chicago*, "In June when the Fair was in full swing, Mr. Burnham's duty to it ceased and he came back to his own office. As agreed, four years before, Dwight was to leave the office in December and begin private practice." Knowing Perkins intended to leave, Burnham asked Ernest Graham, Charles Atwood, and E.C. Shankland to be his partners. Clearly, it would have been awkward for Perkins to continue in a position that gave him more authority than Burnham's new partners.

Perkins's first commission was the Stevens Point Normal School in Wisconsin, which was probably done in part while he was still in Burnham's office. When he left, it was with George W. Selby, who had also worked for Burnham. They opened their practice in the Marshal Field Annex Building, a Burnham & Company commission. It was here that they prepared the drawings for Steinway Hall.

The Steinway Hall building was built rapidly, and it was reported that the firm of Perkins & Selby opened a new office on

May 1 of 1895 in suite 1107 of the building. Hasbrouck wrote, "the partnership was apparently not successful ... The office at 1107 Steinway Hall was a small room on the east side of the eleventh floor with its own winding staircase to the loft above ...[3] It seems that Perkins had intended to move into Steinway Hall from the beginning. The stair from room 1107 was probably built during construction of the building. He was one of the first tenants to move in."[4] In addition to the stairway connecting room 1107 to the loft, Perkins revised the original building plans to add skylights to the attic loft. Later windows were added to provide additional light to the eastern part of the loft space.

The main tenant for the new Temple Music Building to be called Steinway Hall, was to be Lyon, Potter & Company, the Chicago distributors for Steinway Pianos. In William Steinway's diary he records the following from the Board of Directors minutes for February 24, 1894: "Resolved that the name Steinway Hall be applied to the Hall or building recently erected by the Temple Music Building Co. of Chicago, Illinois on Van Buren Street between Wabash and Michigan Avenue, Chicago, be given to Lyon, Potter & Company our present dealers in Chicago."[5] The first six stories of the building were occupied by Lyon, Potter & Company's piano showrooms and their offices. The upper five floors above the showrooms, office, and auditorium contained office space plus studios for musicians. There were two halls, one occupying the second and third stories for recital and lectures, and a second, smaller lecture and recital hall on the seventh floor.

The top floor would come to be occupied almost entirely by architect's offices, beginning with Perkins in room 1107 and then Pond & Pond in 1108.

Perkins would have been in Steinway Hall for almost two years before he was joined by Spencer, Hunt, and Wright. Wright suggests in *An Autobiography* that they all moved in together shortly after the building was completed, "Dwight had a loft in his new Steinway Hall building—too large for him. So we

---

3 It was also possible to get to the loft from a public staircase on the west side of the main corridor.

4 Hasbrouck, *The Chicago Architectural Club*, p.213.

5 From William Steinway, diaries, http://americanhistory.si.edu/steinwaydiary. Quoted in Kris Hartzell, "Steinway Hall," unpublished paper, November 2012.

5.004. Perkins and Selby. Steinway Hall. Chicago, Il. 1895. Main Recital Hall.

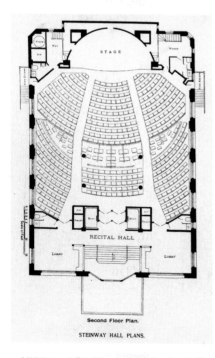

5.005. Steinway Hall. 2nd-Floor plan showing Main Recital Hall.

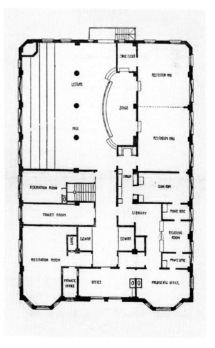

5.006. Steinway Hall. 7th-Floor Lecture Hall.

formed a group—outer office in common—workrooms screened apart in the loft of Steinway Hall."[6] Before Wright, Spencer, and Hunt arrived Perkins occupied the loft space where he employed Francis W. Kirkpatrick, Henry F. Holt, and Marion Mahony Perkins's cousin, both of whom went to work for Perkins's after graduating from MIT. Holt prepared the rendering of Steinway Hall that was used in the Lyon, Potter & Company's newspaper advertisements. During these two years, despite the depression, Perkins had at least twelve commissions divided almost equally between commercial and residential work.

In 1895 *The Critic* published a lengthy description of the building, "The recent opening of Steinway Hall is important to the city because we have long needed here a small place for lectures and chamber concerts ... the new hall seats about 700 and stands the test of sound perfectly. Its arrangement is capital with one gallery and a line of boxes behind the parquet; the decorations are most felicitous ... Mr. Dwight H. Perkins is the architect of the Hall and the high building in Van Buren Street which contains it. The design of the exterior is excellent in its simplicity

---

6 Frank Lloyd Wright, *An Autobiography*, 1938, p.128.

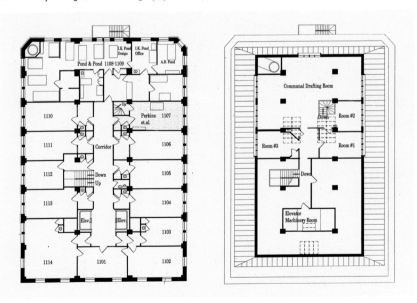

5.007. Steinway Hall. Plans of 11th and 12th floor (shared loft). Drawn by David Waldo for Wilbert Hasbrouck.

and imposing strength ... Mr. Perkins is a young architect, who since he can do work of this kind, deserves to be known.[7]

In the Spring of 1897, Perkins invited his friends to join him, as reported in *The Economist* from March 13, 1897, "D.H. Perkins, secretary of the Illinois Chapter of the American Institute of Architect, the founder of what promises to be a very interesting colony of young architects who have established themselves in the upper stories of Steinway Hall. It will be recalled that Mr. Perkins was for many years with Mr. Burnham and left to practice on his own account, the most important building he has thus far designed being Steinway Hall. Here he established his own office, and during the past winter has rearranged the rear of the eleventh story, which with the attic above, afford unusually attractive and commodious office for a number of other architects. The idea embraces a good-sized reception room with doors leading to the private offices of the architects, the same has been adopted in some of the large buildings by the medical profession. Among those who have offices here are Robert C. Spencer, who was successful some time ago in winning a scholarship which afforded him a year's travel in Europe; Myron Hunt, who was until recently with Shepley, Rutan & Coolidge; and Frank L. Wright. The reception room has a floor of mosaic, is brightly lighted and has a telephone room to the side, and the offices are furnished in keeping with the ideas of the occupants. On the floor above they have their separate drafting rooms, divided by movable partitions so they can be taken down and replaced within a very short time, when the occupants desire to give exhibitions. They have also a photographic dark room, which comprises part of the equipment. Adjoining the establishment referred to on the third floor (sic) a suite is being beautifully finished for Messrs. Pond & Pond, architects who are now in the Venetian building. Their suite embraces four or five rooms and is distinct from the others."[8]

Repeating this story, the Sunday *Chicago Inter Ocean*[9] for May 2, 1897, in their Chicago real estate section wrote, "an

---

7 *The Critic: A Weekly Review of Literature and the Arts*, Vol. XXIII, No.692, N. Y., May 25, 1895, p.10.

8 *The Economist*, Chicago: The Economist Publishing Company, March 13, 1897, p.287.

9 *The Inter Ocean* was a Chicago daily newspaper published from 1865 to 1914; originally called the *Chicago Republican*, it was renamed the *Inter Ocean* in 1872.

interesting experiment in architectural practice has recently been inaugurated in Steinway Hall by four young men, R.C. Spencer, who took the Rotch traveling scholarship in 1888: Frank Wright, who was formerly with Adler & Sullivan: Myron Hunt, who came from the office of Shepley, Rutan & Coolidge, and Dwight Heald Perkins, from the office of D.H. Burnham. These young men, believing in the principles of cooperation rather than in the idea of competition, have united in a general office, the expenses of which are prorated according to the amount of use each one makes of the telephone, typewriter, etc. Uniting in this way upon impersonal expenses, they keep their private offices and their practice absolutely individual. It is essentially a co-operative scheme and they are in no sense partners. At the same time they have the advantage of great reductions in rent and running expenses. This, however, is not the greatest advantage which they feel that they gain by the arrangement. Convinced that the time has come when Chicago is ready to demand more artistic work as well as buildings which will meet every demand of utility, they have set themselves high standards, which by mutual criticisms and encouragement they strive to maintain. The pecuniary advantage derived from co-operation they feel to be insignificant besides the benefit of the inspiration coming from association with each other and contact with each other's ideas. This experiment is certainly worth a trial and there seems every reason for prophesying for it a brilliant success. It is evidence of a progressive spirit and is along general lines of social evolution." We hear the expression of the goal of the collaborative circle, perhaps as voiced by Spencer or Perkins to the author of the article, "*the benefit of the inspiration coming from association with each other and contact with each other's ideas.*"

In his memoir the sculptor Richard Bock wrote, "Early in March of 1896 I received a letter from the architect Dwight Heald Perkins asking me to call at his office in the Steinway Building in regard to some work."[10] Perkins had the commission for the Machinery and Electricity building at the Trans-Mississippi Exposition in Omaha and wanted to include sculptural groupings at the building's corners. The following year, Bock would begin his long collaboration with Wright. He wrote, "Our

---

10 Bock, *Memoirs of an American Artist*, p.57.

5.008. Dwight Perkins. Machinery and Electrical Building. Trans-Mississippi Exposition. 1898.

working association began in the Steinway Hall Building where a group of similar souls in architecture had built their respective nests. Among them were Wright, who was always the dominant character wherever he was; Dwight Heald Perkins, who had been the architect for the Steinway Hall Building and had leased the loft on the upper floor and then sublet it to the other aspiring young architects including Myron Hunt, who I recall soon left for California; Arthur Huen, a very attractive personality; Robert Spencer, an artistic chap, soaring in the clouds; Tomlins, [Henry Webster Tomlinson] who had the misfortune of working with Wright and being unhappy and grumbling about him to me; and a draughtsman named Probst who was working with Perkins, and later became a well-known architect."[11] Probst was to become a partner in the firm of Graham, Anderson, Probst & White, a successor firm to D.H. Burnham & Company. Probst probably worked for Perkins in Burnham's office before leaving to work in Steinway Hall.

Spencer, Wright, and Hunt arrived in Steinway Hall, all fairly new to the practice of architecture, all of about the same age—29–30—with Spencer the oldest at 32. Along with Perkins they were ready to develop a shared vision of architecture, all having worked for acknowledged leaders in the profession, knowing each other professionally and socially, and, except for Wright, sharing similar educational backgrounds.

---

11 Ibid., p.67.

Numerous architects would list their address as Steinway Hall, many working for Perkins, Wright, Spencer, and Hunt as shared employees or working on their own commissions in the studio loft. Wright remembered that among those who joined them in the loft, "George Dean was another and Hugh Garden. Burch Long was a young and talented 'renderer' at this time and we took him into the Steinway loft with us."[12] Long had worked for Wright when he was in the Schiller Building. Wright had had a shared office there, in room 1501, with his friend Cecil Corwin, who he knew from J.L. Silsbee's office. Wright was in the Schiller Building from 1893 until his move to Steinway Hall. Robert Spencer also had an office in the Schiller building in room 1505.

According to Eleanor Perkins's biography of her father, Jules Guerin, the famous renderer, remembered for his illustrations for the 1909 Plan for Chicago, also worked in the Steinway Hall loft. Webster Tomlinson, briefly Wright's partner, credited as having collaborated on a series of residential commissions, was in Steinway Hall, although business directories list him, along with Wright, in room 1106 rather than 1107 for the year 1901. Tomlinson remained in Steinway Hall and in 1909 listed his address as room 809 which was Herman Von Holst's office.

Also, in the Steinway Hall loft were Adamo Boari and Arthur H. Niemz. Niemz had worked with Dankmar Adler. Boari came to Chicago in 1892 from Italy and worked for D.H. Burnham on the World's Fair. He moved into the Steinway Hall loft at the same time as Spencer, Wright, and Hunt. It is possible that Perkins knew him through Daniel Burnham as well as from the Chicago Architectural Club. He did work for Wright from time to time and Wilbert Hasbrouck has identified published renderings of Wright's buildings that were done by Boari. He worked in the loft until 1904 when he moved to Mexico after winning the competition for the Mexico City Opera House. Wright described Boari in 1957 as, "I remember an ebullient Italian, Boari by name, who won the competition to build the National Grand Opera House in Mexico City. He came into our attic space, temporarily, to make

---

12 Frank Lloyd Wright, *An Autobiography*, 1932, p.128. Arthur Dean listed his office in Steinway Hall, but George Dean is at 218 La Salle Street. Hugh Garden lists his office at 362 Ontario Street from 1896–1911, not in Steinway Hall, suggesting that Wright's memory might have been mistaken and that Garden only freelanced for him doing renderings. Beginning in 1897 Edward and Frank Garden, Hugh Garden's brothers, also list their offices at 362 Ontario Street.

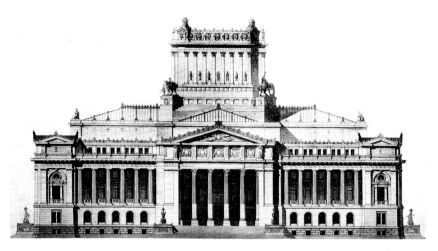

5.009. Adamo Boari. Mexican National Capital Competition. 1900.

plans for that edifice. He was far from all of us but observing, curious and humorous. He would look at something I was doing and say with a good natured grunt, 'Huh, temperance-architecture!' turn on his heel with another grunt and go back to his Italian Renaissance 'gorge' as I called it in retaliation."[13] Wright suggests that Boari wasn't really a part of their group in spite of the time he spent with them in Steinway Hall.

In *A Testament* (1957) Wright offered the following description of his move to Steinway Hall, "I with those nearest me rented a vacant loft in Steinway Hall; a building Dwight Perkins had built. But Spencer, Perkins, Hunt and Birch Long (clever boy renderer) moved in with me. Together we subdivided the big attic into studio-like draughting rooms. We felt the big attic especially appropriate for our purpose. We each had a share in a receptionist and stenographer in common as "office force" on the floor below, trying to please us all. The entrance door panel was a single sheet of clear plate glass, the second one in existence, like the entrance door to the Schiller offices, with all our names thereon in the same kind of gold letters." Wright describes himself as the central figure. "I ... patiently worked on their plans when I could be helpful. My most enthusiastic advocate, young Myron Hunt [Hunt was one year older than

---

13 Wright, *A Testament*, p.35.

5.010. Myron Hunt. Catherine White House. Evanston, Il. 1898.
The second-floor loggia shown glass enclosed has been opened and restored.

Wright], was first among them to set up in Evanston, Illinois, as a 'modern,' with the building of the White House. That was a characteristic instance. I believe myself helpful to them all."[14] The house Wright refers to is the double house Hunt designed for Catherine White the widow of lawyer Hugh White and her niece in Evanston, Illinois in 1897. Perhaps this statement is the source of the questioned attribution of the design which is often credited to Wright.

Of the original occupants of Perkins's collaborative space, Spencer moved into Steinway Hall in 1897 and formed a partnership with Horace Powers in 1905. The firm of Spencer and Powers was listed as practicing in 1107 Steinway Hall.

Wright moved into Steinway Hall in 1897, listing his office as 1107, the eleventh-floor office and twelfth-floor loft drafting room. In 1897 Wright was working on his design for glass tiles for the Luxfer Prism Company in Steinway Hall. However, later that year he moved his office to the eleventh floor of the Rookery building adjacent to the Luxfer Prism offices. The 1898 *Chicago Business Directory* lists Wright in room 1123 of the Rookery. After his move Wright produced a small printed announcement noting that thereafter his studio would be in Oak Park, except between the hours of twelve o'clock and two, when he would be at his downtown office in room 1119 of the Rookery. The brochure noted that the Rookery office was strictly "for business

---

14 Ibid., p.34–35.

purposes, consultation and matters in connection with superintendence."[15] In 1901 Wright formed a partnership with Webster Tomlinson and moved back to Steinway Hall. They were in room 1106 adjacent to Perkins, Spencer, and Hunt. Wright is listed in Chicago Business Directories as being a tenant of 1106 from 1901 through 1907. While Wright's design work was being done in the Oak Park Studio, he was spending many of his afternoons in Steinway Hall, meeting with his clients who worked downtown. He certainly would have had continued interaction with his friends in the loft.

Dwight Perkins moved out of Steinway Hall in 1906, when he became the chief architect for the Chicago Board of Education, a position he held until 1910. He didn't return to Steinway Hall until the late 1920s as part of a partnership he formed with Melville, Clarke, Chatten, and Hammond. Chatten and Hammond had been on the eleventh floor in room 1112. Myron Hunt moved into Steinway Hall in 1897 and left for California in 1903. Adamo Boari moved into the Steinway Building in 1897 and then left in 1903 after winning the competition for Mexican National Capital Building and receiving the commission for the Mexico City Opera House, the Palacio de Bellas Artes.[16]

The second architectural office to locate in Steinway Hall was Pond & Pond. They moved there in 1895 occupying rooms 1108 and 1109 next to the first floor of Perkins's collaborative office. Pond & Pond had the longest tenancy remaining in the Steinway Hall until 1923.

Perhaps the best description of working in Steinway Hall and the ambience there comes to us is from a letter written by Roy A. Lippincott who would have been working for Herman Von Holst at the time. Lippincott married Walter Burley Griffin's sister and went to Australia with Griffin and Mahony in 1914 after they won the competition for the design of the capital city of Canberra. The letter describes Steinway Hall sometime after Wright departed, as Wright is not mentioned. The letter was written to Mark L. Peisch in 1954 and it is quoted in his book *The*

---

15 Hasbrouck, *The Chicago Architectural Club*, p.217.

16 Adamo Boari was born in Ferrara, Italy in 1863 and studied at the University of Bologna. He went to the United States from South America to work on the World's Fair. In 1898 and, 1899 while still in Chicago he built several churches in Mexico City along with the Templo Expiatorio and the Palacio Postal. He then returned to Mexico City in 1903-04. In 1916 he returned to Italy and was the architect of the new theater of Ferrara. He died in Rome in 1928.

Chicago School of Architecture. Lippincott wrote, "In Steinway Hall was a congeries of architects. Arthur Heun, society man and conservative, Webster Tomlinson, interested in slide rule computations for the design of concrete beams, the Pond brothers,

I.K. [Irving Kane Pond] one time president of the A.I.A. and A.B. [Irving's brother Allen Bartlet Pond], bachelors who had their offices near the top of the building and roamed through all the offices as though they owned them, to the delight of the real owners. My introduction to I.K. was one day when Von [von Holst] was out, and he came into the office, mounted my drafting board and standing on his hands with feet in the air gave me a criticism of the work thereon. Up in the penthouse Robert Spencer and Horace Powers had an attractive office which was shared by Walter Griffin and in which the Federal Capital [Canberra] drawings were made … We were all good friends, in and out of each other's offices, as though they were our own. We all knew about the work the others were doing, [and] worked for each other from time to time as pressures necessitated."[17]

5.011. Irving K. Pond. 1927. Pond was an athlete and amateur acrobat who often did back flips to amuse onlookers even when he was in his 70s.

Among the other important architects who worked in the Steinway Hall loft was Marion Mahony, mentioned above. Her enormous importance to Wright's practice is still being reassessed. She graduated from MIT in 1894, the second woman in the United States to receive an architectural degree. After graduating she went to work for her first cousin Dwight Perkins in the Marshall Field Annex building. She wrote in *The Magic of America*, an account of her life, "One year in the office of D.H. Perkins getting

17 Peisch, Mark L., *The Chicago School of Architecture, Early Followers of Sullivan and Wright*, New York: Random House, 1964, p.37.

out at that time the working drawings of Steinway Hall, with the whole drafting force lending me a hand to put me through my paces, gave me a sound foundation in that field. At the end of that year with a drop in the pressure of office work I was dropped and went into the offices of F.L. Wright ... A rendered drawing of one of Spencer's houses was pinned up on Wright's office wall."[18] She worked for Wright in his first office in the Schiller Building in 1895 and moved with Wright to Steinway Hall in 1897. In 1898 she moved to Wright's Oak Park Studio. While Wright would later characterize his employees as young draftsmen who he trained, Mahony, his most important employee, was quite accomplished. She was the first woman to pass the architectural licensing exam in Illinois in 1898.[19] When she went to work for Wright, she was a knowledgeable professional. Her future husband, Walter Burley Griffin, who had graduated from the University of Illinois in 1899 went to work in Steinway Hall doing work for both Spencer, Perkins, and for Adamo Boari. While working for Perkins in 1900, Paul Kruty credits Griffin with the design of Perkins's cottage on Bustin's Island in Maine,[20] although the plan is identical to one of Spencer's *Ladies' Home Journal* houses, which wasn't published the following year. He then worked for Tomlinson in Steinway Hall, taking the licensing exam in 1901 and moving to Wright's Oak Park Studio that same year. After he left Wright in the spring of 1906 to establish his own practice, Griffin moved back into Steinway Hall where he also did work for Dwight Perkins, while Marion Mahony continued to work at Wright's Oak Park Studio part time.

When Wright left Chicago for Europe in 1909, Mahony and Herman Horst von Holst, working from Steinway Hall, would take over completing Wright's projects then under contract. Before that, Von Holst is listed as having an office in room 907, Steinway Hall in 1909. In 1911 Mahony married Walter Burley Griffin. Working with him in Steinway Hall, they won the design competition for the Australia's new capital city of Canberra in

18 Marion Mahony Griffin, *The Magic of America*, electronic edition, p.30, Section IV. The online version of the copy in the possession of the Art Institute of Chicago. Paul Kurty speculates that this rendering would have been the Stanley Grepe House (1894) an influence on Wright's Nathan Moore House (1895).

19 This was the first year the exam was given under Illinois' new licensing law.

20 Kruty, Paul, "A Prairie-School House in Coastal Maine," *Nineteenth Century*. Vol. 27, no.2, fall 2007, Victorian Society in America.

1911. They then moved their office briefly to the top floor of the Monroe Building, before leaving for Australia in 1914.[21]

About Steinway Hall Mahony would write, "A considerable number of the young Chicago School of Architecture had already made similar use of attic space in the Steinway Hall building of Dwight Perkins. A considerable number of the young Chicago School moved in here, Spencer, Powers, Griffin, Wright, Bowrie [she probably is referring to Boari], Hunt, etc. Wright whose early work was without distinction was only just out of Sullivan's office and only now was following the Japanese emphasis of the horizontal line which had considerable influence on the whole group."[22]

Lastly, while they were not part of the group in room 1107 and the loft, Irving and his brother Allen Pond were important residents of Steinway Hall. They occupied rooms 1108 and 1109 which they moved into in 1895 shortly after Perkins moved into his loft space. Their offices occupied the entire north end of the building with their entryway directly adjacent to Perkins, et. al. in room 1107. Irving Pond who was an original founder of the Chicago Architectural Sketch Club would later be national president of the American Institute of Architects. While he was a generation older than the architects in Perkins's loft, he was an active, prominent, and well respected, member of the architectural community. Pond & Pond were influenced by the Arts and Crafts movement and their work was considered "progressive." In his autobiography, Irving Pond doesn't specifically discuss his interaction with the architects in Perkins's loft, but there is every reason to believe that they were aware of each other's work. The most interesting comparison between projects from this period would be the possible influence that Pond's work had on Wright's commission for Unity Temple built in 1904.

In addition to the development of Unitarian worship spaces and meeting halls,[23] it is possible that Pond's 1895 University Congregational Church built in Chicago's Hyde Park was an influence on Wright's future design for Unity Temple. Its interior

---

21 Barry Byrne who worked for Walter Burley Griffin and Marion Mahony Griffin took over the lease of their space in the Monroe Building

22 Marion Mahony Griffin, *The Magic of America*, electronic edition, p.83, Section IV: "The Individual Battle."

23 For a discussion see Siry, Joseph M., *Unity Temple, Frank Lloyd Wright and Architecture for Liberal Religion*, Cambridge: the Press Syndicate of the University of Cambridge, 1996.

development may have also further influenced Wrights interest in the spatial development of cruciform plans. Wright could have known the building, as his house for Isadore Heller would have been under construction in Hyde Park at the time Pond's church was being completed.[24]

---

24 Pointed out to the author by David Swan.

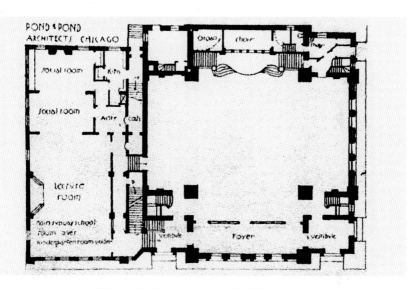

5.012. Pond and Pond. University Congregational Church. Chicago, Il. 1895.

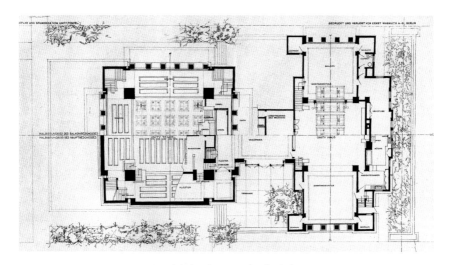

5.013. Frank Lloyd Wright. Unity Temple. Oak Park, Il. 1906.

5.0014 and 5.0015. Pond. University Congregational Church. Chicago, Il. 1895.

Pond's was an influential voice among Chicago's younger architects, and he published articles and books on architectural history and theory. He was a near contemporary of Sullivan's, but not a follower. We know from *The Autobiography of Irving K. Pond: The Sons of Mary and Elihu*, that he found Wright arrogant and egotistical. Philosophically, Pond felt that architecture should not be a literal interpretation of nature, and that Sullivan's organic architecture was best understood as a metaphor for the development of a building's parts from the concept of the entire structure. About ornament, he wrote, derisively, "I gave up, in so far as seemed possible, the use of applied ornament until such time as I should have evolved an ornament which would fit into my social philosophy and into the structural and aesthetic integrity of my design ... I saw even then the falsity underlying the proposition that horizontality should mark the architecture of the prairie because it reflected the horizontality of the region," and more derisively he wrote, "no real soul-satisfying architecture or theory of architecture, ever was evolved in the mind of a man who confused his love of nature with his theory of architectural design and sought to embrace both in any arrangement of pussy willow branches in a Japanese vase."[25]

Even with Wright's withdrawal to the Studio in Oak Park and Perkins absence while at the Chicago Board of Education, Roy Lippincott's letter indicates that Steinway Hall remained a place of collaborative work and intellectual interaction. Beyond the weekly meetings of the Chicago Architectural Club, these

25 Pond, Irving K., David Swan and Tatum, Terry ed., *The Autobiography of Irving K. Pond, The Sons of Mary and Elihu*, Oak Park: The Hyoogen Press Inc., 2009, p.166–67.

men were in daily contact with one another. They shared ideas and were aware of what each was designing. They often shared employees who would have transferred not only technical knowledge but design ideas. They had formed a community around Steinway Hall and the Chicago Architectural Club. It was a community that grew to encompass younger Chicago architects who were excited about the changes taking place in their profession.

Chapter 5

THE LUXFER PRISM COMPETITION*

❝ *We may live to see many a building built of glass from grade to roof … the walls, the ornaments, the gutters, the ridges, the tiles … in short the whole exteriors.*

Daniel Burnham, 1887[1]

❝ *Experience has demonstrated that all spaces within the enclosure of four walls which are not well lighted by sunshine, or at least direct daylight are in office buildings non-productive … it is necessary to know by experiment to what depth from the front wall daylight will reach.*

**John Wellborn Root,
in "A Great Architectural Problem"**

In the 1890s Chicago was in the forefront of skyscraper design. For the development of commercial buildings, the problem of getting light to penetrate building interiors was a problem perhaps as important as the development of the steel frame. Wright's residential client William Winslow[2] and their mutual friend Edward Waller were part owners of a company that made a glass tile designed to refract light into the interiors of buildings. Winslow hired Wright, who was working in Steinway Hall, to do design for his glass tile company. Although Wright would soon move into the Rookery Building to be near the headquarters of Winslow's glass tile company, this interlude would have an impact on the design work being done in the loft studio at Steinway Hall.

Winslow had met James Gray Pennycuick, an inventor born in England and living in Boston. Pennycuick patented a new type

* For additional general information about Luxfer Glass Prisms see, Neuman, Dietrich, "Triumph in Lighting," Nielsen, David, *Bruno Taut's Design Inspiration for the Glashau,s;* and Crew, Henry, *Pocket* handbook of *Electro-Glazed Luxfer Prisms.*

1 Daniel Burnham. Fourth Annual meeting of the Illinois State Association, AIA June 1887, p.88.

2 Winslow purchased the property for his River Forest House from Edward Waller. Winslow was the developer of the Steinway Hall building. For a brief biography see Eaton, Leonard, *Two Chicago Architects and Their Clients: Frank Lloyd Wright and Howard Van Doren Shaw,* Cambridge: MIT Press, 1969.

of glass tile with light-refracting prismatic ridges designed to direct sunlight into dark building interiors.[3] Originally the tiles were assembled into metal frames, but Winslow invented a way to connect them together into panels without conventional adhesives or mechanical fasteners. This was done through an "electro-glazing" process that Winslow patented. The prisms were placed between thin copper strips and exposed to an electrolytic bath of copper sulfate for two days, bonding them together into large sheets. In 1896, Winslow became a major shareholder in Penycuick's Radiating Light Company which was renamed the Luxfer Prism Company that same year. "Lux," meaning light and "fer" from "ferre," meaning to carry or bear. In 1897 the *Inland Architect* wrote about this new product describing it, "as one of the most remarkable improvements of the century in its bearing on practical architecture."

The new company was well capitalized and well promoted with prominent Chicago businessmen such as Cyrus H.

---

3 Pennycuick's prism tiles were initially 4x4 inches, had a flat side 3/32 inches thick, and had 20 triangular ribs per tile, which were 3/32 inches thick.

6.001. Magazine advertisement for Luxfer Prisms. 1896.

McCormick, Charles H. Wacker, and Levi Z. Leiter, along with Winslow and Waller as investors. Winslow sat on the board of directors. Waller had been one of the developers of the Rookery Building where the offices of the Luxfer Prism Company were located. John M. Ewen acted as president of the Luxfer Prism Company, while also serving as president of the George A. Fuller Company. The Fuller Company was an important Chicago construction firm and the general contractor that built Steinway Hall for William Winslow, its developer. Previously, Ewen had been Burnham & Root's chief engineer.

When Winslow and Wright met, Wright was working on Sullivan's ornamental schemes for the Auditorium Theater. In 1897 Winslow hired him initially to design decorative patterns for Luxfer glass tiles. The idea was to take the Luxfer glass tiles out of the realm of industrial and factory buildings by giving them a decorative pattern on their exterior face, making them desirable for use in store fronts and commercial building lobbies. Wright's designs recall the decorative terra cotta work being used on

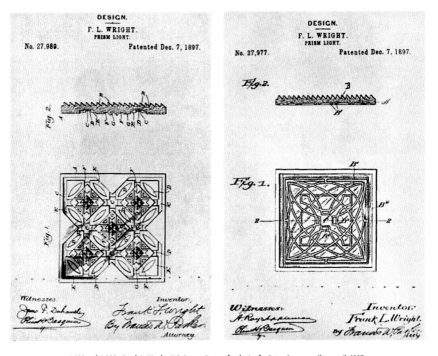

6.002 and 6.003. Frank L. Wright. U.S. Design Patents for the Luxfer Prism Company. Chicago, Il. 1897.

building fronts. On December 7, 1897 he filed for 41 different US "design" patents on behalf of the Luxfer Prism Company. All were for decorative designs for their glass tiles. The patterns were geometric, many with curving flower motifs radiating out from the center. They were reminiscent of Wright's other early decorative work. Sullivan's ornament had been a reinvention of leafy Romanesque motifs built outward from a center. Wright's designs were geometrized to an even greater extent.

At this same time the Luxfer Prism Company also hired Northwestern University physics professor, Henry Crew, the head of the University's Physics Department and his assistant Olin Basquin. They were asked to optimize the light refracting performance of Luxfer tiles. Their work resulted in a number of US patents filed at the same time as Wright's.[4] Crew and Basquin developed mathematical formulas for the angles of prism facets based on the distance the light was to be projected from the surface of the tile. Together they edited a 287-page handbook published in 1898 with technical information, installation drawings, tables based on their calculations, and photographs of building installations throughout the country.

In spite of the camaraderie and intellectual support he had in Steinway Hall, in 1898, Wright moved his Chicago office into the Rookery Building. The Luxfer Prism Company occupied suite 1129 there from 1897 to 1901 with Wright on the same floor in suite 1119. At this time both William Winslow and Edward Waller also maintained offices in the Rookery building. It is probable that Winslow and Waller asked Wright to relocate to have him close at hand, perhaps giving him the office space for free or at a reduced rent. Wright's move was also an indication of his developing relationship with the Luxfer Prism Company and what was no doubt a lucrative arrangement for Wright as their consultant. He would later write, "A contract with the Luxfer Prism Company of Chicago as consulting engineer for making prism-glass installations in office buildings throughout the country had enabled me to build the workroom—I then called it a 'studio'—next to the little Oak Park dwelling place built by means of my contract with

---

4 In 1897 the company filed for a total of 162 different mechanical and design patents related to the manufacture and use of their prism tiles.

Adler and Sullivan."[5] In the 1898 Chicago Architectural Club's annual exhibition and catalog Wright exhibited "An example of elctro-glazing for the American Luxfer Prism Co.," and then in 1899, "Three examples of Luxfer Electro-Glazed Art Glass." The work exhibited was credited to the Luxfer Prism Company rather than to Wright and the exhibition catalogs for these years don't include illustrations of Wright's drawings. During this period, it is possible that Wright's work for Luxfer occupied most of his time.[6]

One of the typical ways in which corporate and civic clients solicited building designs and hired architects in the first decades of the twentieth century was through architectural competitions. Building commissions, educational scholarships, and travelling fellowships were often awarded in this way. The Chicago Architectural Club and its Boston, New York, and other metropolitan counterparts held regular competitions for their members that resulted in modest monetary awards and the prominent exhibition of the winning designs. For young architects just beginning their careers, the architectural competition was a way to gain professional recognition as well as clients. In his capacity as a consultant to the Luxfer Prism Company, Wright was also hired to help promote the use of their products in commercial buildings. So, it may have been Wright who conceived the idea of an architectural competition for the Luxfer Prism Company.

The January 1898 *Inland Architect and News Record* carried an announcement that read, "The American Luxfer Prism Company have organized a competition among architects and draftsmen that presents many interesting features. ... [The] company desires from the architects of America competitive designs setting forth

---

5 Wright, *An Autobiography*, p.136.

6 During this period, Wright's other commissions were houses for Rollin Furbeck (1897), Joseph Husser (1899), a residential remodeling for Edward C. Waller, and a small building for the River Forest Golf Club (1898), of which he was a member. This is far less than he had produced in previous years. Perhaps indicating the almost exclusive nature of Wright's Luxfer contract. Manson reiterates, "The contract Wright negotiated in 1895 with the American Luxfer Prism Company to popularize a new type of fenestration gave him the necessary extra money to add to the house along Chicago Avenue." According to Manson, Wright designed a, "projected office building in Chicago for the American Luxfer Prism Company, whose date is fixed by a document at Taliesin: 1894. This was just a few months before Wright negotiated a contract with the company to act as their architectural consultant" (Manson, *Frank Lloyd Wright to 1910*, p.88). These dates are called into question by the fact that the Luxfer Prism Glass Company wasn't founded in Chicago until 1896. Manson's dates are based on a handwritten note in the corner of an elevation study for a Luxfer building dated 1894–95. The date that Manson saw was probably written by Wright in the 1920s or later. According to Bruce Brooks Pfeiffer, Wright would frequently take out old drawings that lacked title blocks and write identifying notes and dates on them.

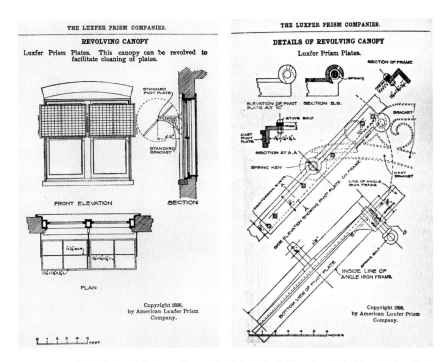

6.004 A & B Design for a Luxfer Prism Window Awning. Illustrations from Pocket Handbook of Electro-Glazed Luxfer Prisms. 1898. Pages 56-57.

in a definite and comprehensive manner new possibilities in the use of Luxfer prisms as a building material ... The nature of these designs should be both practical and artistic." Five thousand dollars in total was to be awarded as a $2,000 first prize, a $1,000 second prize, a $500 third prize, and with fourth and fifth place receiving $300 and $200 respectively and an additional ten designs awarded $100 each. These were sizable sums at a time when draftsmen made $20 to $30 per week. The competition program, while not specifying the type or use of the building to be designed, referred competitors to the company's *Pocket hand-book of Electro-Glazed Luxfer Prisms,* containing drawings, technical information, and suggested uses that included installation of glass tiles used in window transoms and their use in building canopies.

Finally, the awards were to be made, "on March 21, 1898, by a jury of well-known architects and experts," to be announced at a later time. Surprisingly in May, two months after the awards were to have been made, the *Inland Architect* announced that the time period for the competition was to be extended to June 15th. The notice read that, "the reason for this action is that it has become very apparent that the time previously allotted has not been sufficient for the architects desiring to compete to satisfactorily investigate and study the possibilities of daylight illumination in relation to architectural design. ... [The] committee of Award selected by the American Luxfer Prism Company to pass upon the merits of the designs submitted in competition ... have decided not to examine the designs on file, but to give additional time until June 15. (signed) D.H. Burnham, W.L.B. Jenney, William Holabird, Frank L. Wright, and Henry Crew.

It is probable that the time was extended because only a few architects chose to enter the competition despite the generous prize money. This could also have been because of the somewhat ambiguous program and its totally open requirements, which were lacking any specificity as to the building's use or size. If the competition was Wright's idea, perhaps before it was deemed a promotional failure, Wright felt the need to drum up interest among his colleagues at Steinway Hall.

Unlike present day competitions, the original announcement carried no provision prohibiting employees and consultants of the Luxfer Prism Company or their families from entering. The notice for "An Interesting Competition" ran on page 63 of the January 1898 *Inland Architect*, with the note, that "the accompanying studies are suggestions for the use of Luxfer prisms in connection with the steel frame of commercial buildings." A description of a "Study for Luxfer Prism Building Design No.2" and Design No.1 (listed in that order) are on p.64 listed under "Our Illustrations." The format of the *Inland Architect*, like many architectural publications at that time, was to follow the magazine's text with a section of full-page illustrations. There was no indication as to the identity of the designer, Luxfer's employee Frank Wright. It seems curious that a competition intended to solicit new, original, and artistic, uses for a building product would be accompanied by such specific designs suggestions. The two published designs were also accompanied by technical descriptions of how the Luxfer tiles were to be used. This was a specific requirement for competition submissions suggesting that Wright had intended to enter the competition.

Wilbert Hasbrouck thought that Wright was hired by the Luxfer Prism Company to produce designs for "prototypical business buildings" using Luxfer prisms.[7] He suggests that this was the source of the two designs published in the *Inland Architect* accompanying the competition's announcement. This doesn't correspond to Wright's description of his work for the company "as a consulting engineer for making prism glass installations in office buildings throughout the country." Wright's description would suggest that he was aiding other architects to incorporate prism tiles into their plans. We know from the dates of Wright's patents that these designs would have been done in Steinway Hall, perhaps the two competition renderings for Wright's Luxfer office buildings may have been done there as well.

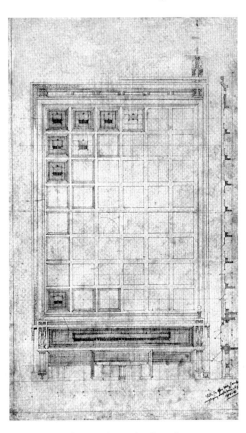

6.005. Design Elevation and section of Wright's Luxfer Design No. 1.

The rendering of Design No. 1 was prepared from an elevation study and accompanying wall section probably done by Wright late in 1897. Wright published this drawing in *A Testament* (1957) and it was used by Arthur Drexler in 1962 in the catalog that accompanied *The Drawings of Frank Lloyd Wright* at the Museum of Modern Art.

Wright's own early residential renderings were all line drawings in the style of J.L. Silsbee. The two renderings published in the *Inland Architect* are not by Wright's hand and were probably done by Birch Burdette Long in Steinway Hall. There were a number of young architects who routinely did renderings for hire including Wright's friend Robert Spencer. When Wright first moved into Steinway Hall, Birch Burdette Long, worked for him. Long was a gifted renderer who is identified as the delineator of many of the works published in

7 Hasbrouck, *The Chicago Architectural Club*, p.217.

the Chicago Architectural Club yearly exhibition catalogs. Long was later described in 1914 in the *Brickbuilder's* series "Monographs on Architectural Renderers": "he began his work as a draftsman in one of the Chicago offices, soon after the beginning of his career, and worked for some time under Frank Lloyd Wright, doing renderings for other men concurrently."[8] The fully rendered Luxfer drawings were probably done in Steinway Hall and would have certainly been seen by the architects in Perkins's loft. They also might have known about the Luxfer Competition even though it had yet to be announced.

Wright's biographer Robert Twombly suggests that Wright entered the competition and then withdrew when he was put on

---

8 *Brickbuilder*, on "Birch Burdette Long," 1914, Vol. 23, p.274-76.

6.006. Frank L. Wright. Design No.1 (left) and Design No.2 (right).
Renderings. Luxfer Prism Competition. The Inland Archtiect and News Record. 1898.

the competitions' jury.[9] It is unlikely that Wright's drawings were anything but the result of his desire to win the competition. With Wright's entry withdrawn, the deadline extended, and Wright on the jury, Wright's colleagues in Steinway Hall could have felt it worthwhile to prepare entries.

The style of Wright's two designs suggest that they were intended to appeal to likely choices for jury members. The first, a "Study for Luxfer Prism Building Design No.1" is for a steel frame building with an 11-foot floor height and an 11-foot module in plan. The building's gridded façade has a horizontally articulated two-story base and a horizontally fenestrated attic story terminating the building. The first story shows clear glazed store fronts with transom panels of Luxfer glass divided into three equal bays by the building's expressed structural columns. "The structural members in the first and second stories are screened by the prism surfaces which are carried in front of them" according to Wright's description in the *Inland Architect*. The central entry bay has a canopy of Luxfer glass tiles like the ones shown in the Luxfer handbook. The second floor shows a horizontal strip of clear glass with a prism glass canopy. Above, the structural bays are subdivided to create a square grid infilled with a sub-grid of 16 square tiles. In each bay a central window is shown as clear glass surrounded by Luxfer prisms with a projecting canopy of Luxfer tiles. According to Wright's description, "The openings in the center of the plate which are shown, about four feet square, are protected by a light canopy filled with prisms which permits a view of the street, and further increases the light." The entry front of the building is framed by corner columns continuous from top to bottom. While the square grid and corner finials atop the building are unusual, the building itself fits comfortably within the genre of "Chicago Frame" buildings as seen in the work of Jenney, Holabird and Roche, and Daniel Burnham.

Design No. 2, which is rarely reproduced in discussions of Wright's work is overtly Sullivanesque. In it the two-story base has a continuous row of canopies on both floors and is framed by

9 In his 1979 biography of Frank Lloyd Wright, Robert Twombly wrote, "In 1898 he [Wright] submitted a drawing to the Luxfer Prism Company's $2,000 contest for an office building but withdrew it when he, along with Daniel H. Burnham, W.L.B. Jenny, and William Holabird, were placed on the judging panel. Although Robert C. Spencer Jr., eventually won, Wright's scheme was published anonymously in the Inland Architect." Twombly, *Frank Lloyd Wright. His Life and His Architecture*, p.35.

a rectangular surround probably to be of ornamented terra cotta surmounted by vertical finials at each of the building's column bays. Above this, the base is given its own attic. Here the windows are horizontal strips. The typical office floors and their windows are grouped into five vertically articulated bays with the mullions between windows extending the entire height of the building's midsection emphasizing a vertical reading of the whole in the manner of Sullivan's office buildings. The windows within each bay are divided into thirds by vertical mullions, which also terminate in finials. The building's top is its most Sullivanesque feature. It is capped by a decorative frame on top of the five square bays. Each bay with a square window surrounded by a round frame of decorative molded terra cotta. The cornice is suggestive of Sullivan Guaranty building. Each of the typical office windows are shown divided in half horizontally suggesting clear glass above, allowing for views out and Luxfer tile sash below.

When Wright began preparing these designs, he would not have known the jury members who were yet to be selected. It is probable that as Luxfer's architectural consultant Wright would have been asked for recommendations. Any list of the best-known Chicago architects would certainly have included Daniel Burnham, William Le Baron Jenny, William Holabird and his partner Martin Roche, and, of course, Louis Sullivan. By preparing two different solutions incorporating prism glass tiles, Wright produced building designs calculated to appeal to the design preferences of those he thought might be selected as jury members.

When the winning designs were finally announced, first prize was awarded to Robert Spencer, the second prize went to Adamo Boari, and the third prize was awarded to S.S. Beman. The winning drawings were published in the September 1898 issue of the *Inland Architect*.

Robert Spencer's winning entry is a mixed-use structure with retail on the ground floor and offices above. Although no typical upper-floor plan was published the assumption is that like Burnham and Root's Rookery building (where Luxfer Prism had its offices), the upper offices ringed a light court as the square building design has an unusually large floor plate. Spencer wrote, "The use of Luxfer Prisms would make it possible to adequately daylight interior spaces further removed from the exterior walls than in a conventional office structure … Offices throughout the building have been arranged in double series, all interior offices receiving ample daylight transmitted by prisms, giving largely increased rentable areas … The ground floor has wide interior shopping streets skylit by vaults of decoratively colored Luxfer Prisms." His idea for the vaults was to eliminate the framing that supported the glass in conventional skylights. Spencer continued, "It will be seen that this idea opens up some interesting possibilities for electro-glazing, and that the entire vault structure is built up and knit together on this principle, the hexagon being selected as the unit because of its fitness for a cellular fabric or shell."[10]

The exterior of Spencer's design is a grid infilled with sash combining clear glass and an upper panel of Luxfer Prisms that slides vertically. The building has a clear expression of its

---

10 *Inland Architect*, September 1898, vol. XXXII, no.2, p.15–16, text plus unpaginated illustrations.

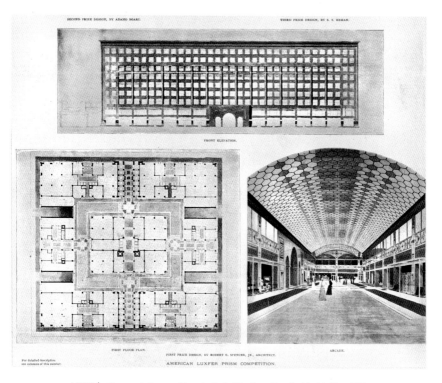

6.007. Robert Spencer winning competition entry. Luxfer Prism Competition. The Inland Architect. 1898.

structural frame at every other bay. The central 14 bays are slightly set back. The two outer bays on the ends of the façade and the top two floors have square windows divided much like Wright's Design No. 1. These show what looks like a central square glass sash. Were these like Wright's design to be surrounded by Luxfer Prisms? Were Wright and Spencer suggesting an alternative to the "Chicago Window" that would have utilized Luxfer prism glass tiles?

At nine stories, the rendering of Spencer's building suggests a warehouse. It was probably not Spencer's use of an expressed frame and prism panels, but, his proposal for a continuous vault of prism tiles lighting the interior arcade that garnered him the first prize. It is improbable that the electro-glazed tiles could have spanned this distance or supported much very weight. In the absence of a building cross section there is no way to know if Spencer's Luxfer Prism vaults were proposed as actual skylights or lay-lights below a skylight at the top of an interior court.

Adamo Boari's second place entry was far more interesting than either Wright's or Spencer's designs. Dietrich Neumann has pointed out that it was, " Much more radical than Wright's proposals for the Luxfer Prism building, the Boari drawings actually represent what seems to be the first design for a virtual glass curtain wall for a skyscraper, and certainly deserved the attention of later critics concerning themselves with the search for a predecessor of the modern office building."[11] Boari did two designs, the first for a 10-story structure and then a later design for a 24-story tower, not entered in the competition. It was the 10-story design that was given an award and published in *Inland Architect*.

Boari's winning entry shows an office building with prism glass walls bookended by expressed corner columns. What is possibly a five-bay structure (no plan was published) has columns expressed the full height of the building in two outboard locations framing a wide center section of all glass with glass awning windows at each floor. At the bottom of the building the curtain wall flares out, as shown in the building wall section to form a canopy of prism glass, an extension of the glass wall above. The

---

11 Detrich Neumann,"The Century's Triumph in Lighting: The Luxfer Companies and Their Contribution to Early Modern Architecture," *Journal of the Society of Architectural Historians*, Vol. 54, no.1, March 1995, p.33 and footnote 50 on p.50 re: Grant Manson letters to Reinhold Publishing Company.

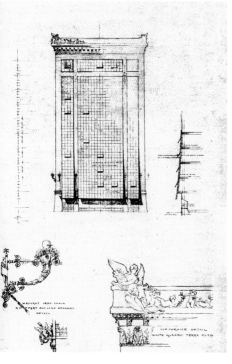

6.008. Adamo Boari. Second-place entry to the Luxfer Prism Competition. The Inland Architect. 1898.

6.009. Adamo Boari. Second project for a Luxfer Prism Building. Chicago Architectural Club Exhibition. 1899.

idea of extending the bottom edge of a curtain wall to form an entry canopy is a feature found in contemporary 21st-century glass buildings including Chicago's Spertus Museum on South Michigan Avenue.

In the brief description of his entry, Boari wrote, "Our effort has been to use the Iridian Prism as the whole surface." Boari's drawing shows columns topped by Corinthian column capitols and a decorative cornice with sculpted corner angels whose wings suggest acroteria. The decorative work on Boari's design was probably intended to be glazed terra cotta like the Reliance building (1895). The terra cotta tiles along with the prism glass would have given the building a unique reflective quality.

The second of Boari's designs was included in the Chicago Architectural Club's annual exhibit and published in the 1899 exhibition catalog. It carried the idea of the all glass curtain wall even further. The published perspective shows a freestanding building made up of five round towers clustered together on a tapered base and clad entirely in glass tiles. The tower is free standing on a pedestrian plaza in the center of a wide city street.

Depicted behind it, across the street, is Boari's winning competition design.

The second design recalls Chicago's Gothic Water Tower, which sits in the center of Michigan Avenue (then Pine Street). That Boari's site is an idealized version of Michigan Avenue is further suggested by the silhouetted structure on the right of the drawing. Its classical profile suggests that it is the Art Institute of Chicago, where Boari's drawing was exhibited. The Art Institute is also recognizable by the lion sculptures that still flank the building's Michigan Avenue entrance.

Wright would publish his "Design No. 1" in 1938 in the *Architectural Forum*. Grant Mansion, referring to the drawing in a letter to his publisher, describes how in 1957 he had to keep Wright from erasing and altering the Luxfer drawing before it was to be photographed to be included in Manson's book *Frank Lloyd Wright to 1910*. Wright did alter the drawing removing the corner finials and both modernizing and simplifying the building's cornice before publishing it in *A Testament* where he claimed that it was prescient of the architecture that would follow. The drawing was republished various times, including in Arthur Drexler's catalog to the 1962 exhibit of Wright's drawings at the Museum of Modern Art. By contrast, Boari's design is all but lost to history.

What the Spencer and Wright schemes share is the idea of the window as infill to a grid rather than as a hole in a wall surface. While the ubiquitous bay and corner windows of the day may have suggested glass volumes, it is not until much later in his career that Wright explored the idea of a glazing system that created volumic forms as he did at Fallingwater and the Johnson Wax Building. However, none of Wright's later projects using curtain walls are without a strong horizontal expression of floor levels. Does Wright's research tower at Johnson's Wax owe something to the rounded, glass corners and diaphanous skin of Boari's second Luxfer design? Would Boari's drawings have come to mind when Wright considered glazing the building with Luxfer prisms before deciding on pyrex tubing?[12]

Perhaps an even more interesting postscript to Wright's Luxfer Design No. 1 is its similarity to Wright's proposed 15-story building for the Guggenheim Museum designed near the end of

---

12 See, Jonathan Lipman, *Frank Lloyd Wright and the Johnson Wax Building*, 1986, p.65.

6.010. Frank Lloyd Wright. "Modern Gallery" Guggenheim Museum.
New York, N.Y. revised 1951-54.

6.011. Frank Lloyd Wright.
Luxfer Prism Building Design No. 1. 1897.

his career. In 1951, as one of many revisions to his plans for the
Guggenheim Museum, Wright proposed a narrow slab building
that could be built over the two-story office structure located
at the east edge of the museum's site. It would have contained
income-producing rental apartments. The façade facing Central
Park would have had a square grid infilled with fixed windows
surrounding a square central operating sash. Like his Luxfer
building the square grid and square windows made this design
unlike any of the other tower projects Wright designed throughout his career.

Sullivan's tall buildings suppressed the horizontal reading
of floors to express window and spandrel panels in vertical
strips. The expressed structural grid that typified the Chicago
School was often the module of the actual structure infilled
with windows. However, both Wright and Spencer in their
Luxfer building designs had no reservations about subdivid-
ing the structural module into a smaller grid as Sullivan had
done. This idea, the creation of an apparent structure as the
visual organizer of both surface and window openings can also
be seen in both Spencer and Wright's use of timbering in their

residential work. A Sullivanesque treatment can also be seen in the window arrangement of Wright and Perkins's early designs for the Abraham Lincoln Center, in Wright's Larkin building, in Unity Temple, and in Perkins's school designs for the Chicago Board of Education.

For the architects of Steinway Hall, window locations were the result of architectural form or structure. Windows were voids between horizontal or vertical elements, or voids between juxtaposed solid volumes. This was a principle abstracted from architectural history through the tenets of Pure Design, explored in their architecture, discussed over their drawings, at lunch, and discussed at meetings of The Chicago Architectural Club.

Chapter 6

THE ABRAHAM
LINCOLN CENTER

Not usually thought of as an example of design collaboration, the Abraham Lincoln Center in Chicago is considered to be Wright's design, with the final built version by Dwight Perkins. This was due to Wright's falling out with the client, his uncle. The project was under design for over three years and no doubt involved an ongoing discussion and collaboration between Wright and Perkins on the building's architectural design and planning issues. Their mutual involvement in the building's design, particularly the treatment of its exterior walls, may be seen in subsequent designs by both Wright and Perkins.

By 1890, Frank Lloyd Wright's uncle the Reverend Jenkin Lloyd Jones and his burgeoning congregation had outgrown the All Soul's Church building which J.L. Silsbee had designed for them. Expanding or building a new church was contemplated and Jones told Silsbee that while any project was a few years off, "I shall certainly talk to you about it and give you all the chance I can."[1] Jones wanted to build a larger church, but also wanted it to be an assembly hall combined with a non-denominational community center based on the model of the settlement house. Like Hull House, which was built by his friend Jane Addams, he wanted to provide community services to his congregation and the surrounding neighborhood. By the fall of 1892 Jones had formulated the uses he wanted included in his building. It was to contain recreational facilities such as a gymnasium and bowling alley, an auditorium, a library and reading rooms, a kindergarten, a manual training school, and space for homemaking classes. In addition to these Jones wanted to include income producing rental space for professionals, and studio spaces for artists.

The *All Souls Church Annual* for 1893–94 included a perspective drawing for a seven-story building, which remarkably prefigures aspects of the designs to be prepared between 1898 and 1903 by Wright and Perkins. While the architect of the design was not identified, based on features of the drawing, including the diagonal brick diapering of the top story, the building might have been a preliminary design prepared by Pond & Pond. Irving

---

1 Jones Collection, Meadville-Lombard, Jones letter Book. December 9, 1891. Quoted in Joseph Siry, "The Abraham Lincoln Center in Chicago," JSAH, September 1991, p.237.

7.001. Preliminary Project for All Souls Building. 1892-93, from All Souls Annual, 1893-94.

and Allen Pond were considered both socially and architecturally progressive. They were the architects of Hull House, whose various additions had similar diagonal brick patterning on their top floors. This was a signature feature of many of Pond & Pond's buildings.

Adler and Sullivan's Jewish Training School on Chicago's west side near Hull House was also a possible model for Jenkins's vision for the new All Souls. While it did not contain a worship space, only classrooms for vocational training, Jones would later commend the homemaking classrooms to Wright and Perkins in a letter dated January 2, 1902. The Training School was built by Jones's good friend Rabbi Dr. Emil Hirsch, a cofounder with Jones of the Congress of Liberal Religious Societies in 1894.[2]

In November of 1892 Jenkins approached Dwight Perkins—a member of his congregation—who was still working in D.H. Burnham's office at the time and asked him to look at and comment on the plans he had for his new All Souls Building. Perkins, who had joined the congregation in 1884, three years before Wright became a member, declined. He wrote to Jones

---

2 Ibid., p.240.

7.002. Adler and Sullivan. Hebrew Manual Training School. Chicago, Il. 1889-1990.

that, "I of course want to be the architect of that building, doing it through Mr. Burnham ... it is hardly right for me to examine another architect's plans while I am a possible competitor."[3] Wright's son Lloyd remembers that his father began working on a new All Souls building in 1888 while still with Adler and Sullivan.[4] Silsbee's All Souls church was completed in 1886 and it is highly unlikely that Jones was contemplating the need for additional space for the activities of his ministry at this early date. Further calling the 1888 date into question, Wright who began his independent practice in 1893, wrote to his uncle in May of 1894, "How about the plans for the new building? Am I to get a chance with the rest of the boys, or is it an open and shut walk away for Silsbee ... I do not want to let any architect walk off with a building with which an uncle of mine is so closely concerned, without making some desperate effort to meet things halfway."[5] It is unclear what would constitute "desperate" efforts. "Meeting

3 Letter from Perkins to Jones, November 11, 1892 in the Jones Collection University of Chicago, Box III, folder 10. Quoted in Siry, Op. cit., p.243.
4 Lloyd Wright, My Father Who is On Earth, 1946, p.20-21.
5 Wright to Jones, letter dated May 15, 1894. Jones Collection, University of Chicago, Box IV, Folder 4. Quoted in Siry, Op. cit., p.243.

things halfway" may have been a reference to a history of disagreements Wright had had with his uncle including his original decision to move from Wisconsin to Chicago to apprentice as an architect rather than pursue an education.

In 1897 Perkins remembers that he and Wright began working together on All Souls. This was the same year that Wright moved into Steinway Hall. In November of 1898, the following year, Perkins and Wright were announced In the *Brickbuilder* as the architects for the All Souls project. "Dwight H. Perkins and Frank L. Wright are associate architects for a new church of special interest."[6]

With Perkins's name listed first, several possibilities exist. Wright had just moved into Perkins's office space. Perhaps the commission was given to Perkins by the Reverend Jones with the condition that his nephew be included. At this time, Wright's own practice was entirely residential. He had worked on larger buildings for Adler and Sullivan, including the Auditorium and Schiller buildings. Both were multi-use buildings that included auditoriums, but Wright had done nothing comparable on his own. It was Perkins who had experience with larger buildings in his own practice. Steinway Hall had showrooms, office space, and a second-floor concert hall. It was a building whose combination of uses was not unlike what the Reverend Jones was envisioning for his new All Souls project. If the commission was offered to Wright, he may have needed to partner with Perkins as a way of reassuring his uncle that he could produce a technically competent design for such a complex undertaking.

The original announcement in the *Brickbuilder* was not accompanied by any illustrations. The following year, 1899, the *Brickbuilder,* in a section entitled "Brick and Terra-Cotta Work in American and Foreign Cities," carried a description of the building: "The erection of a novel building will soon be begun by the congregation of All Souls Unitarian Church whose pastor is the Rev. Jenkin Lloyd Jones. All precedents have been ignored and a building has been designed to meet in the simplest, quietest, and most natural way the peculiar conditions imposed upon these architects." According to the article, the "peculiar conditions" were the mixed-use functions that the building was

---

6 *Brickbuilder*, VII, November 1898, p.240. The 1897 date is cited by Grant Manson.

to accommodate, not the austere design criteria Jones would impose. "The exterior walls ... will be solid brick construction, and the general scheme is dignified and plain, almost to severity, depending chiefly for its effectiveness upon largeness and coherence of composition and refinement of the very sparing detail," ending with, "Frank Lloyd Wright and Dwight Heald Perkins are the associated architects."[7] This constituted a reversal of the name order of their association, something Perkins must have agreed to suggesting that the early designs submitted were largely Wright's.

While the *Brickbuilder* never published drawings of the All Souls building, the description may have been supplied by the architects. It reflects the plans and rendering that they exhibited at the Chicago Architectural Club in April of 1900. The exhibit catalog also included photographs and plans for Wright's Oak Park studio, a few of his house designs and a rendering captioned, "All Souls Building. Chicago. Frank Lloyd Wright and Dwight Heald Perkins, Architects, Associated." That June, Robert Spencer's article in the *Architectural Review* on Wright's work included the same rendering. Spencer wrote, describing the buildings program and its appearance, "the building as a whole is characterized by an austere repression of decorative detail, and with its rifted outer wall of solid brick construction sprung from a broad stylobate, its powerfully stiffened corner piers and clean cornice reduced to a mere molded coping, it will stand like a great rock as a landmark of progress in practical Christianity and art."[8] Spencer makes no mention of his friend Dwight Perkins as associated architect.

The resemblance to Sullivan's Wainwright building has been pointed out by historians starting with Grant Manson who wrote, "It is, furthermore, a Sullivanesque office building, looking very much like Sullivan's famous Wainwright Building in St. Louis, of 1891."[9]

Historian Joseph Siry points out that, "In 1892 Jones had envisioned that 'the building would be really the first of its kind in the world,' as if its designer would be asked to create

---

7 Brickbuilder, VIII, January 1899, p.17–18.

8 Spencer, "The Work of Frank Lloyd Wright," The Architectural Review, June 1900, p.71.

9 Manson, Frank Lloyd Wright to 1910, 1958, p.158.

7.003. Adler and Sullivan. Wainwright Building. St. Louis, Mo. 1891.

7.004. Wright and Perkins. All Souls' Abraham Lincoln Center project. Chicago, Il. 1900.

an architectural prototype for the new program of the institutional church. Ten years later, in 1902 before actual construction began, Jones' structure was termed 'a unique building' in the February 8, 1902 issue of *Construction News*, as if it had no typological precedent."[10] In spite of both Wright and Perkins's views about the use of precedent, in the absence of one, they chose to express the building's primary function as the rental office space of its upper floors. They used Louis Sullivan's solution to the "tall office building," tightly spaced vertical piers. This choice for the buildings' exterior's design gave no expression to the building's most important space, the auditorium planned for religious services. In that way it was like Perkins's design for Steinway Hall where neither the second-floor recital hall or the seventh-floor auditorium are given expression on the exterior.

Jones decided that the building should be called the Abraham Lincoln Center instead of All Souls because the new institution was to be incorporated as an educational organization legally

---

10 *Construction News*, Feb. 8, 1902, p.88. Siry, op. cit., p.248.

separate from All Souls Church.[11] The Reverend had served in the Union Army during the Civil War and was a great admirer of Lincoln, who he felt exemplified his own ideal of an inclusive view of humanity. In a sermon published in *Unity 55* (February 16, 1905) Jones said that Lincoln was, "the greatest and noblest and dearest of Americans who ever lived, a man who represented national and civic interests and ... who has already won his place in the heart of the representatives of all creeds."[12]

The rest of the Lloyd Jones family shared this admiration for Lincoln and Frank Lloyd Wright was born Frank Lincoln Wright. He changed his middle name to Lloyd, after he moved to Chicago further identifying with his mother's family, the Lloyd Joneses. Chicago historian Tim Samuelson has suggested that Wright may have adopted Lloyd as his middle name sometime in 1897 about the time he moved into Steinway Hall. This is based on the dated drawings of the Isadore Heller House, with early drawings signed "Frank L. Wright, Architect, Chicago," and the later ones signed "Frank Lloyd Wright."

By 1901 Jones and William Kent, the head of the All Souls building committee, had reservations about Wright and Perkins's design. They arranged for the distinguished New York architect Ernest Flagg to review the plans. In March 1901 Flagg responded that the plans were "orderly, logical, and convenient as far as I am able to judge," but, "In regard to the decorative clothing of the plan, I think it might be improved. The exterior does not tell the story of the interior, there is nothing to indicate the presence of the great hall, and the general appearance is heavy and forbidding."[13] In May of that year, Jones wrote to his nephew, "I do believe that somehow the auditorium ought to shine on the outside." Jones goes on to suggest the expression of the auditorium by a band of horizontal windows or "an eyebrow over it."[14] From this point in the design process, Jones actively insists that Wright and Perkins incorporate specific architectural features that

---

11 Siry, op. cit., p.242.

12 Quoted in Siry, op. cit., p.242, and in Johnson, *Frank Lloyd Wright: Early Years*, p.166.

13 Flagg's letter to Wright and Perkins of March 20, 1901 in the Jones Collection at the Meadville-Lombard Theological School, Chicago. Quoted in Siry, op. cit., p.249.

14 Jones letter to Wright, May 8, 1901. Jones Letter Book 13, Jones Collection, Meadville-Lombard. Quoted in Siry, op. cit., p.249.

were a part of his vision for a dignified, simple, and economically constructed building.

Jones continued to press his nephew for revisions. The 1902 drawings of a smaller version were exhibited at the Chicago Architectural Club's annual exhibition. A new rendering was included in the exhibition catalog that devoted 14 pages to Wright's work. The height of the building was reduced from nine to six stories. Some of the floors of rental space were eliminated and the pastor's study, the library, offices, and the Unity Club were relocated to the first floor. The auditorium still occupied the second and third floors and was expressed by vertical groupings of windows. The typical upper floors still had windows divided by pilasters. These extended to the fourth floor where they were terminated by a row of recessed windows that were referred to as a "loggia" in the original plans. While still Sullivanesque, the building's expression was at Jones's request simpler and more horizontal.

7.005. Wright and Perkins. Abraham Lincoln Center project. Chicago, Il. 1902.

At this point Jones still objected to many of the features of the exterior design, asking that horizontal lines be carried around the corners and that the Wright "throw away those short pillars...that give the loggia effect to the upper story, and bring the windows out flush ... In wintertime those ledges will simply catch snow drifts and form icicles to stain the walls below and crack them ... I believe you can scrape off several thousand dollars' worth of minor lines, counting the four sides, and still retain the major lines or something better."[15] William Kent, then took the plans back to Ernest Flagg who now described the building as, "a nightmare" and "wasteful in cost of construction and maintenance." It is possible that Flagg's about face with respect to the design was motivated by the belief that he could steal the commission from the two less known and less experienced Chicago architects. Flagg and his associate Walter Chambers offered to do sketches for an alternate design at no charge. Kent also consulted the Ponds who apparently felt that the cost estimate Wright and Perkins had prepared was too low. At Jones's urging Wright and Perkins were kept as the architects for the project, but, were asked to submit a simpler, less expensive version of the building by the end of the summer of 1902. They were directed to eliminate the "loggia and the corner columns," which according to Kent's letter to the architects, "must be wiped off."[16] Jones exhorted, "I have pled for simple lines, plain exterior, for artistic and ethical reasons as well as economic ... Schools, orders and styles of architecture to the winds; the only radical architect is the architect who is free to use whatever serves his purpose in any way he can ... I want no more debating exercises over the history and philosophy of architecture. I want a building."[17] For Jones, Wright and Perkins were not radical enough to set aside their preconceived notions of architectural design and the precedent of Louis Sullivan's forms and ornamentation.

Another version of the design was illustrated in an unidentified and undated newspaper clipping, from the Perkins Papers

---

15 Jones letter to Wright, January 13, 1902. Letter Book 9, Jones Collection, Meadville-Lombard. Quoted in Siry, op, cit., p.252.

16 Letter from Kent to Wright and Perkins, July 21, 1902, Jones Collection, Meadville-Lombard. Quoted in Siry, op. cit., p.253.

17 Jones letter to Wright and Perkins, August 2 ,1902, Jones Collection Meadville-Lombard. Quoted in Siry, op. cit., p.253.

at the Chicago History Museum.[18] It seems to show a modification of the 1902 project that simplifies the building's corners and better expresses the auditorium. This is done by grouping the auditoriums' windows and the first-floor entry together as a base for the windows above. The upper floor windows are still grouped between vertical piers terminated by column capitals. The top floor is still articulated, however, the recessed "loggia," to which Jones adamantly objected, has been eliminated. The elimination of the "loggia" probably dates the drawing sometime after July of 1902.

A further design revision was published in the *All Souls Church Twentieth Annual* for 1903. It shows the most interesting of all the projects Wright and Perkins prepared. The window treatment remains, the unbroken band of attic is eliminated, and the brick corners are kept as simple piers. The main floor and the auditorium space above it are collected into a strong central element by shallow brick piers that carry a horizontal band of masonry capped by a string course. This acts as a sill and as a base to three stories of identical windows between vertical piers.

PROPOSED CHURCH EDIFICE FOR REV. JENKIN LLOYD JONES

7.006. Wright and Perkins. Abraham Lincoln Center project. Chicago, Il. No date.

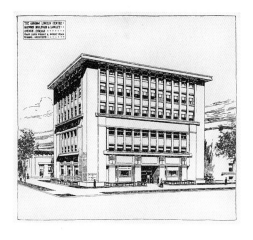

7.007. Wright and Perkins. Abraham Lincoln Center project. Chicago, Il. 1903.

18 Eric Emmett Davis, *Dwight Heald Perkins: Social Consciousness and Prairie School Architecture.* Gallery 400 University of Illinois at Chicago, April 1989.

The building also seems to have been lowered by one story. The cornice is a flat projecting cap that sits atop the four full height corner piers and is perhaps the most dramatic change along with the building's squat proportions and horizontality that give it a distinct "Prairie School" look.

The new plans pleased Jones, but he was still dissatisfied with the complexity of the building's exterior. Kent was displeased that the drawings were not complete enough to be given to contractors for pricing. At this point Jones and Kent asked Perkins to take responsibility for completing the drawings. Jones still wanted all the vertical piers and columns eliminated from the exterior. He noted that, "the simplicity of the building which I wanted was not in accordance with the architectural ambitions of Perkins and Wright, and it was because of this divergence that the matter was taken out of their hands and put in Perkins' hands—because he was willing to embody my ideas, and not his."[19] Wright's sister Maginel Barney would write, "When Frank became an architect, Uncle Jenk asked him to design the church for him. It was a mistake; those two were never meant to build together, they couldn't agree on anything."[20]

Perkins, with Wright's acquiescence, entered into a contract with the building committee to complete the drawings and details. Contained in Perkins's contract was a statement that his work would include the design of an, "elevation satisfactory to Jenkins Lloyd Jones." Perkins wrote, "Your plea for simple monochrome and for economy, straightforward design in every phase pleased me."[21] Jones continued to press Perkins who finally felt that the building's exterior design was so compromised and severe that he wrote to Jones saying he wanted every drawing to carry a note stating, "Designed in accordance with specific directions given by Jenkin Lloyd Jones and against the protest of D.H. Perkins."[22] In spite of this, Perkins fulfilled the terms of his contract and supervised the buildings construction.

---

19 Jones letter from August 19, 1903 to L.J. Lamson. Jones Letter Book 17, Jones Collection, Meadville-Lombard. Quoted in Siry, op. cit., p.258.

20 Maginel Wright Barney, *The Valley of the God-Almighty Joneses*, p.100.

21 Perkins letter to Jones, July 14, 1903. Jones Collection, Meadville-Lombard. Quoted in Siry, op. cit., p.258.

22 Perkins letter to Jones, July 14, 1903. Jones Collection, Meadville-Lombard. Quoted in Siry, op. cit., p.258.

7.008. Dwight Perkins. Abraham Lincoln Center. Chicago, Il. 1905. At right J. L. Silsbee's All Souls Church. Chicago, Il. 1886.

The Center was opened for Easter in 1905. Wright attended the service with his mother and sister, Maginel, who wrote in 1986, "I will never forget Frank's white, furious face the Sunday the Church was dedicated, when he saw printed on the announcement. 'Architect, Frank Lloyd Wright.' Mother, who had had a difficult time to persuade him to come at all, had all she could do to keep him in his seat. I think Uncle Jenk thought he was doing Frank justice. After all, the original plans were his."[23] In 1955 Wright wrote to the director of the Abraham Lincoln Center on the occasion of the Center's 50th anniversary, "it was my first commission for so large a building. The interior is mine, but the exterior belongs to my uncle Jenkins Lloyd Jones and Dwight Perkins."[24]

A rendering of Wright's auditorium interior is credited to Birch Burdette Long, suggesting that Wright continued to work with Perkins on the project in Steinway Hall, not at his Oak Park

---

23 Barney, op. cit., p.100-1.
24 Frank Lloyd Wright, letter to Curtis W. Reese, Unity CXLI, March-April 1955, p.15. Quoted in Siry, op. cit., p.235.

Studio. Long's rendering seems prophetic for the future development of Unity Temple, a project for which both Wright and Perkins were separately interviewed. In spite of Wright's assertion, the Lincoln Center's Auditorium, as built, has none of the characteristics of his work.

While the exterior is as severe as Perkins had feared, the building deserves reconsideration independent of either Wright or Perkins's later work; later written assessments; or the descriptions of their disappointment in the project. The building, as

7009. Wright and Perkins. Birch Long's rendering of Abraham Lincoln Center Auditorium. Chicago, Il. 1903.

7.010. Dwight Perkins Abraham Lincoln Center Auditorium as built. Chicago, Il. 1905.

built, is a well-proportioned block, perhaps compromised only by the bands of darker brick that Jones requested. These wrap the corners and unnecessarily subdivide the building horizontally. While they divide the building into legible zones according to their function, the changes in window size and pattern also accomplish this. The individual windows of the upper three stories are grouped to be read as both horizontal bands and as vertical stacks that correspond to the larger groupings of window on the first three floors. While the windows on the upper floors are a constant width, those on the top floor are shorter in height, subtly suggesting perspectival diminution rather than reading as a separate attic floor. Thus, the building's success is surely to be found in Perkins deft composition of the window openings and the proportion of the remaining brick surfaces.

As in the 1900 and 1902 schemes, the facade is capped by a story-high horizontal band of unbroken brick equal in width to the brick corner piers. Like the earlier schemes the building is still terminated by a shallow projecting cornice. On the first floor, slightly battered walls allow the grouping of three windows to either side of the main entrance to appear recessed reinforcing their reading while still being set in the same surface as all the windows above. Only the entry way is recessed into the volume of the building. On the second and third floor the auditorium is clearly expressed by windows tied together with spandrel panels between vertical mullions. The subdivision of the building into a base with repetitive windows above is created by the broad brick piers forming three bays.

On the main facade these brick piers are relieved by narrow slot windows centered on the piers that flank the entry way. These tall, narrow slot windows are reminiscent of the 18th Street facade of Richardson's Glessner house built in 1887 in Chicago or of the narrow-recessed windows that flank the bays of John Wellborn Root's Monadnock Building built in 1892. Like the Monadnock, the Lincoln Center was the only other totally unornamented brick building in Chicago, excluding industrial buildings or warehouses. Root's building was devoid of ornament because his client Peter Brooks of Boston insisted on it. He believed that ornament was costly, collected dirt, and served no practical purpose. Like Jenkin Lloyd Jones in his correspondence with Wright and Perkins, Brook's letters to Burnham and

Root contained specific practical and aesthetic instructions that he insisted they follow. Brooks wrote to his Chicago agent, Owen Aldis, "I would request an avoidance of ornamentation ... rely upon the effect of solidity and strength, or a design that will produce that effect, rather than ornament for a notable appearance." and, "My notion is to have no projecting surfaces or indentations, but to have everything flush, or flat and smooth ... projections mean dirt."[25]

Unlike All Souls, Brooks's building was not to be built as cheaply as possible and Root was able to use molded brick shapes and undulating bay windows to create this commercial masterpiece. Root, like Sullivan was admired by Perkins, Wright, and their generation. He would write prophetically, "The value of plain surfaces in every building is not to be overestimated. Strive for them, and when the fates place at your disposal a good generous sweep of masonry, accept it frankly and thank God."[26] This progressive idea was echoed by Sullivan himself writing about ornament in the *Engineering Magazine* for August 1892. Sullivan argued for the integral nature of ornament and surface but conceded, "I should say that it would be greatly for our aesthetic good if we should refrain entirely from the use of ornament for a period of years, in order that our thought might concentrate acutely upon the production of buildings well formed and comely in the nude ... for we shall have discerned the limitations as well as the great value of unadorned masses."

When John Wellborn Root passed away suddenly in 1891, there were a number of major buildings on the drawing boards at Burnham and Root. These included the Monadnock. Perkins had been Root's principal assistant. With Burnham absent from his downtown office and working full time at the temporary office in Jackson Park for the Chicago World's Fair, it was Perkins who was responsible for running the practice. He would have played an important role in the realization of the Monadnock Building. This is confirmed by Perkins's daughter Elenore who suggests

25 Letters from April 15 and May 6, 1884. Quoted in Hoffmann, *The Architecture of John Wellborn Root*. These letters no longer exist. They were destroyed by the successor firm to Aldis's in the 1980s.
26 Paper read to the Chicago Sketch Club and published in the *Inland Architect and Builder*, January 1887. Also reprinted in Hoffman, ed., *The Meaning of Architecture, Buildings and Writings by John Wellborn Root*.

that her father was instrumental in the buildings design.[27] Perkins's role in the design of the Monadnock is also confirmed by his son Lawrence Perkins in his 1986 oral history for the Art Institute of Chicago. The Monadnock Building was admired by younger architects and Barry Byrne would later recall Wright saying that, Root, had he lived to continue in his later course, could have been, "the greatest of them all."[28] Years later Wright would suggest in his 1949 book on Sullivan, *Genius and the Mobocracy*, that the divisions of the Wainwright Building's facades were artificial and, "John Root's Monadnock was a noble building. It was later but even further along."[29]

Wright believed the Wainwright Building was a typological solution to the organization of repetitive windows in tall commercial buildings. Having worked on the Wainwright Building, Wright may have felt partially responsible for the idea of organizing the windows of the facade between vertical piers. It may have been his Uncle Jenkin's insistence on the elimination of this feature that convinced Wright he could no longer be involved in the Abraham Lincoln Center's design. While Jones considered the piers unnecessary ornamentation, Wright and Perkins would have considered them the major design idea for the building's exterior. In 1924, Wright wrote about his time working for Sullivan, "When he brought in the board with the motive of the Wainwright Building outlined in profile and in scheme upon it and threw it down on my table ... the 'skyscraper' as a new thing beneath the sun, an entity with virtue, individuality and beauty in all its wonder was born."[30] The grouping together of the windows in a democratic representation of the individual presence would later be lauded as an expression of verticality or "loftiness." The dilemma for Wright was clearly, that in giving poetic expression to the "skyscraper," the Wainwright's facade, like the eclecticism the Steinway architects

27 Eleanor Perkins, *Perkins of Chicago*, p.60.

28 Donald Hoffman, *The Architecture of John Wellborn Root*, p.163.

29 Quoted Hoffman, op. cit., p.163, and Wright, *Genius and the Mobocracy*, p.75. The exact Wright quote about the Wainwright in *Genius and the Mobocracy* is, "nobly tall instead of a simpering superimposition of several or many low buildings to arrive at height in the manner that 'skyscrapers' were being practiced by his contemporaries? By all except one: John Root. Root's Monadnock was a noble building. It was later but even further along. The Wainwright went very far—a splendid performance on the record for all time. Although the frontal divisions were still artificial."

30 Frank Lloyd Wright, "Louis H. Sullivan-His Work," *Architectural Record 56.* No.1, July 1924, p.28-32.

decried, was a sham disguising the nature of the structure that made the building's height possible.

Burnham and Root's Rialto Building of 1886 and their American Bank Building in Kansas City, or George Edbrooke's 1887 Willoughby Building in Chicago are all early examples of tall buildings with windows set between vertical piers. These might serve to put Sullivan's Wainwright Building in context, suggesting that the use of vertical piers as a design device on tall commercial and institutional buildings was already in use rather than Sullivan's invention. Contrary to the horizontal expression of the structural bay favored by Jenney and by Holabird and Roche, Sullivan's tall buildings suppressed a reading of the structural frame. Sullivan favored the expression of a tall building's loftiness. For Wright and Perkins the generally accepted idea regarding meaning in architecture was that verticality was an expression of human "aspiration." This was an idea that could have seemed appropriate to both the religious and humanistic ideals they felt the All Souls building should symbolize.[31] This idea, verticality as an expression of aspiration, along with their admiration for Sullivan's work, may further explain why Wright and Perkins clung to the division of the building's surfaces by piers in the face of Jenkin Lloyd Jones's objections.

---

31 Wright, *An Autobiography*, 1932, p.155; 1957, p.19. In *An Autobiography*, Wright states, "certain geometric forms have come to symbolize for us and potentially to suggest certain human ideas ... as for instance: the circle, infinity; the triangle, structural unity; the spire, aspiration; the spiral, organic progress; the square integrity."

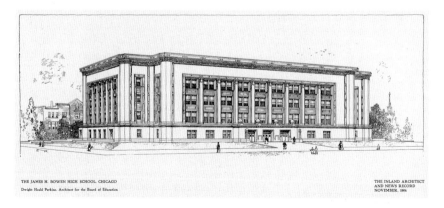

THE JAMES H. BOWEN HIGH SCHOOL, CHICAGO
Dwight Heald Perkins, Architect for the Board of Education

THE INLAND ARCHITECT
AND NEWS RECORD
NOVEMBER, 1906

7.011. Dwight Perkins. Preliminary Design for the James H. Bowen High School. Chicago, Il. 1906.
As built (1910) it was similar to the Carl Schurz High School.

Perkins collaboration with Wright on the earlier designs for the Abraham Lincoln Center would have a profound impact on the school designs he would produce as Chief Architect for the Chicago Board of Education from 1906 to 1911. This is evident in his design for the James H. Bowen High School in Chicago, published in the *Inland Architect* for November of 1906. The elevations are reminiscent of the version of the Lincoln Center illustrated in the newspaper clipping from the Perkins collection at the Chicago History Museum entitled, "Proposed Church Edifice for Rev. Jenkin Lloyd Jones." In Perkins's school design, not only are the corners emphasized, but they are re-entrant, providing space for additional windows.

The influence of the Abraham Lincoln Center can also be seen in Perkins's design for the Grover Cleveland High School of 1911. The grouping of windows between vertical piers, the suggestion of an attic floor by the setback of the vertical piers, and the duplication of the width of the corner piers as a horizontal cornice band, all recall aspects of the 1902 "All Souls" project.

Donald Leslie Johnson suggests that both Wright and Perkins learned from the Lincoln Center as a design exercise. He wrote, "His [Perkins] 1906 design for the John B. Rogers school had an exterior character that, in spite of his published disgust

7.012. Dwight Perkins. Grover Cleveland Elementary School. Chicago, Il. 1911.

7.013. Dwight Perkins. Proposed Commercial high school building for the Chicago Board of Education. Chicago, Il. 1908.

7.014. Spencer and Perkins. Design for an Auditorium. Chicago, Il. 1902.

of Reverend Jones's reductive lesson for Lincoln Center of just a couple of years earlier, was well learnt."[32] Perhaps an even greater resemblance to the earlier (and taller) Lincoln Center designs was Perkins's 1908 proposal for a high-rise "commercial high school building" for Harrison Street and Plymouth Court in Chicago.[33]

Among the important contributions Perkins made to school design, as already noted, was the incorporation of auditoriums in the Chicago Public Schools he designed. Perkins had given much thought to the design of these spaces, beginning with the auditoria incorporated into Steinway Hall, the Abraham Lincoln Center's auditorium, and his unidentified collaboration for an auditorium designed with Robert Spencer, published in the Chicago Architectural Club Annual for 1902. In his project with Spencer, the influence for the proscenium opening seems to have been Alder and Sullivan's use of telescoping forms to enhance the acoustical properties of the hall. Like the Concert Hall in his Steinway Hall building the back wall of the stage is curved to reflect sound.

---

32 Johnson, *Frank Lloyd Wright: The Early Years*, p.117-18.

33 Published in the *Annual Report of the Board*, 1908-9. A second slightly modified version was presented the following year.

Like Perkins's subsequent design work, the Abraham Lincoln Center's designs with windows between vertical piers was the aesthetic solution that Wright would employ on his 1906 Larkin Building. The Larkin Building's design was prepared while he was still working on the Abraham Lincoln Center. At the Larkin Building, not only are the windows grouped between piers, but as in the 1902 Lincoln Center exterior the vertical stacks of windows terminate in a setback like the "loggias" Jones eliminated. Grouping windows between vertical piers was also used in Wright's E-Z Polish factory of 1905 done for the brother of Darwin Martin for whom he had designed the Larkin Building in Buffalo. A letter from Darwin Martin to John Larkin dated March 30, 1903 reports on his first interview with Wright suggesting that, "The $500,000 Wainwright Building and the Union Trust Building of St. Louis ... were, I inferred from Mr. Wright, largely his creations."[34]

While the Abraham Lincoln Center was for Perkins, among the tallest building he would build, Wright continued to be occupied by the problem of the tall building; Sullivan's aesthetic

---

34 Jack Quinan, *Frank Lloyd Wright's Larkin Building: Myth and Fact*, Appendix C, p.131.

7015. Frank Lloyd Wright. Larkin Building Buffalo, N.Y. 1903.

solution; and his ambivalence about Sullivan's choice to suppress the true expression of the building's structure.

In 1914, Wright displayed a plaster model at the Chicago Architectural Club's 27th annual exhibition titled "Office Building, San Francisco." It was a vertically extended reworking of the 1903 design for the Abraham Lincoln Center project. For Wright, the San Francisco project was an opportunity to solve the problem of the Wainwright Building's aesthetic expression, on which Wright and Perkins had modeled their earlier designs.

Wright's office building project was a design for a new building for Claus Spreckels, the son of John D. Spreckels, the owner of the *San Francisco Call*, the city's morning newspaper. The project has been represented as a collaboration with Harrison Albright, a San Francisco architect who had done work for John Spreckels. It is unclear whether Spreckels ever saw Wright's design. Wright's son John, who wanted to enter the architectural profession, had taken a job with Albright. According to John, "His work is all reinforced concrete and he takes nothing under $1,000,000."[35] Wright had built Unity Temple and the E-Z Polish factory in concrete. The possibility of building a skyscraper in concrete and creating an exposed concrete exterior wall of structural columns may have been seen by Wright as a solution to Sullivan's brick pier facade, hung on a metal frame that it did not express. In his 1901 Hull House Lecture—"The Art and Craft of the Machine"—he wrote about an "art torn and hung upon the steel frame of commerce, a forlorn head on a pike." Suggesting that he believed Sullivan's brick piers to be as dishonest as the applied cladding of a *Beaux-Arts* skyscraper.

In the Call Building project, the building's narrow width would have allowed the concrete floor slabs to span the dimension between the exterior walls. These were to be comprised of closely spaced concrete columns. The short ends of the building would have acted as shear walls. Placing the stair towers at the corners of the plan as he had done in the Larkin Building and Unity Temple and expressing them as solid volumes allowed his tower to have solid corners. However, these were a real expression of the use behind them, unlike the Lincoln Center designs or

---

35 John Lloyd Wright, letter, July 19, 1912 quoted in Hoffman, *Frank Lloyd Wright, Louis Sullivan and the Skyscraper*, p.48.

the Wainwright Building. This can be understood by comparing the plans of these buildings. Like the Wainwright, Wright articulated the attic floor with a stringcourse and then capped the entire building with a flat cornice like Sullivan's or his and Perkins's 1903 project for the Lincoln Center. The cornice, like the brim of a hat, has a greatly exaggerated projection at the short ends of the building where the ground floor entrances were to be located. While the Call Building has been compared to both Unity Temple and the Larkin Building, its real antecedent is Wright and Perkins's early designs for the Abraham Lincoln Center, particularly their 1903 project.

7.016. Frank Lloyd Wright. Call Building project. San Francisco, Ca. 1912.

The idea of the wall dissolved into a series of piers was an idea that would dominate Wright's work. He explored this idea in a number of houses from this period and its development should also be considered as a step beyond his and Spencer's use of half timbering to regulate the location of windows in their residential work. This use of a row of multiple piers was certainly not a new concept, Alberti had written centuries earlier that, "a Row of Columns being indeed nothing else but a Wall open and discontinued in several places."[36] This is perhaps an apt description of Wright's plan for the Martin House at Buffalo of 1904.

The design of the Abraham Lincoln Center was important to Wright's development. In 1907 he chose to exhibit a five-year-old plaster model of the 1902 scheme for the Abraham Lincoln Center along with his newer work in the Chicago Architectural

---

36 Alberti, *Ten Book on Architecture*, London: Tiranti, 1965, p.14.

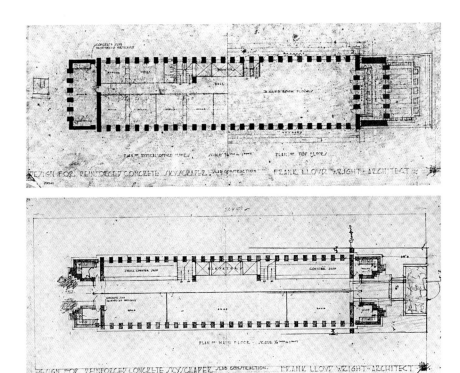

7.017. Frank Lloyd Wright. Call Building project. Ground and Top floor Plans. San Francisco, Ca. 1912

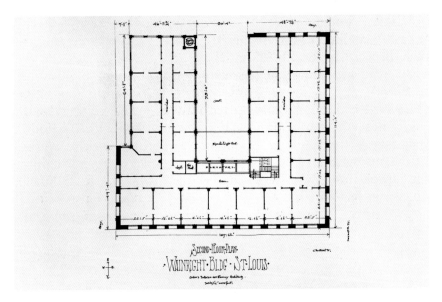

7018. Adler and Sullivan. Wainwright Building. Plan. St. Louis, Mo. 1891.

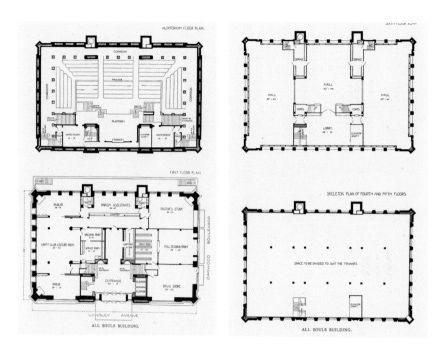

7.019. Wright and Perkins. Abraham Lincoln Center. Ground Floor Plan and 2nd and 3rd floor Auditorium Plan. Chicago, Il.

7.020. Wright and Perkins. Abraham Lincoln Center. Upper floor plans. Chicago, Il.

Club's annual exhibit. Later he would include the Call Building to represent his solution to the vertical expression of a tall building. He exhibited a plaster model of the Call Building in the Chicago Architectural Club's exhibition for 1914. Wright would include the Call Building model in retrospectives such as the 1930 traveling exhibition organized by the Architectural League of New York, an exhibit of his work from 1893 to 1930. Later, in 1939–40, the Call Building model was rebuilt in wood with slight design modifications. This second model was included in "Sixty Years of Living Architecture" at New York's Guggenheim Museum in 1953. That Wright would continue to exhibit these projects suggests their importance. It was the design of the Abraham Lincoln Center that would shape his early institutional and commercial designs as well as Dwight Perkins schools.

Chapter 7

SPENCER, WRIGHT, AND THE LADIES' HOME JOURNAL*

❝ *America consequently produced her most*
original monuments where one after all might
have expected to find them: in the homes of
individual men.

Vincent Scully Jr., The Shingle Style

T he *Oak Park Reporter* for May 3, 1900, noted that,
"R.C. Spencer has returned from Philadelphia Thurs-
day. He was called there by the editors of the *Ladies'*
Home Journal and has been engaged by them to write a series
of articles on architecture for publication."[1] The articles referred
to were probably the series of model farmhouses designed by
Spencer and published between 1900 and 1901. In March of that
year Spencer had published an article entitled *"The Farmhouse*
Problem" in the 13th Annual Chicago Architectural Club Catalog.
The essay was accompanied by two designs for farmhouses and
it is entirely possible that he could have taken this work with
him to Philadelphia for his meeting with the Journal's editor
Edward Bok.

Wright's projects for the *Ladies' Home Journal*—"A Home in
a Prairie Town" (February, 1901) and "A Small House with 'Lots
of room in It' (July 1901)"—are generally considered breakthrough designs and the first appearance of the Prairie House.
Robert Spencer has never been adequately acknowledged as a
collaborator in the creation of certain ideas this work embodied. Without question the commission for Wright's *Ladies' Home*
Journal houses came through Spencer. Not only were Wright
and Spencer working side by side in Steinway Hall, but Wright
would describe Spencer as his closest friend and confidant
after the departure of Cecil Corwin. Before moving to Steinway
Hall, Wright's and Spencer's offices had been side by side in
the Schiller Building. In *A Testament* Wright remembers, "Bob

---

* In addition to notes below also see Lehland Roth's article "Getting the Houses to the People,"
Edward Bok *Ladies' Home Journal*, and the "Ideal House" in Perspectives in *Vernacular*
Architecture, 1991.
1 Quoted in Kruty, *Prelude to the Prairie Style*, p.54, footnote 4.

and I were often seen together, at times even borrowing each other's Bohemian manners and costumes, so that Chicago conformists working in other offices seeing us arm in arm down the street, would say in derision, 'There goes God Almighty, with his Jesus Christ.'"[2] A comparison of their work for the *Ladies' Home Journal* suggests at the very least an exchange of ideas and cross-fertilization, if not a collaboration. For them, publishing their work in the *Ladies' Home Journal* offered the opportunity for their designs and ideas to reach an audience well beyond the architectural journals of the day.

At the beginning of the 20th century the *Ladies' Home Journal* had the largest circulation and was the most influential of the magazines devoted to improving the American home. It was read by over a million subscribers. It's editor Edward Bok, in his 1921 autobiography, written in the third person, tells us about his decision to publish designs for model houses: "he travelled through the United States, he was appalled. ... Where the houses were not positively ugly, they were, to him repellently ornate ... Bok found out that these small householders never employed an architect, but that the houses were put up by builders from their own plans. Bok felt a keen desire to take hold of the small American house and make it architecturally better."[3]

Cyrus Curtis of the Curtis Publishing Company was the owner and publisher of the *Ladies' Home Journal.* In 1889 he hired Bok, his future son-in-law, to replace his wife as the editor. In December of 1895 Bok published the first installment in a series of model house designs that would continue until his retirement in 1919. The first installment was titled "A $3500 Suburban House." The article featured an English Tudor home designed by a fashionable young Philadelphia architect, William L. Price, who the following year would design a house for Bok and his new wife in suburban Merion, Pennsylvania. Price had worked for Frank Furness during the 1870s and was influenced by the English Arts and Crafts movement and its ideal of simplification. In 1901 he founded a crafts community, the Rose Valley

---

2 Wright, *A Testament*, 1957, p.34. We don't know which role Wright cast himself in, but it was probably as god, with Spencer as the messianic proponent of his ideas. He would later write, "I saw the architect as savior of the culture of modern American society ... savior now as for all civilization here-to-fore." Wright, op. cit., 1957, p.24.

3 Bok, *The Americanization of Edward Bok. An Autobiography*, p.238.

Association, based on the ideas of C.R. Ashbee. The publication of Price's 1895 design was followed by a second house designed by Ralph Adams Cram. The first series of eight houses was then followed by a second series of nine houses published from July 1897 to June 1898. The designs were offered for sale with the magazine providing drawings, building specifications, and cost estimates from builders in different parts of the country. The plans sold for five dollars a set. While we don't know how much the architects received from the sale of their plans, according to Bok the plans were sold by the thousands.

Initially Bok had difficulty in getting architects to contribute as many believed, "It was 'cheapening' their profession," and "taking bread out of their mouths."[4] However, with the success of this feature and the sale of plans, Bok had no problem getting architects to participate. In his autobiography Bok quotes Stanford White, "I firmly believe that Edward Bok has more completely influenced American domestic architecture for the better than any man in this generation. When he began, I was short-sighted enough to discourage him, and refused to cooperate with him. If Bok came to me now, I would not only make plans for him, but I would waive any fee for them in retribution for my early mistake."[5] In addition to White, Bok's friend Theodore Roosevelt would later write, "Bok is the only man I ever heard of who changed, for the better the architecture of an entire nation, and he did it so quickly and effectively that we didn't know it was begun before it was finished."[6]

By the turn of the century America was amid a period of both social and cultural change that impacted the design of houses for the growing middle class. The sale of house plans was hardly unique, and both plans and precut materials for entire houses were available through various companies and publications. Among these were: Aladdin Homes, their motto being, "built in a day"; Wilson Bungalows; Radford Homes; and Sears and Roebuck, who sold entire precut "kit houses." Later publications such as Gustav Stickley's *Craftsman* magazine also sold house plans. A big difference between the houses offered by the

4 Bok, op. cit., p.241.
5 Bok, op. cit., p.243.
6 Bok, op. cit., p.249.

Ladies' Home Journal and other purveyors of house plans was that Bok sought out well-known designers as well as innovative young architects. Unlike other magazines or house plan companies, Bok's magazine prominently credited architects for their designs, asking each architect to provide a written description of their work for publication.

In 1900 the magazine decided to run two concurrent series, the first illustrating somewhat larger suburban homes and the second devoted to illustrating model farmhouses aimed at the magazine's rural readers. The desire on Bok's part to feature designs for model farmhouses may have reflected the growing interest in the Arts and Crafts movement in America. The ideals of the movement, such as a return to the "simple life" and "handcraft" were still believed to be exemplified by rural America. In the first decade of the 20th century the idea of life on the frontier was part of America's mythology. A return to outdoor living and an appreciation of things "rustic" were being endorsed by Bok's friend Teddy Roosevelt as a respite from city life and industrial capitalism.[7]

In the October 1900 issue of the *Ladies' Home Journal* the magazine announced the beginning of its new suburban house series devoted to "Model Suburban Houses Which Can be Built at Moderate Cost." Designed for them by "the foremost architects of New York, Philadelphia, Boston and Chicago," who, "will prepare the plans and estimates for these houses." The announcement, which ran at the front of the magazine didn't mention the farmhouse series which ran concurrently. Thirteen house designs were published between October 1900 and November 1901. These were designed by Bruce Price, Ralph Adams Cram, Elmer Grey, Wilson Eyre, Robert Spencer, and Frank Lloyd Wright.

Bok had ties to Chicago through his friend Eugene Field, the author and poet, Frances Willard the leader of the temperance movement, as well as Jane Addams, the social reformer whose Hull House was home to the Chicago Arts and Crafts Society. However, it may have been Spencer's article in the *Architectural Review* about the work of Frank Lloyd Wright that could have

---

7 In April of 1900 Roosevelt, then governor of New York, addressed the Hamilton Club of Chicago. His talk, "The Strenuous Life," attacked "ignoble ease," and promoted "the doctrine of the strenuous life, the life of toil and effort, of labor and strife." Quoted in in Thomas, William Price, p.75.

brought the more progressive residential work being done in Chicago, to Bok's attention. In it Spencer had written, "It is a pleasure to see how style may be given in the cheapest structure when dull or useless precedent is abandoned, and materials are handled not merely with a sound knowledge ... but with a keen poetic insight into the subtle sources of beauty," and "These houses, ... express clearly and consistently certain ideas of home and of quiet, simple home life, and are solutions of problems which have been developing slowly among our people of the intelligent middle class. ... the homes of the people should receive the best thought and effort of those who have not yet been drugged by material success into a state of *blaise* indifference to small things."[8]

Spencer was clearly expressing the same ideas that Bok was promoting, and it is entirely possible that William L. Price, Edward Bok's architect, called Bok's attention to Spencer's writing. Price, as Bok's architect, would have had an influence on Bok's model house program and could have played a prominent role in Bok's selection of architects. Reflecting Price's importance to Bok's agenda, in 1895 the Curtis Publishing Company printed *Model Houses for Little Money*, a book of small house designs by Price. The book used as its introduction, the text of his 1895 article a *"$3500 Suburban House"* written for the *Ladies' Home Journal.*

Price was an advocate for the simplification of the American house. He would have been aware of work being done in Chicago as an invited participant in The Chicago Architectural Club's 1897 (10th Annual) exhibit. Along with Chicago work, by this time, the club's yearly exhibits included projects by other architects from across the country. Price could have also called Bok's attention to Spencer's article in the Chicago Architectural Club's Annual for 1900 on the "Farmhouse Problem" as well as his article on the "American Farmhouse" in the September 1900 issue of the *Brickbuilder.* These arguments for the redesign of the American farmhouse may have been the impetus for Bok's inclusion of farmhouse designs in his publication.

Edward Bok's ideas aligned perfectly with Spencer and Wright's residential agenda. Bok called for the simplification of

---

8 Spencer, "The Work of Frank Lloyd Wright," the *Architectural Review*, June 1900, p.62.

the house, the elimination of "useless" ornament, provision of cross ventilation, and the elimination of unnecessary rooms such as the parlor, as a way to create the affordable small houses he wished to make available to the public. Bok asked, "that each plan published should provide for two essentials: "in place of the American parlor ... a useless room, should be substituted either a living-room or a library," and that, "every servant's room should have two windows to insure cross ventilation,"[9] reflecting Bok's concern as a social reformer. However, many of the plans published in the Ladies' Home Journal still had the rooms conventionally found in American houses, eliminating the entry hall or stair hall to make for a more compact layout. Bruce Price's "Georgian House for Seven Thousand Dollars," in the October 1900 issue had an entry and stair hall with a room labeled "parlor" to the right. Charles Kent and Frank Mead's Art and Crafts design, a "Quaint, Old-Fashioned House for $6,600," has a large hall as its primary living space that included the main stair and a fireplace nook. However, it still provided a separate dining room. By contrast, all of Spencer's designs featured a single large space, essentially combining living room and dining room and providing a compact functional kitchen, embracing the simplifications Bok called for. It is possible that Bok may have thought about including designs for farmhouses as a way to move beyond the tendency of East Coast architects to simply produce smaller versions of Georgian and Colonial houses with their well-known arrangement of interior spaces.

An early Wright biographer, Grant Manson suggests that, "There can be no argument, however about the date of the two model houses which Wright drew up sometime in 1900 for the Curtis Publishing Company of Philadelphia ... in The Ladies' Home Journal in February and July respectively, of 1901. In these designs, Wright officially unveiled the Prairie House, and the title of the first of the two presentations was 'A Home in a Prairie Town.'"[10]

It is interesting to compare the principal elevation and the plans of Spencer's "A Southern Farmhouse to Cost $3,000" published in January of 1901 to the principal elevation of Wright's

---

9 Bok, op. cit., p.241.
10 Manson, Frank Lloyd Wright to 1910, p.103.

8.001. Robert Spencer." A Southern Farmhouse." Project. Ladies Home Journal. 1901.

8.002. Frank Lloyd Wright." A Home in a Prairie Town." Project. Ladies Home Journal. 1901.

8.003. Frank Lloyd Wright. Ward Willits House, Highland Park, Il. 1902.

design for "A Home in a Prairie Town," which appeared the following month. Spencer's design should also be compared to the Ward Willits House of 1902.

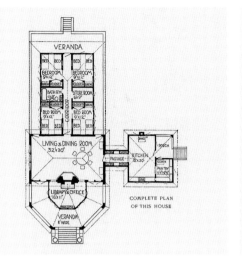

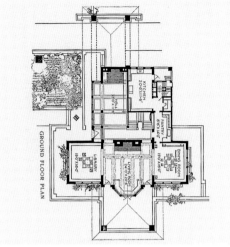

8.004. Robert Spencer. "A Southern Farmhouse."
Project. Plan. Ladies Home Journal. 1901.

8.005. Frank Lloyd Wright. "Home in a Prairie Town."
Project. Plan. Ladies Home Journal. 1901.

Spencer's one-story farmhouse elevation with its double-height living and dining space is similar in overall massing to Wright's January 1901 design and to his 1902 Willits House. Of interest is the window treatment on the side of the main block of Spencer's Farmhouse compared to that of the Willits House. In both, the first- and second-story windows are grouped vertically. Unlike Wright's earlier Nathan Moore House, the Willits House is the first occurrence in his work of timbering only used to order and visually connect windows. Wright's interest in half-timbering as a design device and its use in the Nathan Moore House was probably derived from Spencer's Grepe House of 1894.[11]

Spencer's "Southern Farmhouse" adheres to the old regional custom of locating the kitchen in an attached dependency. Wright's house is two stories, but what is of interest is the development of the main living spaces in both Spencer and in Wright's plans. In each case the plan is "T" shaped with the living space extended by a covered porch. In each a glazed bay window extends under the porch flanked on either side by French doors. While Wright interconnects a library, a dining space, and the central living room, Spencer combines all the living functions into one two-story space extending to the underside of a hipped roof.

---

11 Kruty, "Wright, Spencer and the Casement Window," p.107.

Spencer's design for "A Brick and Shingle Farmhouse" published in February 1901 is the most compact of all the model houses that Bok published. While it has a steep shingled roof and shingled walls, its plan was an important moment for the architects of Steinway Hall. It incorporated an original planning feature that Wright would later utilize in his smaller cubic houses. Spencer combined the entry vestibule and the first landing of the principal stair that went up through the house. Wright's 1903 house designed for Robert Lamp, his childhood friend, is almost identical in plan. In the Lamp House the stair arrives at a landing behind the fireplace in the main living space, an arrangement which is identical to Spencer's 1901 farmhouse design. Further, Wright's places the kitchen and other features in the same relationship to the principal living space. Unlike Spencer's plan, the Lamp House stair is not pulled out of the house's cubic volume to form an entry feature and create a more spacious entryway. This was a feature that Wright would later incorporate into his work. When Spencer's design was done in the studio loft at Steinway Hall, Perkins, Walter Burley Griffin, and Marion Mahony were all still in residence and Wright was splitting his time between Oak Park and his Steinway Hall office. Wright's "A Fireproof House for $5000" published in 1907 is almost identical to Spencer's 1901 plan, with the entry to the house directly into the stair which proceeds up to the main floor and then up through the house. In Spencer's farmhouse the protruding stair volume is a prominent feature of the front façade. An articulated stair volume is an element that Spencer would use in many of his subsequent houses. The main room of Spencer's farmhouse faces away from the proposed approach drive and ascending the stair arrives at an enclosed vestibule. In Wright's plan the stair arrives directly in the main living space, a superior arrangement, but orients this space to the street rather than to a private rear yard. Wright would use this plan for his 1907, Stephen Hunt House in LaGrange, Illinois, with the exterior also based on his *Ladies' Home Journal* house. This plan was also the basis of Wright's 1908 Stockman House in Mason City, Iowa and then with slight variations, the Green House of 1912 in Aurora, Illinois, the Bach House of 1915 in Chicago, and the Ross House also built in 1915 in Glencoe, Illinois.

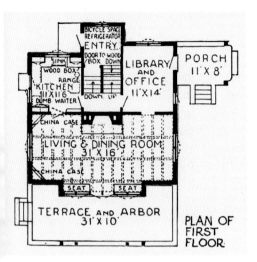

8.006. Robert Spencer." A Brick and Shingled Farmhouse." Project. Ladies Home Journal. 1901.

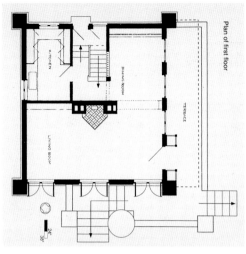

8.007. Frank Lloyd Wright. Robert Lamp House. Madison, Wisc. 1903.

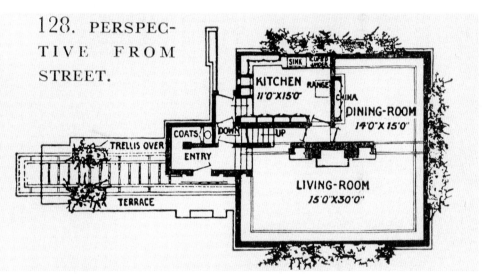

8.008. Frank Lloyd Wright. "A Fireproof House for $5000." Project. Ladies Home Journal. 1907.

Further suggesting the possibility of collaborative inter-actions, Spencer's plan for "A Brick and Shingled Farmhouse" is related to a small vacation cottage built by Dwight Perkins. While the project was included in the Chicago Architectural Club's catalog for 1902, its design predates Spencer's. Exhibited as a "Cottage on Bustin's Island, Casco Bay," Maine, it began con-struction in May of 1900.[12] It featured a single large living room

12 Kruty, "A Prairie School House in Coastal Maine," p.12–17. Kruty established the cottages' date of construction.

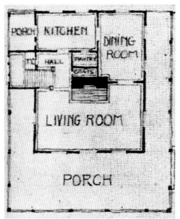

8.009. Dwight Perkins. Cottage on Bustin's Island. Casco Bay, Me. Plan. 1900.

8.010. Dwight Perkins. Cottage on Bustin's Island. Casco Bay, Me. 1900.

with a fireplace centered on the back wall and the stair pulled out of the square floor plan. The relationship of the stair to the fireplace and living room is nearly identical to Wright's "A Fireproof House" of 1907. Unlike either Spencer or Wright's designs the main block of Perkins's house is surrounded by a porch on three sides accessed through French doors. The entry into the cottage is from the porch through the living room, a major difference from Spencer's design and its inventive use of the stair's landing as the entryway.

Historian Paul Kruty, speculates that, Perkins who was busy at the time with large institutional commissions, could have turned the design over to Walter Burley Griffin. In May of 1900 Griffin was still working for Perkins. Griffin didn't leave to work for Wright in his Oak Park Studio until 1901 and it is certainly possible that he worked on the cottage. The client, Ella Gould, was an old friend of Perkins's who he had known from his time in Boston, when they both rented rooms in the same boarding house. It is unlikely, given his personal relationship to the client, that he would have entirely delegated the design to Griffin. If Griffin worked on the cottage for Perkins, he could have brought this planning idea to Wright's Studio when he went to work there. Was Perkins's cottage the source of Spencer's farmhouse and was Spencer's farmhouse then the source of Wright's design for the Lamp House of 1903? Given the dates of these projects, one conclusion could be that this unique plan was jointly developed by Perkins, Spencer, Griffin, and Wright.

The idea of eliminating the entry hall by combining it with the landing of the main stair was a feature of several of Spencer's

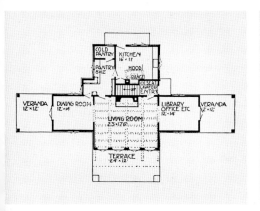

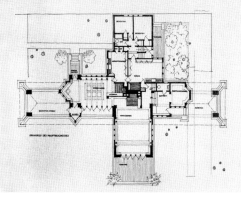

8.011. Robert Spencer. "A Shingled Farmhouse for $2700."
Project. Ladies Home Journal. 1901. Plan.

8.012. Frank Lloyd Wright.
Ward Willits House. Highland Park, Il. 1902. Plan.

other designs for the *Ladies' Home Journal*. "A Northern Farm-house to Cost $3000" in the December 1900 issue features a stone-clad first floor and a half timbered second floor. It has a protruding stair that arrives directly in the combined living and dining space. "A Small Farmhouse that Can be Enlarged" published in June of 1901 is a version of this same cube house that can be elongated with the addition of a living room space with three more bedrooms above it. The original living room is converted into a dining room. The treatment of the projecting stair tower, its stepping windows and covered entryway is like Spencer's later work such as his 1906 Magnus House in Winnetka, Illinois.

Another example of the reciprocal influences exhibited in Spencer and Wright's *Ladies' Home Journal* houses may be seen in a comparison of the cruciform plan for Spencer's March 1901 "A Shingled Farmhouse for $2700" and Wright's plan for the 1902 Ward Willits House. This similarity was first pointed out by H. Allen Brooks in his book *The Prairie School*.[13] This plan is also,

13 Brooks wrote, "Wright's own work ... augmented, perhaps by the stimulation he received form his colleagues at Steinway Hall, came rapidly to maturity after 1900. Most notable were his projects for the *Ladies' Home Journal*, published in February and July 1901 ... Concurrently, seven Model Farmhouses by Robert Spencer were published in the same journal, and one of these ... was distinguished by its open, cruciform plan and uninterrupted flow of space along the horizontal axis. ... [O]ne initially assumes that Spencer utilized Wright's idea for the massing and organization of interior space—while rejecting Wright's vocabulary of form. ... [An] unanticipated possibility exists, therefore, that Spencer's designs came first and acted as a catalyst for Wright, helping him achieve a synthesis in his own designs ... This is possible as Spencer's 'A Shingled Farmhouse' was exhibited at the Chicago Architectural Club in March 1900, and apparently precedes Wright's designs." H. Allen Brooks, *Prairie School*, p.58–59. Spencer's plan was drawn and published before Wright began the design of the Willits house in 1902. We now know that Ward Willits purchased the land early in 1902 and Wright completed the construction drawings in June of 1902. See *Johnson, Frank Lloyd Wright: Early Years*. p.183. "Wright & Tomlinson, Architects, Wright was the designer; linens dated 1 June 1902, revised November 1902 and January 1903." Even so, Brook's supposition is a standard of art and architectural history that tracks sequential influences and sources rather than assuming the collaborative creation of ideas.

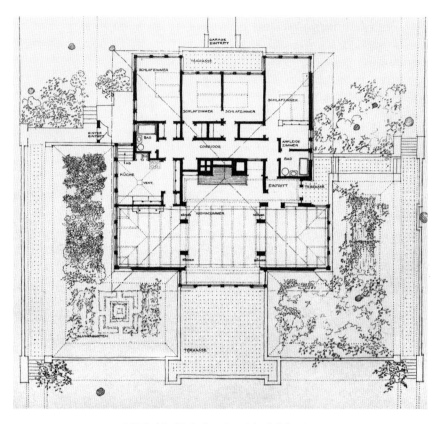

8.013. Frank Lloyd Wright. Cheney House. Oak Park, Il. Plan. 1903.

arguably the source of many of Wright's cruciform plans such as that of the 1903 Cheney House. Neil Levine has also pointed out the similarities between the Willits House plan and the ground-floor plan of Wright's "A Small House with Lots of Room in It" published in the July 1901 issue of the *Ladies' Home Journal*.

In both the "Shingled Farmhouse for $2700" and the layout of the Willits House, the principal spaces are in the form of a cross. In both, the back arm of the plan is devoted to service functions, kitchen, and pantry, and in the case of Wright's more elaborate design, also the servant's bedrooms and bath. In Spencer's design the three arms that contain the principal ground-floor living spaces are each extended by a covered porch, providing varying degrees of connection between interior and exterior. This is a function of the rows of French doors that open the living rooms to the outside. In both cases the end of the living room has French doors and the flanking wings only have windows. This gives the living rooms a greater sense of connection to the outside in each plan.

In Wright's Ward Willits House, as in his *Ladies' Home Journal* "Fireproof House," the living room faces the front of the house and the street. In the Ward Willits House the main entrance is under a *porte-cochere* while Spencer's farmhouse plan shifts the entry and the main stair into the service arm of the house. One major difference is in the connection between adjacent spaces. When the corners of Wright's living room and dining room are open to each other, they create a very different spatial connection than Spencer's design, which connects to adjacent spaces through wide central openings. In Spencer's plan the fireplace is a part of the back wall of the space with openings to the entry hall and to the pantry on either side of it. In Wright's Ward Willits House, half walls extend from the fireplace suggesting directional movement around it into the adjacent spaces, beginning to create a pin-wheel effect. The fireplace, rather than being the center of the room as in Spencer's design, becomes the center of Wright's entire house.

The Cheney House of 1903, even more than the Willits House, seems clearly inspired by the plan of Spencer's shingled farmhouse. The Cheney House, which is only one story, is a much simpler structure. The location of the entry along the back surface of the library wing and the kitchen's location are similar in both plans. However, the "service" areas behind the central fireplace are expanded to include the house's bedrooms. While the plan connections between the dining room, living room, and library are similar in plan, Wright's spatial development brilliantly connects the rooms by sliding the ceiling over a lower band of trim that forms part of the bookcases and piers dividing the rooms. It is also worth remembering that Spencer's and Wright's plans have entirely different orientations with respect to the street, how they are approached, and the location of private yard space.

Unlike the Prairie School architects, Robert Spencer's work was always clearly distinguishable from Wright's. He continued to use gabled rather than low hipped roofs and to use half timbering to organize windows and panelize exterior surfaces.

Many of the important aspects of Spencer and Wright's model house designs, particularly the spatial interconnection of

8.014. Spencer and Powers. Denkmann Residence. Rock Island, Illinois. 1909-11.

living spaces, were logical extensions and perhaps the culmination of design trends that grew out of the Queen Anne and Shingle-style houses of the 1880s and '90s. These, in turn, were related to social changes affecting the growing informality of family life. John Wellborn Root's article, "The City House in the West" pointed out these developments years before Spencer and Wright's *Ladies' Home Journal* model houses began to appear. He wrote, "One feature in the plans of Western city dwelling must be clearly defined. This is their openness ... while in the general plan, rooms are more closely related, openings between rooms wider, and single swinging-doors less frequent. Several dwellings in Chicago have no doors whatever in the first story, except those at the entrance and between the dining room and butler's pantry ... it is also true that life in the West is less conventional, freer, less restrained by artificial restrictions than in older communities, and the true nature of people and things is perhaps more frankly expressed."[14]

---

14 Root, "The City House in the West," in *Scribner's Magazine*, October 1890. Reprinted in Hoffman, ed., *The Meaning of Architecture, Buildings and Writings by John Wellborn Root.*

Clearly the ideas behind this new residential work were the result of collaboration and cross-fertilization. It was the *Ladies' Home Journal*, with its enormous readership, that introduced the Prairie House to America, not the publication of Wright's work in architectural journals. Yet, Wright wanted to make it clear that he was the source of all these new ideas, "A small clique formed about me, myself naturally the leader."[15] That Wright wanted to take credit for everything he touched has been acknowledged for many years.[16]

Wright and Spencer would have discussed their respective designs for the *Ladies' Home Journal*. Common to their designs was the "great room"—combining primary living functions with the hearth at its' center[17] and an unprecedented connection to the outside. They would have been excited at the opportunity to present these ideas to such a large forum. The publication of their house designs in the *Ladies' Home Journal*, must have seemed to them, like an ideal way to promote both themselves and their larger cause shared by the magazine's editor—the transformation of the contemporary American house.

As Teddy Roosevelt suggested, Bock, by promoting the ideas and designs of Price, Spencer, Wright, and other young architects, changed "the architecture of an entire nation." These changes were observed by Henry James in 1906 in *The American Scene*. James was one of the most influential novelists of his generation and had lived in England for many years. He wrote, "My visit to America had been the first possible to me for nearly a quarter of a century ... I was to return with much of the freshness of eye." James observed the changes in residential architecture and its implication for social mores. Describing what we now call the *open plan*, he wrote about the lack of separation between rooms, as "a strange perversity" testifying to the prevailing "conception

---

15 Wright, A Testament, 1957, p.34.

16 See Richard Bock, Memoirs of an American Artist, p.90. Wright's friend and collaborator, the sculptor Richard Bock tells the following story, "I was commissioned to design a drinking fountain 'for man and beast' ... for Oak Park ... I showed my design to Frank and asked how he liked it. He looked at it at length with approval, then he made a suggestion, sketching a rectangular opening just above the drinking trough. 'Now Dicky,' he said, 'you've got something.' The only difficulty was that now he began to lay claim to the whole project ... This fountain is still claimed for Wright by some writers about his work."

17 Levine, The Architecture of Frank Lloyd Wright, p.31. Levine identifies (as did Norris Kelly Smith) the central hearth as an important symbolic feature of domesticity. Levine called it the "essential element of representation and family unity."

of life." Further, he understood that architects were striving to create a fluid connection between the spaces inside and outside of their houses. He wrote, "The instinct is ... that of minimizing, for any interior ... each sign by which it may be known from an exterior ... Thus, we see systematized the indefinite extension of all spaces and the definite merging of all functions; the enlargement of every opening, the exaggeration of every passage, the substitution of gaping arches and far perspectives and resounding voids for enclosing walls."[18]While James clearly laments the changes that have taken place in America, he correctly observes their embodiment in a new type of American residential architecture.

Thomas Tallmadge, the Chicago architect and historian, in his 1927 book *The Story of Architecture in America*, writing in retrospect, also commented on these changes to the American house. He wrote, assessing the impact of Wright, Spencer, and the Prairie School architects, "Be it said here that if these independents did nothing else, they at least revolutionized the planning of the small house. There was no such thing as a sensible and scientific plan for a small house thirty years ago. Most of the conveniences that make for economical housekeeping and convenient living which we take for granted today date from that period."[19] And, it could be said, continue to shape the planning of American houses today.

---

18 Henry James, *The American Scene*, Las Vegas: Lits, 2010, reprint, p.72.
19 Tallmadge, *The Story of Architecture in America*, p.232.

Chapter 8

SPENCER AND WRIGHT: ARCHITECTURAL PRINCIPLES

" *Of the group, George R. Dean. Robert C.*
Spencer Jr., Dwight Perkins, and Frank Lloyd
Wright were all outspoken, and highly literate.
Literate enough, in fact, to have recorded many of
the seminal ideas propagated by the group. Each
of these men found time to record his thoughts
and, in many cases, to get his words into print.

Hasbrouck[1]

In *Michelangelo, Drawing and the Invention of Architecture* Cammy Brothers writes, "Michelangelo is too often
studied in precisely the terms that he defined rather
than in relation to the culture from which he emerged."[2] This
has often been the case in evaluating works of genius. It is certainly true that for more than half a century Wright defined the
terms by which his work and architectural ideas were understood. How his work was viewed, and its origin stories began
with Robert Spencer's 1900 article on Wright in the *Architectural Review.* The main points of which were echoed for years by
Frank Lloyd Wright. Reading both Spencer and Wright, suggests
that their early writings may have grown out of a collaborative
attempt to codify their architectural ideas.

In the June of 1900 issue of the *Architectural Review* Robert
Spencer published the first extensive description of Frank Lloyd
Wright's work and of the ideas underlying the architecture that
Wright, along with his Steinway Hall colleagues, was developing. Wright had built more than Spencer or Hunt and Perkins's
practice at this point was primarily institutional and commercial. Wright's work, which was rapidly reaching maturity, served
as the best examples of their ideas about architecture. The publication of Spencer's article appeared just three and a half months
after the Chicago Architectural Club's 13th Annual exhibit at the
Art Institute on March 20—an exhibit that provided Wright with

1 Hasbrouck, *The Chicago Architectural Club*, p.257.
2 Cammy Brothers, *Michelangelo, Drawing and the Invention of Architecture*, p.48.

his own separate gallery space. Dwight Perkins edited the catalog of the exhibit that grouped together Wright's work on ten consecutive pages, its first major appearance in print. Additionally, the work of the Steinway Hall architects was well represented. For them, controlling this publication was the opportunity to put forward and illustrate a polemic.

Spencer's article in the *Architectural Review,* was the first national publication of Wright's work and, like the Architectural Club's catalog, was illustrated by photographs, plans, elevations, and perspective drawings. Among the buildings and projects shown were Wright's home and studio; the Winslow House and barn; The Waller dining room; the unbuilt Orrin Goan House; the Bagley, Heller, Frubeck, Harlan, and Moore houses; the Francis and Francisco Terrace apartments; a Municipal Boat House for Madison, Wisconsin; and an early design for the Abraham Lincoln Center. About these Spencer wrote, "It is not my purposed to criticize the works shown here, except as it may seem needful to do so in order to bring out clearly the real nature and significance of each … *they embody new thought and new ideas"* (Italics added).

It is instructive to compare Spencer's 1900 article to Wright's early published writing and lectures. Particularly to his 1908 article in the *Architectural Record,* "In the Cause of Architecture," in which Wright lays out the key points of his work. In it he also acknowledges the formative influence exerted by Sullivan as well as his own contemporaries. He writes, "I well remember how 'the message' burned within me, how I longed for comradeship until I began to know the younger men and how welcome was Robert Spencer and then Myron Hunt, and Dwight Perkins, Arthur Heun, George Dean and Hugh Garden. Inspiring days they were, I am sure, for all of us."[3]

Spencer in his 1900 article establishes not only many of the points later listed by Wright in his 1908 article but provides key interpretations of Wright's work and of his early influences. These would become the cornerstones of what was to be written or said about Wright until the second half of the twentieth century. These included such staples of Wright's biography as the influence of his kindergarten training with Froebel blocks.

---

3 Wright, "In the Cause of Architecture" (1908) in Twombly, *Essential Texts,* p.84.

Spencer writes, "As a child in Boston he was given by his mother the benefit of the Froebel system of training the eyes to see, the brain to think and the hands to do. To this early training as a beginning she ascribes his instinctive grasps of the niceties of line, form and color." It seems likely that Spencer may have gotten this information from Wright, not his mother, in spite of writing, "she ascribes." Personal details such as this would certainly suggest Wright's participation with the intention of promoting a specific understanding of his work and of his and Spencer's jointly held views about contemporary architecture.[4]

Spencer's article, by suggesting the role of early childhood education and Froebel blocks in the shaping of Wright's architectural work, was clearly promoting his belief in the importance of the theory of Pure Design. Pure Design was being espoused as a way to educate artists, architects, and even young school children. It was an idea put forward by Arthur Wesley Dow, Denman Waldo Ross, and Ross's student Emil Lorch, who taught architecture at the school of the Chicago Art Institute beginning in 1899.[5] Pure Design proposed the study of abstract form and composition emphasizing, as Ross wrote, "the forms of Order, in the modes of Harmony, of Balance, or Rhythm."[6]

Key words, phrases, ideas, and even entire arguments seem to characterize the writing of both Spencer and Wright during this early period.

Spencer's 1900 article begins, not with a discussion of Wright's work, but by setting forth an argument that builds on Sullivan's call for the development of an original American architecture. Spencer writes, "The last year of the century finds the majority of our prominent and successful architects still busily engaged in the transplanting of exotics. From every fashionable foreign source the outward forms of the various styles and periods are being 'adapted,' plagiarized or caricatured according to the caliber and taste of the individual designer." Wright lectured on the same theme discussing the idea of "borrowed finery" in his 1896 talk to the University Guild in Evanston,

---

4 Both Manson & Hitchcock acknowledged Wright's participation in their books about his work.

5 Marie Frank, "The Theory of Pure Design and American Architectural Education in the Early Twentieth Century," JSAH v.67, n.2 June 2008, p.249-73.

6 Denman Waldo Ross, "Design as a Science," *Proceedings of the American Academy of Arts and Sciences* XXXVI, no. 21, March 1901, p.374.

Illinois. His first published article, "The Architect," was adapted from a paper presented to the second annual convention of the Architectural League of America, held in Chicago at the Art Institute. In it Wright bridles against the commercialization of the architectural profession. His comments were published in the *Brickbuilder* for June of 1900 at the same time that Spencer's article appeared in the *Architectural Review*. Writing about his professional peers, Wright notes that the architect, "has dragged his ancient monuments to the marketplace ... He has degenerated to a fakir[7] who flatters thin business imbecility with 'Art architecture shop fronts' worn in the fashion of old 'dickie' or panders to silly women his little artistic sweets." He continues, architecture becomes "a 'thing' to be applied like a poultice or a porous plaster." Both Spencer and Wright are addressing their fellow architects, and both are decrying contemporary eclecticism. Spencer in direct but measured terms, Wright in insults. Neither is expressing an original sentiment, but rather one that was growing in favor among younger architects in Chicago under the influence of Louis Sullivan.

Describing Wright's Oak Park studio, Spencer wrote (italics added), "The nervous, commercial atmosphere of the average architect's *plan factory* is entirely absent." The term plan factory was a label for the commercial architect's office and occurs several times in Wright's 1900 article "The Architect." He wrote, "Do you wonder at the prestige of the *plan factory* when architecture has become a commodity."[8] Other examples of the occurrence of identical language and expressions are to be found. Spencer writes in 1900, "When these houses were tortured with the universal *plinth and corner block trim*, his [Wright's] scheme of simple, plastic trim originated and quieted the cut, *butt and slash* of conventional practice." In 1908 Wright wrote, "These interiors were always slaughtered with the *butt and slash* of the old *plinth and corner block trim,* of dubious origin, and finally smothered with horrible millinery."[9]

---

7 Wright, who selected words carefully, does not mean faker, but he may be referring to Muslim Sufi monks known as dancing, whirling, or howling dervishes because of their rituals.

8 Italics added. Wright, "The Architect," the *Brickbuilder*, 9, June 1900; see also Twombly, *Essential Texts*, p.27.

9 Italics added. Wright, "In the Cause of Architecture," the *Architectural Record*, 23, March 1908; see also Twombly, ed., *Frank Lloyd Wright, Essential Texts*, p.87.

While these terms may have been jargon used in the loft of Steinway Hall, further expressive similarities may be seen in the description of the relationship of architecture to nature. Borrowing from Sullivan, Spencer applies the term "organic," to describe Wright's work. A comparison of Spencer's 1900 article and Wright's 1908 article and the descriptive language they use follows:

Spencer: "Into these small things it is always possible for the architect to put something of his higher self, something which will give grace, meaning and beauty to the simplest combination of humble material, just as the tiny flower expresses in exquisite and organic form and detail the life-principle and life-purpose of the humblest weed."

Wright: "Primarily, Nature furnished the material for architectural motifs out of which the architectural forms as we know them today have been developed ... her wealth of suggestion is inexhaustible; her riches greater than any man's desire."

Spencer: "Organically related in general scheme and smallest detail to the building as a whole."

Wright: "A sense of the organic is indispensable to an architect ... A knowledge of the relations of form and function lies at the root of his practice; where else can he find the pertinent object Nature so readily furnishes?"

Spencer: "All art influences must bear closely upon the common people ... if we are to have a real basis for a great national architecture. Our beautiful buildings ... must be the natural bloom of a hardy native growth with its roots deep in the soil."

In 1900 Spencer put forth principles of building illustrated by Wright's work. These would become the descriptive origins for Wright's discussions of his own work and would be repeated by several generations of biographers and critics. Wright's propositions set forth in 1908 *In the Cause of Architecture* were abbreviated and presented in outline form. They are summarized here in his words and compared to Spencer's article using the descriptive categories identified by Spencer rather than Wright's numbering system and outline format of 1908:

Spencer on Simplicity and the Organic: "A certain simple power of an organic nature that seems to have as much right to its place and is as much part of the site as the tree. The analogy begins there and continues, for the details of the house are as much in their place and as consistent in themselves and in relation to each other, as the whole house is to its surroundings." (It should be noted that Spencer's is perhaps the earliest and best definition of Sullivan's use of the idea of organic when understood as a metaphor for a design process that relates the parts of a building to the whole.)

Wright on Simplicity and the Organic: "Simplicity and Repose are qualities that measure the true value of any work of art ... a wildflower is truly simple ... I have endeavored in this work to establish a harmonious relationship between ground plan and elevation of these buildings, considering the one as a solution and the other an expression of the conditions of a problem of which the whole is a product. I have tried to establish an organic integrity to begin with, forming the basis for the subsequent working out of a significant grammatical expression and making the whole, as nearly as I could, consistent."

Spencer on Horizontality: "Mr. Wright has an evident love for the horizontal dimension and the horizontal line, he seldom employs it except in sympathy with masses in which the horizontal dimension exceeds the vertical."

Wright on Horizontality: "We of the Middle West are living on the prairie ... Hence gently sloping roofs, low proportions ... low terraces and out-reaching walls sequestering private gardens."

Spencer on the Relationship to the Ground: "There is almost invariably a base or stylobate of sufficient size to unify his masses and support the spring of the building from the ground with which it seems firmly and broadly associated ... You do not feel that these buildings have been dropped accidentally upon the ground or into holes in the earth dug carelessly."

Wright on the Relationship to the Ground: "A building should appear to grow easily from its site and be shaped to harmonize with its surroundings if Nature is manifest there, and if not try to make it as quiet, substantial and organic as She would have been were the opportunity Hers."

Spencer on Walls: "In the treatment of his walls the ruling idea is that of a plain or subordinately treated surface between two terminals."

Spencer on Openings: "Openings are few and wide in mullioned groups or sunny bays. An expanse of blank wall, out of which are punched at regular intervals a lot of openings all alike, each treated with a neat little architrave, has no interest for the maker of these plans unless there is some general scheme to unite them and produce a more interesting effect than that of a masonry box full of rectangular holes."

Wright on Openings: "'Architecture' chiefly consisted of healing over the edges of the curious collection of holes that had to be cut in the wall for light and air and to permit the occupant to get in or out. ... Openings should occur as integral features of the structure and form, if possible, its natural ornamentation."

Spencer on the Rooms of the house: "for the average home the only rooms upon the ground floor, aside from the working department, should be a hall, a living room and a dining room, all of ample dimensions ... It will be found expressed in various arrangements wherever people who have learned to simplify the art of elegant living have co-operated with architects of intelligence. The movement in this direction began with the advent of wide doorways between the principal rooms and the growing attention paid to the hall."

Wright on the Rooms of the house: "interiors were cut up into box-like compartments ... A building should contain as few rooms as will meet the conditions which give it rise and under which we live, and which the architect should strive continually to simplify ... Beside the entry and necessary work room there need be but three rooms on the ground floor of any house, living room, dining room and kitchen ... really there need be but one room, the living room, with requirements otherwise sequestered from it or screened within it by means of architectural contrivances."

Spencer on Roof Overhangs: "These almost unvarying broad eaves—what is their justification? Aesthetically, they make broad simple roof surfaces compatible with a very pleasing livable arrangement of bays or low windows beneath the roof surfaces which quiet the whole scheme with their unbroken surfaces."

Spencer on Ornament: "Ornament ... is a natural outgrowth of structure an organic part of a whole. ... The building is conceived as a perfect and complete organism. According to this conception there must be an intimate and organic relation between ornament and structure, between surface decoration and decorated surface, ... In this and in all his [Wright's] ornament there is evidence of wise and thoughtful planning, of the same synthetic method which successfully develops the ground plan of a great building."[10] (This last statement is perhaps a way of understanding what Wright took from his time working for Sullivan.)

Wright on Ornament: "Decoration is dangerous unless you understand it thoroughly and are satisfied that it means something good in the scheme as a whole, for the present you are usually better off without it."

Spencer on Color: "The rigid austerity of the mass, however, will be softened and balanced by the warmth of color, a rich dull tan, which will glow from its varied surfaces."

Wright on Color: "Colors require the same conventionalizing process to make them fit to live with that natural forms do; so go to the woods and fields for color schemes. Use the soft, warm, optimistic tones of earth and autumn leaves ... Bring out the nature of materials."

Spencer on Spatial and Volumetric development: "It is one of the faults of the average 'drawing board architect' that he neglects or forgets the third dimension in his buildings."

Concluding his article of 1900, Spencer suggests that like Sullivan, Wright is a leader, "in the present movement for a living, national architecture ... Mr. Wright has been doing for the typical residence and apartment house what Sullivan has done for the theatre and office building."

Although Spencer's description of Wright's work may have been formulated in discussions with Wright, by 1908 Wright felt the need to claim that the ideas underlying his houses were his and his alone. In 1908 a full issue of the *Architectural Record* was devoted to Wright, which included as a theoretical introduction, Wright's essay "In the Cause of Architecture." It was followed by 56 pages illustrating his work. In it he wrote, "In 1894 ... I formulated the following 'Propositions.' I set them down here much

---

10 A number of authors have suggested the relationship of the principles of the design of ornament to the design of floor plans. See particularly David Van Zanten's *Sullivan's City* and Thomas Beeby's "The Grammar of Ornament/Ornament as Grammar."

as they were written then." Wright is claiming the primacy of his ideas. They did not appear in his writings or lectures before Spencer's 1900 article. For Wright, he had "set them down" not in words but in his built work. The Winslow House was built in 1894, about which Spencer wrote, "the Winslow House, is more than worth a pilgrimage to see. In fact, it is the broadest, the most characteristic and the most completely satisfying thing that he has done." Perhaps, because Spencer had suggested that this was Wright's most characteristic early work, Wright could claim that it was here that he first "set down" his propositions, in spite of the dramatic differences between the Winslow House and his work after 1901.

The "propositions" that Wright ascribes to the Winslow House are in his written description of it published in the 1910 Wasmuth Portfolio, *Aussgefuhrte Bauten und Entwurfe von Frank Lloyd Wright*. The first plate was a street-level perspective of the Winslow House. Wright's description is as follows: "Many of the features which have since characterized this work originated in this house. The setting of the basement outside the main walls of the house to form a preparation for the projecting sill courses; the division of the exterior wall surface into body and frieze, changing the material above the second story sill line, the wide level eaves, with low sloping roofs; the one massive chimney; and the feeling for contrast between plain wall surface and richly decorated and concentrated masses; the use of the window as a decorative feature in itself; the lines of the building extending into the grounds, the low walls and parterre utilized to associate it with its site."

These "propositions," are from Wright's 1908 article. He felt the need to restate them in nearly identical form in *An Auto-biography* (1932), in *The Natural House* (1954), and then in an extended and modified form in *A Testament* (1957). Wright wanted to establish these ideas as being present in his earlier work. This could explain why so many Wright historians insist on calling the Winslow House the first Prairie House in spite of the dramatic visual differences between it, his *Ladies' Home Journal* houses, the Willits House, and his work after 1902.

One wonders if Wright would have attributed so much importance to the Winslow House, derivative of the exterior of Sullivan's Charnley House, but for Spencer's accolades. The nature of Sullivan and Wright's joint contributions to the design of the Charnley house has been discussed in Richard Longstreth's *The Charnley House*. Longstreth writes, "But the house for James and Helen Charnley was a special case. Sullivan's close friendship with the couple, the prestigious location of their site, and the publicity the firm sought for the project all suggest that this was an important commission that would not have been simply turned over to an assistant, no matter how gifted that individual."[11] The formality of the exterior is so different from Wright's early work or projects he would have worked on in Silsbee's office that it is more likely that Sullivan was the designer of the house's exterior with Wright creating the interior detailing and the sky-lit stair. After 1893, when Wright began his independent practice, it is possible that Wright was representing the design of the Charnley House as his own when he was approached by perspective clients. Orrin Goan and William Winslow could have known and admired the Charnley House, even asking Wright for a similar design.

That these design ideas can be seen in other progressive work of the time has been pointed out by Paul Kruty who writes, "The Charnley house was created during a period of rapid formal change in American architecture, as symmetry and simplification replaced picturesque complexity ... However radical its forms appeared later to architectural historians, the Charnley house would have seemed to be part of this new preference for dignified simplicity in its own day."[12] The Charnley House bears comparison to Pond & Pond's Coonley House of 1888 including the garden wall extending the houses base, the Lynch House of 1891 by Jennie & Mundie and the later Madlener House of 1901 by Schmidt, Garden & Martin all only blocks away from the Charnley House.

---

11 Richard Longstreth, ed., "Afterword: A Case for Collaboration," in *The Charnley House, Louis Sullivan, Frank Lloyd Wright, and the making of Chicago's Gold Coast*, p.193. Also see Paul Sprague, "Who Designed the Charnley House, Louis Henry Sullivan or Frank Lloyd Wright?" in Longstreth. Sprague writes, "Nor would Sullivan or any other respectable architect in Chicago at that time ever have allowed a draftsman, even Frank Lloyd Wright, to design a building for him" (p.134). Sprague discusses the history of Wright's written assertions of authorship of the Charnley House and their acceptance by various early Wright historians. Concluding that it was important to Wright that the Winslow House not be perceived as directly dependent on Sullivan. Sprague quotes a letter from Wright to Lewis Mumford dated April 7, 1931, "The Charnley house in Chicago ... I did at home for Adler and Sullivan to pay my building bills. That house was the forerunner of the Winslow house as you may see if you glance at both together" p.153.

12 Paul Kruty in Longstreth, ed., *The Charnley House*, p.95.

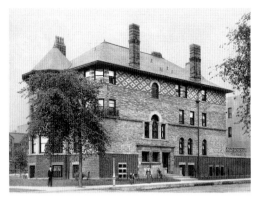

9.001. Pond & Pond. Coonley House. Chicago, Il. 1888.

9.002. Sullivan and Wright. Charnley House. Chicago, Il. 1891.

9.003. Frank Lloyd Wright. Winslow House. River Forest, Il. 1894.

9.004. Jenney & Mundie. Lynch House. Chicago, Il. 1891.

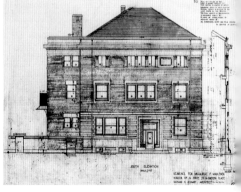

9.005. Richard Schmidt. Madlener House. Il. 1901.

Wright's published articles from this period, largely in architectural journals, were written to promote his work and his underlying ideas. However, it was Spencer who wrote extensively about the adaptation of these ideas to the construction of houses for the growing middle class. Spencer wrote over 50 articles, often published as serial installments. These were primarily for popular magazines such as the *House Beautiful* and *Ladies' Home Journal*, as well as architectural publications such as the *Brickbuilder*, the *Inland Architect*, the *Architectural Review*, and the *Architectural Record*.

Spencer and Wright, in their published articles, were building upon ideas that Sullivan had put forward. They were also expressing commonly held sentiments shared by other members of their collaborative circle in Steinway Hall as well as the younger architects of the Chicago Architectural Club. In calling for reform, Spencer, Wright, George Dean, and Elmer Grey, among others who published their writings, were asking for the development of an indigenous American architecture; suggesting new sources of architectural form; and giving voice to a new generation of architects.

Wright would go on to become one of the 20th centuries most prolific architectural authors. He wrote and published extensively between 1927 and 1932 a period during which he had few architectural commissions. Anthony Alofsin, discussing Wright as an author observed that writing was for him, "a vehicle to sort out and through his ideas, to establish his manifestos and promote his vision ... Books and articles could circulate; buildings rested in place."[13] This could equally describe the written work of Spencer and Wright during their early years together in Steinway Hall.

---

13 Anthony Alofsin, *Wright and New York, The Making of America's Architect*, p.185.

Chapter 9

DENOUEMENT

❝ *A collaborative circle usually begins as a casual
association among acquaintances working
in the same discipline ... then for a variety of
reasons, the members escalate their commitment
to one another and deepen their interdependence
until the circle becomes the center of their creative
lives ... Under some conditions, as the circle
develops, the dynamics of the group transforms
the work of the members. Those who are merely
good at their discipline become masters ... A circle
usually lasts for approximately a decade.*

Michael Farrell[1]

C.R. Ashbee, an important figure in the English Arts
and Crafts movement had visited Chicago on several
occasions, lecturing to the Chicago Architectural
Club and participating in the Club's exhibits. In 1908 Ashbee
visited Chicago and noted in his memoirs that Chicago's great
days in aesthetics were past, that Wright had grown bitter, and
that Louis Sullivan had spent the last years of his life "writing a
dreamy chaotic prose epic."[2]

By 1908, all the original occupants of Room 1107, except
Robert Spencer, had departed from Steinway Hall. Dwight
Perkins was working as chief architect for the Chicago School
Board and was no longer in the loft space he designed. Perkins
is listed in the Chicago Architectural Club Annual at 720 Tribune
Tower, space occupied by the architect's office of the Chicago
Board of Education. He was there until he was dismissed by the
Board of Education in 1911. By 1912 he was in suite 1100 at 6
North Clark Street with his partner John Hamilton. In 1914 his
firm Perkins, Fellows & Hamilton were still at the same address,
but moved to 814 Tower Court in 1918. This was a new building
they built for their use.

---

1 Farrell, *Collaborative Circles*, p.2.

2 *Ashbee Memoirs*, III, p.72–73, quoted in Robert Winter, "American Sheaves from 'CRA and Janet Ashbee,'" JSAH Vol. 30, no.4, December, 1971.

Myron Hunt relocated to Pasadena in 1903 and Adamo Boari moved to Mexico City in 1904. By this time Wright was producing all of his work in his Oak Park Studio, however, he is still listed as having an office in Steinway Hall from 1901 through 1907. Wright was in room 1106, immediately next to the ground-floor entry to the loft, room 1107. While this was his Chicago business office used for meeting with clients, it seems reasonable to assume that he still had some contact with other architects in Steinway Hall. In 1908, he moved his "business office" to the Fine Art Building.

Robert Spencer and his partner Horace Powers practiced in Steinway Hall, with Spencer designing houses and hardware for his Casement Hardware Company of Chicago. They were listed as having offices in Steinway Hall until 1916 when they moved to 10 South La Salle Street, moving to 5 N. LaSalle in 1919. It is not known why they finally left Steinway Hall. Pond & Pond, and Arthur Heun were in residence the longest and were still listed in Steinway Hall in the Chicago Architectural Club's Annual for 1920. By 1909 neither Spencer nor Perkins were active members of the Chicago Architectural Club, although Perkins remained active in the Illinois Society of Architects and the Illinois Chapter of the AIA. Wright was never officially a member of the Chicago Architectural Club nor did he ever join the American Institute of Architects.

In 1909 Wright left his wife and his architectural practice, running off to Europe with the wife of his client Edwin Cheney. Wright had grown dissatisfied with his domestic life as well as his practice which he no longer found challenging. His houses had become perfunctory, and repetitive, utilizing the same plan types and the same vocabulary of forms and materials. In "The Cause of Architecture-Second Paper" Wright noted, "So reaction is essential to progress, and enemies as valuable an asset in any forward movement as friends. ... some time ago this work reached the stage where it sorely needed honest enemies [he means constructive critics] if it was to survive."[3] Neil Levine notes that, "during the years he might have needed it most ... he lacked

---

3 Frank Lloyd Wright, "In the Cause of Architecture-Second Paper," the *Architectural Record*, May 1914, p.407–8.

any meaningful critical discourse with peers and colleagues."[4] While Wright may have felt that he had outgrown his colleagues in Steinway Hall and their discussions of architecture, Wright's employees from his Oak Park Studio described lively discussions, particularly between Wright and Marion Mahony. Yet for Wright, as he often indicated, these would not have been discussions among those he considered equals.

In Europe Wright traveled, met with editors in Berlin about a planned monograph on his work, and finally took up residence with Mamah Cheney in Fiesole. There he worked with his son Lloyd and Taylor Wooley, from his Oak Park Studio, preparing the plates for the Wasmuth Portfolio, *Ausgefubrte Bauten und Entwurfe von Frank Lloyd Wright,* published in Berlin in 1910. The Wasmuth plates were redrawn, all to the same format, from photographs and from original renderings by Marion Mahony and a number of different delineators. Before he left Chicago, Wright contracted with Herman von Holst to complete the commissions in his office while he was away.[5] This, von Holst did, along with Mahony, moving from the Oak Park Studio back to Steinway Hall. Von Holst listed his address as 809 Steinway Hall from 1910 through 1916. In 1916 he had offices at 72 W. Adams Street. Walter Burley Griffin who left Wright's Oak Park Studio in 1906 was listed as having his office in the 12th-floor loft of Steinway Hall from 1909 through 1911, according to the Chicago Central Business and Office Directory. Griffin was there through 1912 when he and Marion Mahony,

---

4 Neil Lavine, *The Architecture of Frank Lloyd Wright,* p.63.

5 The September 1909 contract between Wright and Von Holst is reproduced in full in Anthony Alofsin, *Frank Lloyd Wright: The Lost Years,* p.311–12.

10.001. Robert Spencer (Spencer & Powers). Magnus House. Winnetka, Illinois. 1906.

who he had married, won the competition for the design of the new City of Canberra, Australia.

The work of Mahony, Griffin, Purcell & Elmslie, Tallmadge and Watson, Guenzel & Drummond, along with others who had worked for Wright, would employ the formal vocabulary Wright developed between 1902 to 1909. This was not the case for either Spencer, Hunt, or Perkins. Spencer's work would have its own distinctive characteristics in both its interior planning, massing, roof forms, and use of materials, including his judicious use of timbering. This would prompt William Gray Purcell, Elmslie's partner, to ask, "How could one belong to that crowd up on the top floor of Steinway Hall for so many years and not show it in his work?"[6]

Hunt's Chicago work reflected the same early planning and formal ideas seen in Wright and Spencer's houses; however, his California work would come to embody a strong West Coast influence. His houses and his smaller public buildings would employ his own personal interpretation of regional vernacular, while his more important institutional commissions were often done in a simplified classical style with Spanish influences.

Dwight Perkins's schools and Wright's buildings after 1902 were perhaps the most interesting work done by the Steinway

---

6 *Western Architect*, April 1914, p.192. Reprinted in Brooks, *Prairie School Architecture, Studies from the "Western Architect."*

10.002. Hunt and Grey. Throop Hall at California Institute of Technology. Pasadena, Ca. 1910.

Hall group. Perkins's schools continued to draw upon aspects of Sullivan's buildings and on his and Wright's work on the Abraham Lincoln Center. Like Wright's Larkin Building and Unity Temple, Perkins's schools were simple volumetric compositions with uninterrupted expanses of wall surface and windows organized by vertical piers. Perkins's residential commissions were never typical of the Prairie School. The houses he would do in Evanston were stucco with occasional second floor half timbering. They had a strong demarcation of the second floor topped by low pitched gabled or hipped roofs and employed plan types developed earlier in Steinway Hall by Spencer and Wright. His Joseph Kearney House of 1911 in Evanston, Illinois is a "T" shape in plan with a combined living and dining room and a central hearth. This main space was extended by enclosed sun porches at either end. The stair is tucked behind the fireplace with the butler's pantry and kitchen in the short leg of the "T" with the entire plan echoing Spencer and Wright's *Ladies' Home Journal* houses.

Marion Mahony and Barry Byrne, both suggested later in their careers, that Perkins was not a particularly talented designer. According to David Van Zanten, in an interview conducted in 1965, Barry Byrne told him that Marion Mahony was the designer of Perkins's school buildings. This seems doubtful

10.003. Perkins and Hamilton. Joseph Kearney House. Evanston, Il. 1911.

10.004. Dwight Perkins. Carl Schurz High School. Chicago, Il. 1910.

10.005. Perkins Fellows & Hamilton. Farmers Trust Company. South Bend, Indiana. 1919.

10.006. Perkins Fellows & Hamilton Architect's Office. (Tower Court opposite the Water Tower). Chicago, Il. 1918. Entrance.

10.007 Perkins Fellows & Hamilton Architect's Office. Chicago, Il. 1918.

for many reasons given her employment during this period. She worked for Wright for 13 years beginning in 1895 and remained with him until Wright's departure for Europe in 1909. Barry Byrne, who worked for Wright from 1902 to 1907 said that Marion was "on call" suggesting that she was not always full time in Wright's employ.[7] Byrne left Chicago in 1907, working in Seattle and then southern California returning to Chicago to take over the Griffins's practice when they departed for Australia. Given these dates, his knowledge of any work Mahony did for Perkins, would have been second hand. We know that during the years that she worked for Wright, she did a small number of independent projects including the Church of All Souls in Evanston, built in 1904. It is entirely possible that when she wasn't working for Wright she could have sought work for her cousin Dwight Perkins, helping with the design of schools, although there is no mention of this in her memoir *The Magic of America*, and no surviving records place her in the office of the Chicago Board of Education. If she did work for Perkins on the schools it is possible that like Wright, she claimed authorship for projects she felt she had contributed to.

---

7 From 1965 Byrne interview with David Van Zanten. Unpublished notes.

John L. Hamilton left the architectural office of the Chicago Board of Education in 1905 to form a partnership with Perkins and ran Perkins's private practice at the time Perkins was made the Board's chief architect. Hamilton was active in the Chicago Architectural Club, serving as first vice president in 1903 and president as well as head of the Club's exhibition committee in 1904. Hamilton certainly could have participated in the design of Perkins and Hamilton's private commissions while Perkins worked for the School Board, but he was no longer involved in the design of Chicago Public School buildings. We have a list of architects who served as chief architect for the Board of Education, but no list of architectural employees has survived at the Chicago Board of Education from the time of Perkins's tenure. No one who worked full time for the School Board has subsequently claimed to be the principal designers of the extraordinary school buildings done between 1905 and 1910.

In 1907 Perkins exhibited 13 projects done for the Board of Education, including the Lyman Trumbull School, in the Chicago Architectural Club's annual exhibit. He listed the Board of Education office from which he worked as 720 Tribune Tower. Many of the men who worked under Perkins were also members of the Chicago Architectural Club. Each year the Club's exhibition catalog published the names and addresses of club members. During the years between 1907 and 1910, the following club members listed their address as 720 Tribune Tower: Vernon Behel (1907–10), Salvadore Ciarcoschi (1907–09), Arthur Knox (1909–10), Martin Peterson (1909), Robert Williamson (1907–10), and Otto Silha. Silha, who was quite active in the Chicago Architectural Club, was elected the Club's president in 1913. Arthur Knox won a mention in the *Brickbuilder's* 1906 competition for "An Architectural Faience." Almost all these men remained with the Board of Education after Perkins left and none of them had subsequent private practices of note or built buildings of recognized significance.

We do not know if Spencer and Wright remained friends. Wright makes no mention of it in his autobiography, nor does he write about ever seeing Hunt on any of his various trips to California. There is no record in the Wright Archives at Columbia University of Wright having corresponded with either of them. We know that Wright, after his return to Chicago in 1910, continued to keep a Chicago office first in the Fine Arts Building and then at Orchestra Hall in 1912 and 1913. Once Midway Gardens was under construction, he was commuting by train from Spring Green to Chicago every week. In spite of being ostracized by both Chicago and Oak Park society, we know he remained friends with Dwight Perkins and had apparently gotten past his much earlier feud with Lucy Perkins.[8] Larry Perkins, Dwight's son born in 1907, also became a noted architect of school buildings, founding the firm of Perkins and Will. He remembered that Wright was a frequent dinner guest at their house in Evanston. "Frank frequently came to dinner at our house. All the kids adored him. He would always bring presents for us and play with us before dinner." He further recalled that his father and Frank remained friends because his dad was smart enough to never lend Wright money.[9]

The Steinway Hall group, as Michael Farrell suggests, had lasted less than 10 years. Their work and the work of the Eighteen matured as well as receiving varying levels of professional success and recognition. However, their energy, the level of invention, and engagement was not sustainable. Concurrently, the demise of the "Prairie School," after 1914 was not simply a result of the classicism promoted by the 1893 World's Fair and of changing tastes. It could have also been hastened by the desire of some of the Prairie architects to distance themselves and their work from Wright's marital scandals and by Wright's publicly expressed animosity toward his former friends, collaborators, and "disciples." Wright's initial rift with Marion Mahony was over the desertion of his family and of Catherine Tobin Wright who was her close friend. When Wright finally returned to the United States in 1910, it was only briefly to Chicago, where he was still a social outcast. Wright withdrew to the Lloyd Jones's property in Spring Green, Wisconsin. He was convinced that Von Holtz and Mahony had stolen commissions from him in his absence. He believed that Marion and her husband Walter Burley Griffin cheated him of the commission to design two residential communities in Mason City, Iowa and he believed that the work of all the Prairie School architects was

---

8 In 1903 Lucy had arranged for Wright to lecture to the University Guild of Evanston on, "good taste in home decoration." He insulted the women assembled. Perkins of Chicago, p.97–100.

9 Larry Perkins in conversation with the author, at the University of Illinois, Chicago, c.1980. This is not confirmed by Perkins Oral History done for Art Institute of Chicago. He noted that his mother never forgave Wright for his insults to the Woman's Guild of Evanston and that his parents sided with Kathrine Tobin Wright when Wright left her. The comment about his father never lending money to Wright is in Lawrence Perkins oral history at the Art Institute of Chicago.

derivative of his architecture and his ideas. In his second article titled "In the Cause of Architecture" in 1914,[10] Wright implied that his early colleagues had had no original ideas of their own and were simply his followers. The national press had begun to lump his work together with the other Prairie School architects as simply the new "style of the Midwest." Articles began to appear with pictures of his houses that identified them only as typical Midwestern work, which must have infuriated him. Finally, Wright would suggest in his second *Architectural Record* article, that the work being done by the Prairie School architects was mindless copying, implying that it was no better than the eclectic use of Renaissance precedents that he had fought against. He wrote, "The young work in architecture here in the Middle West, owing to a measure of premature success ... threatens to explode over in pretentious attempts to 'speak the language' ... Half-baked, imitative designs—fictitious semblances—pretentiously put forward ... until utter prostitution results ... my disciples or pupils ... are responsible for worse buildings than nine-tenths of the work done by average architects who are 'good school' ... Personally, I too, am heartily sick of being commercialized and traded in and upon."[11] In the face of such rage and scorn, why would Wright's disciples, pupils, or even colleagues, continue working in his manner?

The philosopher, Alain de Botton writes, "A perverse dogma overtook the architectural profession ... a faith in a necessary connection between architectural greatness and originality. Over the nineteenth century, architects came to be rewarded according to the uniqueness of their work, so that constructing a new house or office in a familiar form grew no less contemptible than plagiarizing a novel or poem."[12] Although this sentiment would continue to pervade the profession throughout the 20th century, by the 1920s, with respect to the Prairie School, public perception had changed. As Meryl Secrest points out, "in the United States the vogue for individuality and original design was being superseded by a revival of the colonial house, the new symbol of genteel culture ...

---

10 Wright, "In the Cause of Architecture: Second Paper," *Architectural Record*, 34, May 1914.

11 By "good school" does Wright mean Beaux-Arts trained? The original version of the text which is quoted here was edited when published in *Frank Lloyd Wright Collected Writings Vol. 1*, p.126. Wright's rant was softened, and the language considerably changed from its original publication in the *Architectural Record*.

12 De Botton, Alain, *The Architecture of Happiness*, New York: Vantage Press, 2008, p.182

publication lent editorial weight to the new view that the words *Americanism* and *democracy* could best be applied to the colonial style, which some wrote, was the only distinctly American one."[13] For all the important architectural inventions that the Steinway Hall architects brought to residential design, ultimately the specific formal language of Wright's houses and the Prairie School was too personal and idiosyncratic to provide an enduring image for the 20th-century American house.

For a brief period, the architects of Steinway Hall came together to question and challenge the architectural profession. They worked, hoping to create an American architecture expressive of the social and cultural changes they were a part of. Their architecture and their writings, when examined side by side, indicate the nature of their work as a collaborative circle. The ideas and the architecture of Spencer, Perkins, and Hunt have been almost totally eclipsed by Wright's career. This suggests a continuing bias in the architectural profession and among architectural historians toward the myth of the lone genius. Recent scholarship, focusing on Wright's early career and influences, has failed to fully examine Wright's collaboration with Robert Spencer and others in the creation of ideas that would be claimed by Wright alone. Wright would maintain that 20th-century architecture was based on his buildings and their impact on the development of European modernism. However, we must finally recognize that the credit for the initial development of many of these ideas should also go to Chicago's cultural milieu, the Eighteen, the architects of Steinway Hall, and the collaborative circle they formed.

---

13 Secrest, *Frank Lloyd Wright. A Biography*, p.234–35. It would be Wright's USONIAN houses of the 1940s that would shape the middle-class residential landscape and what became known as the ranch house that would transform mid-century American residential architecture.

ARCHITECTS WITH OFFICES IN STEINWAY HALL

S teinway Hall opened in 1895. There are several sources of addresses for professional and business offices in Chicago at the turn of the last century. Principle among these are the *Chicago Central Business and Office Building Directory* and *The Lakeside City Directory of Chicago*. *The Lakeside City Directory* variously lists Steinway Hall as 64 E. Van Buren and 17 Van Buren in different years as does the *Chicago Central Business and Office Building Directory*. The later has alphabetical business listings for the entire city as well as listings grouped by profession or occupation. Dwight Perkins is listed at 17 Van Buren for 1896, the first full year Steinway Hall was open.

In the 1903 Directory, in addition to Lyon Potter & Company (later Lyon & Healy) the Chicago Distributor for Steinway Pianos, there are three other companies selling pianos, several other listings for people selling violins and other musical instruments, as well as a listing for a piano tuner. While we have discussed Steinway Hall as a favored location for Chicago architects' offices, it is well to remember that Steinway Hall was originally to be called the "Temple of Music." The 1903 Directory lists 23 people as music or voice teachers, as well as the Chicago Opera School, the Western Conservatory of Music, and the Columbia School of Oratory. Founded in 1890 the Columbia School of Oratory became Columbia College and occupied the seventh floor from 1895 to 1916. The building also included artists, illustrators, a firm of designers and decorators, two tailors, two dressmakers, a dentist's office, six physicians' offices, the Balthazard School of Languages, and the Society for Ethical Culture.

The Chicago Central Business and Office Building Directory's listing for Steinway Hall included the line rendering of the building done for Perkins by Henry Holt, and the following description:

STEINWAY HALL BUILDING: 17 Van Buren Street, Between
Wabash and Michigan Avenues.
Studios overlooking the lake.
An ideal home for musicians and artists.
Removed from the disturbances of cars, yet one of the most
accessible locations in Chicago. The elevated loop and Illinois
Central Ry. Stations and Wabash and State Street cable
cars all being about one block from the building. The build-
ing contains one of the finest halls in the city, with seating

capacity of 750, also a smaller hall seating 300. FARNHAM, WILLOUGHBY & CO. Agents, Atwood Bldg. Tel. Main 4888.

A further source for lists of architects' business addresses was the *Chicago Architectural Club Annual*, which each year included a list of members and their addresses. After 1916, it also included lists of members of the Illinois Society of Architects and the Chicago Chapter of the American Institute of Architects. The AIA and Illinois Society of Architects listings had addresses but not room or suite numbers.

The list below is not necessarily complete for all years from 1895 through 1920, which was the last year directories and catalogs were searched for inclusion. This list is intended to give an idea

11.001. Chicago Central Business and Office Directory. 1903

of which architects were in the building and what their overlapping tenancies were. Many of the names have simply disappeared from Chicago's architectural history while others have remained prominent. Room 1107 and 1200 were the suite of offices shared by Perkins, Spencer, Hunt, Wright, and Boari—among others. The list doesn't differentiate employees from employers. In the list below "NL" indicates that no room number was listed in any of the sources for that particular architect. Several different sources suggest that Jules Guerin, who is remembered today for his beautiful renderings for the Burnham and Bennett Plan for Chicago also was in 1200 Steinway Hall in 1897 although he doesn't show up in any of the directories. According to Dwight Perkins's son Lawrence, Earl Reed—who had worked with his father in Daniel Burnham's office—was also in Steinway Hall although he isn't listed in the directories that were searched. Also, unconfirmed is William Drummond (ca. 1909).

Architects discussed in the text are listed in bold type. For those Steinway Hall architects listed with offices on the 11th or 12th floor see floor plan 5.007 for office locations. The plans show no room 1115 (John Paulding). This may have been a typographic error in the original listing.

Alyea, Thomas	Room 809	1914-1915
Brand, Gustave	Room 514	1906-1909
Boari, Aldamo	Room 1107	1897-1904
Brydges, E.N.	Room (NL)	1918-
Buck, Lawrence	Room 909/910	1906-1911, 1915
Carr, George Wallace	Room 809/1107	1906-1911
Corse, Redmond P.	Room (NL)	1917-1919
Chatten & Hammond	Room 1112	1909-1919 (Melville Chatten, Charles Hammond)
Childs & Smith	Room (NL)	1919- (Frank Childs, William J. Smith)
Clark, Edwin B.	Room 910	1909-1910
Davis, Zachary T.	Room 1109	1909-1917
Dean, Arthur	Room (NL)	1902 (George is at 218 La Salle Street in 1902)
Franklin, Robert	Room (NL)	1919
Fyfe, J.L.	Room 907	1911
Griffin, Walter Burley	Room 1200	1907-1911 (thereafter in the Monroe Building)
Gurein, Jules	Room 1200	1897
Haagen, Paul	Room 801/810	1908-1910 (probably worked for Heun)
Hall, Emery Stanford	Room (NL)	1919
Hodgkins, Howard	Room 1110/606/802	1906-1908
Heun, Arthur	Room 809/810/801	1906-1920 (502 in 1903, 810 after 1914)
Hunt, Myron	Room 1107	1897-1902 (he was at 123 La Salle Street in 1902)
Jensen, Jens	Room 815	1911-
Kohfeld, Walter	Room (NL)	1917-1919

Linke, John	Room 1101	1906-1910
Lippencott, Roy	Room 907	1912-
Long, Birch Burdette	Room 1107	1897-
Loring, Rawson	Room 1114	1912
Martini, Elisabeth	Room (NL)	1917-1918
Matthes, Carl	Room 1112	1917
McBride, E.E.	Room (NL)	1918-1919
Neiemez, Arthur R.	Room 1107	1901-
Paulding, John	Room 1115	1911-
Perkins, Dwight	Room 1107	1895-1907 (Perkins & Selby)
Pond & Pond	Room 1109	1895-1920
Probst, Edward	Room 1200	1896-
Phelps, Wyman A.	Room 805	1909-
Prinderville, Charles	Room 807	1911-1919 Egan and Prinderville 1911-1914)
Rawson, L.A.	Room 1114	1911-
Rich, Charles	Room 1109	1911-
Ritter, Woldeman	Room 1101	1907-
Spencer, Robert C.Jr.	Room 1107	1897-
Spencer & Powers	Room 1107	1906-1918 (Horace Powers)
Tomlinson, Webster	Room 1106/809	1899-1919 (809 in 1916; 1899 from CAC catalog members list)
Viehe-Naess, Ivar	Room (NL)	1917-1919
Von Holst, Herman	Room 907	1909-1913
Warren, William A.	Room 1012	1911-
Waterbury, Charles D.	Room 1017	1911-1917
Wright, Clark	Room 1200	1903-
Wright, Frank L.	Room 1107/1106	1897,1901-1907
Zimmerman, W. Carbys	Room 1101	1901-1920 (with Albert Saxe, Ralph Zimmerman)

Appendix 2

EIGHTEEN ARCHITECTS: DINING AT THE BISMARCK HOTEL

There are two original references to the Eighteen: they are in Wright's *A Testament* from 1957 and in a paper that Robert Spencer delivered to the Illinois Society of Architects in 1939. Spencer said that they "used to meet for some years once a month at the old Bismarck Restaurant for a steak dinner in one of the private rooms ... At these little informal dinners we could discuss our architectural problems and theories."[1] Wright first mentions the Eighteen in 1957: "Before long a little luncheon club formed comprised of..."

Of the eighteen architects that Wright refers to as "a little luncheon club," Wright, only listed nine names in addition to himself: Spencer, (James) Gamble Rogers, Handy and Cady, Dick Schmidt, Hugh Garden, (George) Dean, Perkins, and Shaw. There has been speculation over the years as to the remaining names. In conversation with H. Allen Brooks in 1956 Wright added six more names, making a total of 16, assuming we can rely on Wright's memory 56 years after the fact. These were: Arthur Dean, Alfred Granger, Arthur Heun, Myron Hunt and Irving, and Allen Pond. In addition to those Wright remembered Brooks suggests that Webster Tomlinson probably was part of the group and Wilbert Hasbrouck suggests Hermann von Holst. Robert Twombly writes, "The eighteenth may have been Walter Burley Griffin, Adamo Boari, Birch B. Long or Arthur R. Niemz all tenants at Steinway Hall around this time.[2] Another, possible candidate for the Eighteen, is Francis W. Kirkpatrick, who was president of the Chicago Architectural Club and who worked in Steinway Hall until 1902. He then worked for D.H. Burnham and Company for a year before leaving Chicago for Missouri."[3]

Brooks believed that the group was "unified only by the mutual idealization of simplicity."[4] However, many also shared educational and work experiences.[5] A number of the group of Eighteen and three of the four original occupants of Perkins's

---

1 Quoted in H. Allen Brooks, *The Prairie School*, p.31.

2 Twombly, *Frank Lloyd Wright, His Life and Architecture*, p.55, footnote no. 8.

3 Little is known about Kirkpatrick who was born in Kansas in 1872. Hasbrouck supplies some brief information about him and one photograph of semi-detached houses he designed that were published in the Inland Architect. These bear a passing resemblance to Wright's Gothicized Roloson Apartments of 1894. Wilbert Hasbrouck, *The Chicago Architectural Club*, p.228.

4 Brooks, op. cit., p.47.

5 Litchfield, Master's Thesis, 1994. "Robert C. Spencer Jr. Contributions to the Formation of the Prairie School."

loft in Steinway Hall attended MIT. Depending on their date of matriculation they might have known one another. More importantly, given the short span of time covered, they all would have been educated by the same professors. Probably William Ware and his assistant Eugene Letang, a *diplome of the Ecole des Beaux-Arts,* suggesting that they all shared a classical *Beaux-Arts* training. Louis Sullivan described his Paris *Beaux-Arts* education writing about himself in the third person as, "the theory of the school, which, in his mind settled down to a theory of *plan,* yielding results of extraordinary brilliancy, but which after all, was not the reality he sought, but an abstraction."[6] For the Eighteen, the plan as a generator would lead to a rethinking of the architectural space it implied. In contrast to their classical training many were enamored with the Arts and Crafts movement, late 19th-century romanticism, and picturesque architecture. This was the "simplicity" to which Brooks referred. Many of these men worked in either the Boston or Chicago offices of Shepley, Rutan & Coolidge, or in both. In the firm's Boston office, they would have been exposed to the picturesque work of H.H. Richardson and the Shingle-style architects practicing in Boston. As the successor firm to Richardson's practice they were a prestigious and highly respected firm and during the economic recession of the early 1890s their Chicago office was busy and still hiring architects. Many of the Eighteen could have worked together there on the same projects suggesting another point of overlap and friendship formation. Lastly, after these men started their own practices, many had their offices in Steinway Hall.

Several of the Eighteen are architects that became well known locally and are now frequently cited in books on the history of Chicago architecture. Dwight Perkins and James Gamble Rogers were known nationally having revolutionized, in different ways, the design of school buildings. James Gamble Rogers is credited with literally inventing "collegiate gothic" as a style for university buildings. Howard Van Doren Shaw also enjoyed a national reputation for his residential work and in 1926 received the AIA's Gold Medal, the highest recognition of the American Institute of Architects. Only Wright, ultimately, received international recognition. He was the second member

---

6 Louis H., Sullivan, *The Autobiography of An Idea,* Dover, 2009, p.240.

of the Eighteen to receive the AIA's Gold Medal but not until 1949. In his address at their national convention, Wright, who never deigned to join the AIA, referred to the recognition in his acceptance speech as, "a long time coming." Wright who claimed to prefer "honest arrogance to false humility," told the AIA, "I feel humble and grateful. I don't think humility is a very becoming state for me, but I really feel touched by this token of esteem from the home boys."[7]

Since little is known about many of these architects, brief biographies of each are included. Spencer, Perkins, Hunt, and Wright have been profiled separately in short biographies included in the appendices. The Eighteen architects discussed here (not including those in the Steinway Hall Loft) are: **Arthur Dean, George Dean, Hugh Garden, Alfred Granger, Frank Handy and Jeremiah Cady, Arthur Heun, Herman von Holst, Irving and Allen Pond, James Gamble Rogers, Richard Schmidt, Howard Van Doren Shaw, and Webster Tomlinson.**

The buildings illustrated are from approximately the same period and were chosen to suggest what these men's design work had in common.

Jeremiah Kiersted Cady (1855–1925) and Frank Handy (1847–1929)

Cady was born in Indianapolis, Indiana. He studied architecture at Cornell University, also studying in Europe. In 1883, after working in Cincinnati, he came to Chicago to work in the office of Burnham and Root. In 1887 he formed a partnership with Frank W. Handy in the firm Handy & Cady. He worked with Handy until 1909. At this time, he went into partnership with J. Spencer Crosby and the firm became Cady & Crosby. Cady was the architect of a number of Chicago residences as well as the Teutonic Building of 1894 and the Medical Arts Building in Omaha, Nebraska. He designed bank buildings in La Crosse and Winona, Wisconsin.

Frank Handy was born in Ohio. His father died when he was a child. He entered the profession through an apprenticeship

---

7 Published in the *Journal of the American Institute of Architects,* May 1949. Reprinted in Robert Twombly, ed., *Frank Lloyd Wright, Essential Texts.*

12.001. Handy & Cady. Harper Residence. Evanston, Il. 1893.

12.002. Handy & Cady. Brown Residence. Evanston, Il. 1898.

for a prominent Cincinnati architect, James McLaughlin. This is where he met Jeremiah Cady. After moving to Chicago, Handy lived in Evanston, Illinois.

George S. Dean (1864–1919) and Arthur Dean

George Dean was born in Bombay, India. He came to the United States as a boy with his parents. Dean had some basic training in architecture and then studied at the *Ecole des Beaux-Arts* in Paris. Returning to the United States in 1893 he began work as a draftsman in Minneapolis, Minnesota for W. Channing Whitney. Whitney was a prominent residential architect and an MIT graduate who had worked for William Ralph Emerson and had designed the Minnesota Building at the 1893 Chicago World's Fair. Dean then worked in the Boston office of Shepley, Rutan & Coolidge and was sent to Chicago to work on their Chicago commissions. After the completion of the Art Institute and the Chicago Public Library, Dean opened his own practice and in 1903 he was joined in practice by his brother Arthur. They practiced under the name of Dean and Dean, although the addresses listed in sequential Chicago Architectural Club Catalogs shows the Dean Brothers at different addresses in 1898, at the same address in 1899 and at different addresses again in 1900. George Dean was active in the Chicago Architectural Club and wrote articles about architectural theory and architectural education, published in the *Inland Architect*, the *Brickbuilder*, and the Architectural League of America's annual publication. His article asking if architects should put, "Progress before Precedent," was taken up by the Architectural League of America as their motto.

12.003. George Dean. Dining Hall. Strawberry Island. 1902.

12.004. George Dean. Alpha Delta Phi Chapter House, Cornell University. Ithaca, NY. 1902.

Hugh Mackie Gordon Garden (1873–1961)

Hugh Garden was born in Toronto, Canada in 1873. His family moved to Minneapolis, Minnesota in 1887 and after the death of his father Garden worked as a draftsman to help support his family. He moved to Chicago in the 1880s. There he worked for Shepley, Rutan & Coolidge and Henry Ives Cobb. In 1895 he formed a partnership with Richard Schmidt who would be the principal designer for the firm. In 1906 the firm became Schmidt, Garden & Martin with the addition of Edgar Martin. The partnership lasted almost 20 years. The firm was responsible for the original buildings at Michael Reese Hospital in Chicago, the Montgomery Ward Warehouse, and the Ambassador Hotel. The firm also designed the Julia C. Lathrop Homes, public housing which combined row houses and three-story apartment buildings. It was designed in collaboration with Thomas Tallmadge and Vernon Watson. In 1925 Martin, who left the firm, was replaced by Carl A. Erickson who had been an employee. The firm became Schmidt, Garden & Erickson. Schmidt continued practicing into the 1950s. See biography of Richard Schmidt below.

12.005. Hugh Garden. House. Highland Park, Il. Chicago Architectural Club Annual. 1901.

12.006. Hugh Garden. Frank McNullin House. Highland Park, Il. 1902.

Alfred Hoyt Granger (1867–1939)

Born in Zanesville, Ohio in 1867, Granger was the son of a judge. He graduated from Kenyon College in 1887 and attended one term at MIT, like so many other of his Chicago colleagues. He studied at the *Ecole des Beaux-Arts* in Paris from 1889 to 1891. Granger then worked in the Boston firm of Shepley, Rutan & Coolidge, moving to Chicago in 1891 along with Robert Spencer Jr. when Charles Coolidge set up a Chicago office to work on the commission for the Art Institute of Chicago. He also worked for Jenney and Mundie and was briefly in private practice in Cleveland, Ohio with Frank B. Meade, who he worked with at Jenney and Mundy's office. Granger and Meade did residential architecture. In 1893 Granger returned to Chicago and married Belle Hughitt, one of the daughters of the president of the Chicago and Northwestern Railway. He formed a partnership with his brother-in-law Charles Sumner Frost and they designed stations for the Chicago and Northwestern railway. Frost and Granger built over two hundred railway buildings for their father-in-law and for the Milwaukee Road, The Great Northern, and the Rock Island railroads. They designed more than 50 buildings in Chicago including banks, churches, and hospitals. Frost and Granger built side by side houses for themselves in Lake Forest, Illinois and Granger designed the Lake Forest City Hall and academic buildings for Lake Forest College.

In 1910 Granger moved to Pennsylvania where he practiced with Willam D. Hewitt for 14 years returning to Chicago in 1924 and forming the firm of Granger, Lowe, and Bollenbacher, which later became Granger & Bollenbacher. Granger was active in the AIA serving as president of the Chicago Chapter and he was elected to fellowship in 1926.

12.007. Alfred Granger. Granger Residence. "Woodleigh." Lake Forest, Il. 1897.

In 1922 Granger chaired the jury for the international competition for an office building for the Chicago Tribune newspaper. Granger was the author of a biography of Charles Follen McKim, who he considered to have been his mentor. He also wrote *Chicago Welcomes You*, an architectural guidebook to Chicago and its suburbs published at the time of the 1933 *Chicago Century of Progress*, World's Fair.

In Chicago Granger designed the Northwestern Terminal and the LaSalle Street Station. He also designed Chicago's St. Luke's Hospital (1907), and the Northern Trust Bank Building (1908). Granger died in Chicago in 1939.

12.008. Alfred Granger. Midlothian Golf Club. Midlothian (Blue Island), Il. 1899.

Arthur Heun (1866–1946)

Arthur Heun was born in Saginaw, Michigan in 1866. He began his architectural career as an apprentice to his uncle Volusin Bude, who had an architectural practice in Grand Rapids, Michigan. At the age of 21 he moved to Chicago and worked as a draftsman for Francis Whitehouse, a well-known residential architect and early classicist who did work at the 1893 Chicago World's Fair. Heun worked in Whitehouse's office on residential commissions for prominent clients including

General A.C. McClurg, Colonel J. Mason Loomis, and Barbara Armour. When Whitehouse retired in 1893, Heun took over his practice continuing to design residential architecture. In 1908 he built Melody Farm, a large Italianate estate in Lake Forest, for J. Odgen Amour. He also built houses for William McCormick Blair and for Albert Loeb on Chicago's south side. In addition to residences, he was the architect of Chicago's Casino Club. Heun retired from practice several years before he passed away and spent his last days painting.

12.009. Arthur Heun. "Villa Crest." Manchester, MA. 1900.

12.010. Arthur Heun. Mrs. Charles McGennis House. Lake Forest, Il. 1908.

Herman Valentin von Holst (1874–1955)

Herman von Holst was born in Freiburg, Germany in 1874. He was the son of a well-known historian Hermann Eduard von Holst and of an American mother. In 1891 his family moved to Chicago when his father was made the head of the Department of History at the University of Chicago. Von Holst received a Bachelor of Arts degree from the University of Chicago in 1893 and continued his studies in architecture at MIT graduating in 1896. He then returned to Chicago to work for Shepley, Rutan & Coolidge, where he became their chief draftsman. He left in 1905 to open his own practice with an office in the Rookery Building and then moved to Steinway Hall in 1909. Von Holst was active in the Chicago Architectural Club and served as both treasurer (1905) and then president of the Architectural League of America. He was the author of several books including: *A Study of the Orders* (1906), which he co-authored; *Cyclopedia of Drawing* (1907); and *Modern American Homes* (1912). The later contained work by a number of Prairie School architects as well as houses he designed. He was friendly with John J. Glessner, a cofounder of the International Harvester Company, and his family, who the senior von Holst knew through William Rainey Harper, then-president of the University of Chicago. Von Holst's first commissions in 1905 would come from the Glessners for buildings at their summer estate in New Hampshire. These included a large horse barn, a sawmill, a cow barn, an addition to their daughter Frances Glessner Lee's cottage, and a residence for their son George. He also created a summer estate, nearby, for George Macbeth, a Pittsburgh glass manufacturer who was Mrs. (Frances) Glessner's brother.

Von Holst taught architectural design at the Chicago School of Architecture, at the Art Institute of Chicago, and later in the Department of Architecture at the Armour Institute of Technology, which became the Illinois Institute of Technology. Von Holst is also remembered as the architect who took over Frank Lloyd Wright's practice when Wright left for Europe. Von Holst completed Wright's commissions along with Marian Mahony who served as his principal designer. Upon his return to Chicago, Wright accused von Holst and Mahony of stealing his commissions. Wright never mentioned von Holst again. Von Holst continued to practice in Chicago through the 1920s collaborating with George Grant Elmslie who had worked for Sullivan for many years. They designed a number of commercial and industrial structures including power company buildings and train stations. Von Holst also formed a brief partnership with James L. Fyfe. Von Holst left Chicago for Florida, practicing in the late 1920s in Boca Raton. There he designed a number of Spanish-style houses in a real estate development, called "Floresta" being built by Addison Mizner. Von Holst retired from architectural practice in 1932 and served on the Boca Raton City Council twice between 1937 and 1947 and from 1948 to 1949. He was chairman of the Boca Raton Town Planning Board in 1940. Von Holst died in Boca Raton in 1955.

12.011. Herman Von Holst. George Macbeth Residence Bethlehem, NH. 1905.

12.012. Herman Von Holst. Glessner Residence. Bethlehem, NH. 1905.

Irving Kane Pond (1857–1939) and Allen Bartlet Pond (1858–1929)

The Pond brothers were both born in Ann Arbor, Michigan where they grew up and attended the University of Michigan. After graduation Allen worked as an assistant to his father, who was warden at the Michigan State Prison in Jackson. Irving graduated with a degree in civil engineering and then worked in Chicago for William Le Baron Jenney. He then worked for Solon Spencer Beman who was designing the town of Pullman. The brothers formed a partnership in 1886, practicing together until Allen's death in 1929. The Ponds were best known as the architects of Jane Addams's Hull House Settlement. They designed 10 buildings that formed a complex over an 18-year period as additions to the original 1856 Hull House building. Allen Pond served as the secretary of Hull House beginning in 1895 until his death. In Chicago they built the Baptist Training School for Nurses, the City Club, and a number of Presbyterian churches. They designed university buildings and student unions throughout the Midwest including Perdue, Lake Forest College, and their alma matter—the University of Michigan. Both brothers were active in the Chicago Architectural Club and Irving was a founding member. They were both Fellows of the American Institute of Architects and in 1908 Irving was elected the AIA's national president succeeding New York architect Cass Gilbert. Irving also wrote about architecture for various journals, and in 1918, published *Meaning in Architecture,* a book on his theories of architectural design.

12.013a. Pond and Pond. Elliot Anthony House. Evanston, Il. 1895.

12.013b. Pond and Pond. Elliot Anthony House. Evanston, Il. 1895.

12.014. Pond and Pond. Hull House. Chicago, Il. 1889-1908.

James Gamble Rogers (1867–1947)

James Gamble Rogers was born in Bryan Station, Kentucky. He attended Yale University on a scholarship graduating in 1889 one year ahead of Howard Van Doren Shaw. After graduation he traveled through Europe as part of an American baseball team that introduced the sport to the continent. Returning to Chicago in that same year he worked for William Le Baron Jenney and then for the firm of Burnham and Root. He worked briefly on his own before going to Paris to study at the *Ecole des Beaux-Arts* to further his architectural education. Unlike most Americans who attended the *Ecole* for one or two years, as a finishing school, Rogers spent five years in Paris graduating with a diploma and medals in both architecture and construction. He returned to Chicago in 1897 to establish a private practice designing residences as well as an addition to Burnham and Root's Ashland Block. Rogers married Anne Day, a daughter of Albert Morgan Day who was president of the Chicago Stock Exchange. Day was related to the McCormick family. Anne's sister married Francis C. Farwell, one of Chicago oldest families and one of the largest property owners in Chicago. These connections were the source of Rogers's residential commissions in Lake Forest and some of his later academic buildings, such as the Deering Library and the Sorority Quadrangle at Northwestern University.

In 1905 Rogers moved his office to New York City to design a lavish mansion for Edward Harkness, a part owner of John D. Rockefeller's Standard Oil Company. Rogers is best known for his work at Yale University, the Harkness Memorial Quadrangle, Harkness Tower, and the Sterling Memorial Library as well as Yale's Sterling Law buildings, the Hall of Graduate Studies, and eight residential Colleges. He served as an architectural advisor to Yale and was also responsible for Yale University's master plan in 1924. Harkness frequently made Rogers's employment as architect a precondition of his gift for new academic buildings. Rogers also designed buildings at the University of Chicago, Princeton, and Columbia Universities. All his university buildings were in the Gothic Revival style and he is credited with the development of what became known as "collegiate gothic." He died in New York City in 1947.

12.015. James Gamble Rogers. House. Winthrop Street. Chicago, Il. 1901.

12.016. James Gamble Rogers. Country House. 1902.

12.017. James Gamble Rogers. School of Education. University of Chicago. 1901-04.

Richard Ernest Schmidt (1865–1959)

Richard Schmidt was born in Ebern, Bavaria in 1865. His parents emigrated to America when he was one year old. His father would become a prominent Chicago doctor. In 1883 he attended MIT to study architecture. He returned to Chicago working for Charles Sumner Frost who would later be Alfred Granger's partner. In 1887 he began practicing with Adolph A. Cudell, the architect of Cyrus McCormick's Chicago mansion, and an architect who did work for Chicago's tight-knit German community. By 1895, he was practicing on his own and invited Hugh M. Garden to work with him. Their firm, while they did some residences, designed primarily commercial and public buildings. They were the planners of over 300 hospitals including Michael Reese Hospital in Chicago. Schmidt was the author of a book entitled *The Modern Hospital*.

12.018. Richard Schmidt. House. Buena Park, Chicago, Il. 1902

12.019. Richard Schmidt. Mrs. W. H. Miller House. Mount Morris, Il. 1906.

Howard Van Doren Shaw (1869–1926)

Howard Van Doren Shaw was born in Chicago in 1869. He grew up in the wealthy Prairie Avenue district of Chicago and attended the prestigious Harvard School for boys in Hyde Park on Chicago's south side. Shaw graduated from Yale University in 1890, then studied architecture at MIT graduating in 1892. In Chicago, Shaw worked for Jenney & Mundie before leaving for an extended tour of England, and Europe. His first independent commission, built while he was traveling in Europe, was a summer house in Connecticut for his future father-in-law. Returning home to Chicago he designed a double house in Hyde Park for himself, his new wife, her sister, and his brother-in-law. Shaw built over 20 houses in Hyde Park, as well as the University of Chicago's Quadrangle Club. In 1911, he moved his home to the top floor of the co-operative apartment building he designed on Lake Shore Drive. In addition to his residential commissions he also designed the Mentor office building, 1906, in Chicago's Loop, for the father of a childhood friend. There he located his architectural offices. He designed the Lakeside Press building and a printing press building on the near south side for R.R.

12.020. Howard Van Doren Shaw. Shaw Residence. "Ragdale." Lake Forest, Il. 1897.

12.021. Howard Van Doren Shaw. Market Square. Lake Forest, Il. 1915.

12.022. Howard Van Doren Shaw. Market Square. Lake Forest, Il. 1915.

Donnelley and Sons, the family of his Yale friend Thomas Donnelley, for whom he also built a house in Lake Forest. In 1897 he built his summer house *Ragdale*, now an artist's in-residence colony, in Lake Forest, Illinois. In 1915, he built his masterpiece, Market Square, Lake Forest's town center. Shaw was one of Chicago's best-known residential architects, building houses for the Donnelleys, Swifts, and Ryersons, as well as estate houses across the Midwest. His English-inspired houses shared many interior planning and spatial ideas with other members of the Eighteen, particularly ideas about the connection of interior and exterior space. In 1926 Shaw was awarded the Gold Medal of the American Institute of Architects. He died at the age of 57 that same year.

Henry Webster Tomlinson (1870–1942)

Henry Webster Tomlinson was born in Chicago in 1870. He grew up in Chicago and studied architecture at Cornell University. Tomlinson began work as a draftsman in the office of W.W. Boyington, the architect of the Chicago Water Tower and Chicago's first Board of Trade Building. He was in practice with Frank Lloyd Wright as a partner from 1901 to 1902, managing Wright's Chicago practice in room 1106 Steinway Hall. In references to the work they were doing, he is credited first as an "associate" and then fully as Wright and Tomlinson. From this period there were five houses built in Oak Park, River Forest, Elmhurst, and Sault Ste. Marie, Michigan. Tomlinson went by his middle name and when Wright filed their partnership with the State Board of Examiners, he listed his partner as Webster Tomlinson. The Board had a record for Henry Tomlinson and reportedly refused to allow Tomlinson to practice under a "false name." They then told Wright he could not practice with an unlicensed architect, having no recorded license for Webster Tomlinson, and threatening to revoke Wright's own license.

After his partnership with Wright Tomlinson worked on a number of commercial and industrial commissions including factory buildings and warehouses. From 1904 to 1906 he built two churches in Chicago and a sanitorium in Hinsdale, Illinois. Tomlinson was active in the Chicago Architectural Club and the Architectural League of America. At the Leagues' first meeting he read the opening address written by Louis Sullivan, who was unable to attend. In 1904 he designed the Lake Bluff, Illinois City Hall and several Lake Bluff residences. In addition to these commissions he designed several three-story apartment buildings in Chicago. In 1906 he obtained commissions in South Dakota for a mental hospital and the Yankton County Prison, both he designed as concrete structures. Tomlinson, who was very interested in concrete construction, invented a slide rule for calculating the size of concrete beams based on their spans and the weight they would carry. His slide rule was patented in 1914 and was used by architects, engineers, and bridge manufacturers throughout the country.

In 1918 he moved to Joliet, Illinois to serve as superintendent of construction for work at Statesville Prison designed by W. Carbys Zimmerman, whose office was also on the 11th floor of Steinway Hall. Tomlinson received prison related work in Joliet and in different parts of Illinois. In 1925 he was sent abroad by the State of Illinois to inspect European prisons. Tomlinson built a house for himself in Joliet where he continued to live and build single-family residences until his death in 1942.

12.023. Henry Webster Tomlinson. Lake Bluff, Il. City Hall, 1905.

12.024. Henry Webster Tomlinson. Tomlinson Residence. Joliet, Il. 1918.

ROBERT CLOSSON SPENCER JR.

Robert Spencer was the member of the Steinway Hall collaborative circle, who, with Wright, would jointly work out the principles of their residential architecture. In the early years in Steinway Hall, it was primarily Spencer who would promote these ideas through writing as an important adjunct to the group's individual architectural practices.

Robert Closson Spencer Jr. was born in Milwaukee, Wisconsin in April of 1864. His father ran the Spencerian Business College there. Opened in 1865, it stayed in business for over one hundred years, though not under family ownership, merging with Concordia College's School of Business Administration. There

were also Spencerian Business Colleges in Louisville, Kentucky; Washington, D.C.; Newburgh, New York; and Cleveland, Ohio. Spencer's father served on the Milwaukee School Board and worked with Alexander Graham Bell to develop the first schools for the deaf in Wisconsin. Spencer's grandfather Platt Rogers Spencer was trained as a bookkeeper and became an educator. He opened the first Spencerian Business Schools in Ohio and New York. He was also a calligrapher who developed a handwriting method that he described in a book *The Spencerian System of Penmanship.*[1] Spencerian Script was a style of handwriting used in American primary schools up until the 1920s when

13.001. Robert C. Spencer Jr.

it was replaced by the simpler Palmer Method. Robert Spencer Jr. was known for his focus and organizational skills that were

---

1 In 1889, Robert C. Spencer wrote and printed a "Spencer Family History and Genealogy," which contains several pen and ink drawings by Robert C. Spencer Jr. including a drawing of the house in Newbury, Mass, built in 1650 by John Spencer. The Spencers are descended from Henry Spencer, first earl of Sunderland. His son Robert Spencer bequeathed property in New England to John Spencer. The publication includes a biography and articles by Platt Rogers Spencer, including "The Origin of Spencerian Writing." At the Wisconsin Historical Society.

thought of as family characteristics. These traits were described in a profile of Spencer in the *Brickbuilder* written by his friend Dwight Perkins, "Precision and breath stand out as conspicuous characteristics of the work of Robert Closson Spencer Jr. ... His precision he inherits from his father and from his grandfather, who was the author of the Spencerian System of Penmanship."[2]

Robert Spencer Jr. was educated in the Milwaukee public schools and then attended the University of Wisconsin, where he was one of the founders of the Alpha Lambda chapter of the Sigma Chi fraternity. In 1886 Spencer graduated with a degree in mechanical engineering. We do not know if he knew Frank Lloyd Wright, who was a special student in engineering at the University. Wright was not on campus full time, although he suggests in *An Autobiography* that he had met Spencer. After graduation, Spencer worked as a draftsman for the Milwaukee architect Henry Koch.[3] Deciding that he wanted to be an architect, in 1888 he enrolled in the architecture program at the Massachusetts Institute of Technology. There he studied with Eugene Letang, the first graduate of the *Ecole des Beaux-Arts* to teach in the United States. Spencer's transcript shows that he took courses in freehand drawing, watercolor, the orders of architecture, and architectural history. In Boston he would have been exposed not only to the study of *Beaux-Arts* classicism in school, but to the contemporary work of H.H. Richardson. At that time the MIT campus was on Boylston Street one block from Copley Square, the site of Richardson's Trinity Church (1872–1877). We do not know if he knew either Perkins or Hunt while he was in Boston. He could have met Perkins who remained in Boston after graduation to teach at MIT. Perkins moved back to Chicago in 1888 during Spencer's first year at MIT. He also might have met Myron Hunt who was at MIT from 1890 to 1893. After he graduated, Spencer remained in Boston to work. Both Spencer and Hunt were members of the Sigma Chi fraternity[4] and could have met socially.

---

2 *Brickbuilder*, vol. 24, 1915, p.76.

3 Henry Koch was the designer of a number of public buildings in Milwaukee including the Old City Hall, the Hotel Phister, and the Science Hall at the University of Wisconsin in Madison. He designed 20 court houses and a number of schools in Wisconsin and neighboring states.

4 Spencer belonged to the Alpha Lamda chapter at the University of Wisconsin and then joined the MIT chapter. He is listed as a member of Alpha Theta at MIT in the Sigma Chi Quarterly vol. 14.

After his graduation, in 1889, Spencer took a job with the Boston firm of Wheelwright & Haven.[5] That same year he married Ernestine Elliott. They were married in her hometown of Bath, Maine. Returning to Boston he went to work for Shepley, Rutan & Coolidge—the successors to H.H. Richardson's practice. Spencer entered the firm three years after Richardson's death. At that time the commissions in the office were for the Ames Building in Boston, and the Boston Chamber of Commerce, both designed in the Richardsonian Romanesque style, and a a commission to do a master plan for Stanford University in Palo Alto.

In 1891 Spencer was the 8th winner and first Midwesterner to receive the Rotch Traveling Scholarship from the Boston Society of Architects. The scholarship was open to young professionals working in Massachusetts and awarded a stipend of $2,000 for two years of travel and study abroad. The travelling scholarship was founded in 1884 by Arthur Rotch, a graduate of MIT architecture, class of 1875. It offered the opportunity for American architects to make a "grand tour" of Europe, an experience that had been an obligatory part of European architectural education. The scholarship was in many ways the American equivalent of the *Ecole des Beaux-Arts' Prix de Rome*, a two-year fellowship that included both travel and a residency at the French Academy in Rome. Like the *Prix de Rome*, the Rotch Scholarship required the applicants to compete for the position. They were required to take two three-hour written exams in the history of architecture, architectural theory, building construction, and to make a three-hour drawing from a cast. Applicants were also tested for a knowledge of French. Finalists who passed, then competed in a design competition for "an important monumental building." Like *Prix de Rome* winners, Rotch Scholars were required to document their travel by making freehand as well as measured architectural drawings during their time abroad. These were published and exhibited by the Boston Architectural Club. Today, we know where Spencer went in Europe and England based on his travel drawings, which are in the Architectural Drawing

---

5 Edmund Wheelwright was a well-known Boston architect who graduated from Harvard and MIT and then attended the *Ecole des Beaux-Arts Paris*. He designed Boston public buildings such as the New England Conservatory of Music, the new Opera House, and the State Historic Building in the Fenway.

Collection of the MIT Museum.[6] A number of his drawings that received critical attention were exhibited in both Boston and later in Chicago. These were a series of six watercolors of Renaissance ceilings. They also included imagined restorations of ceilings at the Ducal Palace in Mantua. Dwight Perkins wrote, "The colored drawings of the ceiling of the central dome of the Villa Madonna, Rome, which was published in the Rotch Scholarship Envois, has shown his ability to work and show every detail without the loss of breath. Many acquired breath by elimination, but Robert Spencer never does. He includes everything." These drawings included decorative floral motifs which were to influence Spencer's later decorative designs for the interiors of the Chicago Public Library (1893).

---

6 A list of dated drawings suggest Spencer spent from September 1891 to November of that year in France and from November to August of 1892 in Italy, returning to France and then Germany in the Spring of 1893 and then England in June.

13.002. Robert Spencer. Rotch Watercolor. 1891-92.

13.003. Shepley, Rutan and Coolidge. Chicago Public Library. Chicago, Il. Interior. 1893.

Also included in his travel drawings were watercolors of farmhouses in Siena and Brescia. His watercolors of farmhouses in rural England show half timbering that may have served as the inspiration for the half-timbered houses done early in Spencer's architectural practice.

In the fall of 1893 Spencer returned to Boston and to Shepley, Rutan & Coolidge. In 1891 the firm had won the competition for the Chicago Public Library. This would lead to the commission for a new building for the Chicago Art Institute the following year. The Art Institute had outgrown their Burnham and Root building on south Michigan Avenue. Root had died and Burnham's consuming involvement with the fair probably explains why his firm didn't receive the commission for the Art Institute's new building. With two Chicago commissions in the works, Shepley, Rutan & Coolidge opened a Chicago office in 1893 headed by Charles Coolidge. It was Coolidge who had come to Chicago to supervise the construction of Richardson's Glessner House. Familiar with Chicago, it made sense that Coolidge would run the Chicago office. A nationwide financial panic in 1893 negatively impacted construction in Boston and the firm

13.004. Robert Spencer. Rendering of the "Main Stair for an Art Building." 1891-1893.

13.005. Shepley, Rutan and Coolidge. Art Institute of Chicago. Chicago, Il. Main Stair. 1893.

actively sought work in other cities as well as in Chicago. With little work in Boston, Spencer was sent to Chicago to work on the interior details of the Chicago Public Library and then the Art Institute. At this point, the firm had turned away from Richardsonian Romanesque to embrace Classical architecture. Classicism was being taught in all the schools. It was the dominant architectural language of the Chicago World's Fair and in Boston was to be seen in McKim, Mead & White's influential Boston Public Library.

The Chicago Architectural Club published a catalog of their yearly exhibit for the first time in 1894. Hugh Garden who was working for Shepley, Rutan & Coolidge, was the club's president, and Charles Coolidge served on the jury of Admissions. The exhibit included five projects by Shepley, Rutan & Coolidge, two represented in drawings made by Spencer. These were "A Dwelling House" and "Main Stair for an Art Building." Also included were 12 of Spencer's Rotch Scholarship drawings. The drawing of the "Main Stair" is clearly a design drawing showing the development of the Art Institute's main stair. Just discernable in the center arch of Spencer's drawing is the Louvre's Winged Victory of Samothrace, which would become one of Wright's cherished icons, small scale reproductions of which he placed in many of his houses.

That same year 1894, Spencer left Shepley, Rutan & Coolidge and formed a brief partnership with R.R. Kendall, moving into office space in the Schiller Building adjacent to the office Frank Lloyd Wright shared with Cecil Corwin. With Kendall as his partner, Spencer designed three houses in Evanston including the John Stanley Grepe House, a half-timbered residence across the street from the lake. Done for John Grepe, an Englishman, the house is Tudor Revival, with half timbering and casement windows. Marion Mahony wrote in her memoir that when she began to work for Frank Lloyd Wright in 1895, a rendered drawing of one of Spencer's houses was pinned up on Wright's wall. Given the date this probably would have been the Grepe House,[7] which was clearly an influence on Wright's Nathan Moore House of the following year.

---

7 Paul Kruty, "Wright, Spencer, and the Casement Window," *Winterthur Portfolio*, vol. 30, no. 2/3, 1995.

13.006. Robert Spencer. John Stanley Grepe House. Evanston, Il. 1894.

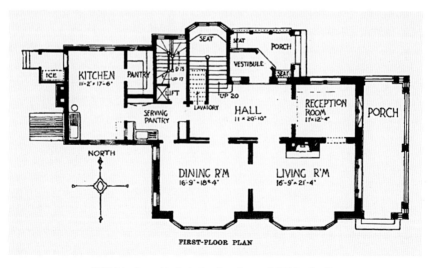

13.007. Robert Spencer. John Stanley Grepe House. Evanston, Il. 1894. First Floor Plan.

While, the plan of the Grepe House is not inventive in its spatial interconnection of rooms, it does provide views of Lake Michigan all the way through the house by aligning door and window openings in the ground-floor rooms. This axial arrangement of room centers and openings would have been a part of Spencer's *Beaux-Arts* training at MIT. Perhaps the most important feature of the house is Spencer's use of vertical timbering to organize the location of windows along with horizontal timbering to tie together the windowsills. While the former comes from the original structural nature of timbering in Tudor construction, the latter, horizontal banding at the sills, was not always the case. Vertical boards used in this way would become a typical feature in both Spencer's and Wright's subsequent work as well as that of the Prairie School architects. In a portfolio of work by Spencer and Powers published in the *Western Architect* in 1914, William Purcell writes, "In these buildings the intent is nothing more than a reasonable desire to panel or divide up an area of wall, or to make the natural panels, which windows are, form a pattern with other panels arranged to suit the fancy."[8]

It is easy to see why Wright admired the Grepe House. The skillful articulation of the entry porch, which opens to the entry and stair hall, marked on the exterior by a two-story glass bay window, suggests Spencer's rapidly maturing talent. The articulated stair would become a feature of Spencer's later work including his designs for model farmhouses. In his 1901 article "Half-Timber and Casement," for the *House Beautiful* magazine Spencer illustrated the entire article with photographs of the Grepe House. He writes about the picturesque qualities of half-timbered, stucco houses and continues to laude picturesque architecture, "The most interesting early works of Richardson, McKim, Peabody, Eyre, Wheelright [sic][9] and Emerson, all lean toward the picturesque and the romantic. Only within the past decade have our famous architects succumbed, almost without exception, to the formal and coldly intellectual spirit of classicism in the designing of country houses ... but something of the freedom and honesty of what for lack of a better name may be

8 Purcell, *Western Architect*, April 1914, p.36. Reprinted in Brooks, ed., *Prairie School Architecture, Studies from the "Western Architect."*
9 Wheelwright for whom he had worked.

called the 'picturesque' in architecture is bound to assert itself in the works of the men who do their own thinking, who love to invent, and scorn mere fashion-mongering."[10] The Grepe House may have also had an influence on Myron Hunt's work at this time. The speculative house he designed in Evanston at 1600 Wesley (1898–99) for Harlow Higinbotham, designed shortly after he moved into Steinway Hall, was Hunt's only half-timber house. Inside the Grepe House, the stairway features horizontal boards the width of each stair riser with reveals between the boards aligning with the stair nosing. This is a feature of the stairways in Myron Hunt's own house of 1896 and the Catherine White double house of 1897 both in Evanston, perhaps a feature borrowed from Spencer.

13.008. Frank Lloyd Wright. Nathan Moore House. Oak Park, Il. 1895.

13.009. Spencer and Powers. Adams House. Indianapolis, In. 1903. Spencer would continue to use half-timbering to organize the windows of his houses

In 1894 Spencer designed two speculative houses in Evanston.[11] They were done for Myron Hunt's good friend and their fellow Sigma Chi brother Charles Wightman. The following year Spencer would build three more houses for Wightman, also at Evanston on Pioneer Road. These were published by Spencer in the *Inland Architect* in May of 1898 and in the *House Beautiful* of August 1901. Spencer published this group of "cottages" again in the *Architectural Record* for August 1912 as part of a seven-part series of articles entitled "Building the House of Moderate Cost."

10 Spencer, "Half-Timber Casements," the *House Beautiful*, 11, no.1, December 1901, p.12–-13.
11 Wightman was a real estate investor who built houses in Evanston and made real estate loans. Wightman was a secretary of the Evanston Savings and Loan and served as an Evanston alderman.

13. 010. Robert Spencer. Speculative Houses for Charles Wightman. Evanston, Il. 1894.

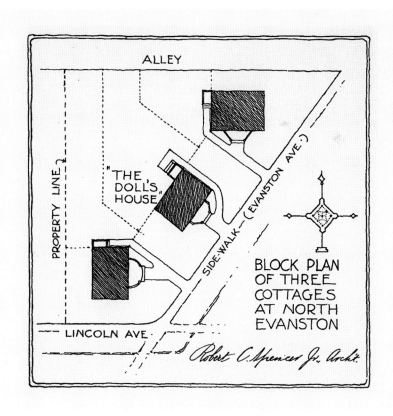

13.011. Robert Spencer. Speculative "Dolls" Houses. Evanston, Il. Site Plan. 1894.

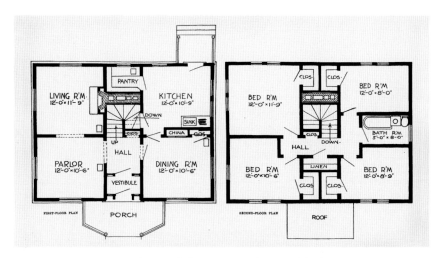

13.012. Robert Spencer. "Dolls Houses." Evanston, Il. 1894. Typical Floor Plans.

In the third article in the series, which included the Wight-man cottages referred to as "Dolls Houses," Spencer wrote, "there are but five or six really more or less distinct types of plan for the house of average size, each susceptible of variations and modifications, which give a new form to the basic idea."[12] He published six floor plans discussing and illustrating variations in stair and fireplace placement, point of entry, and location of principal rooms. Spencer's *Beaux-Arts* education at MIT would have included the idea of building typology.[13] This is possibly the first attempt to consider the application of plan typologies to the design of simple low-cost residences.

In 1896 Wright, with his office still in the Schiller Building adjacent to Robert Spencer's, was asked by his Oak Park friend and neighbor Charles E. Roberts[14] to design speculative houses for an entire city block in Oak Park. The site was six blocks east of Wright's house on Chicago Avenue. Although never built, among the houses Wright designed, one labeled "House

---

12 Spencer, "Building the House of Moderate Cost. The Third Article," the Architectural Record, vol. 32, no.2, August 1912, p.113. In that same article Spencer wrote about the development of a house's exterior, "For broadly speaking, a plan is an elevation ... he [the architect] will always have in mind the general character of his design as he develops his little plan." This idea, linking the plan and elevation, would be expressed by Le Corbusier and other European modernists years later.

13 In 1800 J.N.L. Durand published his compendium of comparative building plans all drawn to the same scale, *Recueil et parallele des edifices de tout genre.*

14 Roberts served on the building committee for Unity Temple when Wright was selected as their architect.

1" is reminiscent of several of his "bootlegged houses of 1892. However, it is Wright's design for "House 3" that seems to owe a debt to his friend Robert Spencer. It has a timbered gable above a bay window like Spencer's Grepe House and the articulated, pavilioned entry porch recalls not only the connected garage of his Moore House, but the gabled entry porch of the Grepe House. This feature is an element that would characterize many of Spencer's subsequent houses from the mid-1890s on.

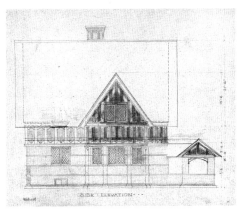

13.013. Frank L. Wright. Charles E. Roberts Speculative Houses. Rigeland (now Oak Park), Il. 1896. Project.

Wrights proposal for Roberts stands in contrast to his later design for a "Home in a Prairie Town" (February 1901), a project that Neil Levine[15] points out introduced Wright's idea of the "Quadruple Block Plan." In this plan, rather than different houses facing the street, as Edward Bok's model house program presumed, Wright proposed four identical houses occupying the corners of a square city block each with a different orientation to the street. Like Wright's plan, Spencer's 1894 development carefully sited houses to offer multiple orientations to the adjacent streets.

The design of modest middle-class residences and what Spencer referred to as "the problem of the farmhouse" would be a continuing theme in his work, beginning with his Rotch Travelling Fellowship and his interest in vernacular farmhouses. Spencer was in sympathy with Edward Bok's crusade for better residential design in the *Ladies' Home Journal* and would design seven model farmhouses for that publication. Reiterating Bok's thinking, which addressed his woman readers, Spencer wrote in the *Architectural Record* in 1912, "It is the wife rather than the husband who has the last word as to what the house shall be, and who is really the owner. Were it not for the women a lot of men would be living in shacks."

---

15 Neil Levine, *The Urbanism of Frank Lloyd Wright*, Princeton: Princeton University Press, 2016, p.42.

In 1896–1897 Spencer moved from the Schiller building into Dwight Perkins's loft on the top floor of Steinway Hall. During that first year in Steinway Hall Spencer designed the Robinson House built in his wife's home town of Bath, Maine. It was Spencer's only completely shingled house. It had an open entry porch with its own gabled roof held up on two rectangular columns. An articulated, gable roofed entry porch would become a feature of most of Spencer's later houses. A similar entry porch can be seen in his 1898 Kelsey House, which was exhibited in the Chicago Architectural Club's exhibition and catalog for that year. The Kelsey House also featured an articulated stair tower in a projecting bay. This would be an important feature in Spencer's designs for the *Ladies' Home Journal* and for many of his later houses.

Spencer's work from his early years in Steinway Hall was mostly residential. However, in 1898, his designs for the Menasha Public Library at Menasha, Wisconsin[16] and the Spencer Memorial Library at Geneva, Ohio were included in the Chicago Architectural Club exhibit and catalog. The Ohio project was named for his grandfather Platt Rogers Spencer, who was a resident of Geneva having moved there in 1810.

---

16 "The Elisha D. Smith Public library was built in 1898. Plans were advertised for in 1897 and from a dozen or more submitted, that of H.J. Van Ryn, of Milwaukee, was accepted." Menasha Press, Semi Centennial Souvenir Edition.

13.014. Robert Spencer. Robinson House. Bath, ME. 1897.

R. C. Spencer, Jr.   *House for H. N. Kelsey on the Sheridan Road at Wilmette*

13.015. Robert Spencer. H. N. Kelsey House. Wilmette, Il. 1898. Rendering.

13.016. Robert Spencer. Kelsey House. Wilmette, Il. 1898. Rendering.

HOUSE OF MISS SUSANNE DENKMAN, ROCK ISLAND, ILL.
Spencer & Powers, Architects, Chicago

13.017. Spencer and Powers. Denkmann-Hauberg House. Rock Island, Il. 1907-1911.

13.018. Spencer and Powers. Spencer rendering of the W. P. Cowan House. Weaton, Il. 1913.

SPENCER MEMORIAL LIBRARY.
Robert C. Spencer, Jr., Architect.

13.019. Robert Spencer. Spencer Memorial Library. Geneva, OH. 1898.

Rob. C. Spencer Jr.   *Menasha Library*

13.020. Robert Spencer. Menasha Library. Menasha, WI. 1898.

In 1905 Spencer formed a partnership with Horace Powers with Spencer serving as the principal designer. Their office was still in the loft of Steinway Hall. That same year Spencer would build a house for his family in River Forest a few miles west of Wright's Oak Park home and studio. There, Spencer designed the Oak Park-River Forest high school. It was done in association with Norman Patten, a resident of Oak Park, who had been the chief architect for the Chicago Board of Education from 1896 to 1898. The building was completed in 1908 and Spencer's son Charles was in the first graduating class.

Beginning with his articles for the *Inland Architect*, the *Ladies' Home Journal,* and his 1900 article in the *Architectural Review* on the work of Frank Lloyd Wright, Spencer wrote continually. He, not Wright, would become a principal spokesman for the architects of Steinway Hall and the Eighteen, articulating their ideas about residential architecture and architectural education. Between 1900 and 1910 Spencer would write articles for both popular and architectural periodicals. These addressed

13.021. Robert Spencer. Spencer Residence. River Forest, Il. 1905.

the design and construction of affordable, aesthetically pleasing suburban and rural houses. Spencer understood that in promoting the architectural ideas of the Steinway Hall group, he was also promoting himself. Addressing the question of how to find an architect he recommended, "Unless you *like* his work, do not patronize an architect, simply because he is an acquaintance or a friend ... The best way to become familiar with the work of many architects is to begin, long before you build, to subscribe to the journals, particularly those published for the profession and which illustrate the work of the best men."[17]

Spencer's articles were often illustrated with his work and that of Spencer and Powers. Occasionally he illustrated the work of Prairie School architects, most frequently that of Walter Burley Griffin, with Wright's work conspicuously absent. Spencer wrote about the importance of residential design, "We who would like to see a constantly rising standard of architectural taste, and a constant widening of public appreciation of good architecture, may well say: 'We care not who designs our churches, courthouses and marts of trade, if we may really *design* the homes of the people.'"[18]

17 Spencer, the *Architectural Record*, 31, 1912, p.614.
18 Spencer, "Building the House of Moderate Cost. The First Article," the *Architectural Record*, 1912, p.609.

13.022. Spencer and Powers. Residence. Chicago Architectural Club Exhibit. 1909.

13.023. Robert Spencer and Norman Patten Associated Architects. Oak Park- River Forest High School. River Forest, Il. 1908.

The Chicago Architectural Club Catalog for 1900 featured Spencer's farmhouse designs as well as a short, illustrated essay "The Farmhouse Problem." Among the drawings exhibited were some that were made for the *Ladies' Home Journal*. That same year Spencer published an article on the "American Farmhouse" in the *Brickbuilder* (September 1900, p.179–86), which he illustrated with his sketches of vernacular American farmhouses and renderings of his designs. Spencer realized that the Farmhouse was an area of residential design never considered by architects. He blamed the lack of good farmhouse design on the Homestead Act of 1862. It provided free tracts of land and promoted the physical isolation of farmers in this county's most rural areas, while architects were concentrated in the cities. Spencer wrote, "The sod house and 'shack' are but temporary makeshift shelters, and the cheap frame house is taking their place ... The unscrupulous plan-merchant, who never lets art interfere with business will continue to be the only architect the farmer knows.[19] ... Altogether, the farmhouse problem in this country is a most interesting one: and as the cheap and temporary houses of the first settlers and their immediate descendants fall into dilapidation and decay, it is to be hoped that we shall enter on an era of more substantial livable and attractive homes for the millions who till the soil and form the backbone of the nation."[20] In his second article on "Houses of Moderate Cost" Spencer noted that, "The modern bungalow makes an ideal farm house."

Spencer was a proponent of casement windows rather than commonly used double-hung windows that he and his colleagues referred to as "guillotines." Spencer wrote two articles

---

19 Spencer, the *Brickbuilder*, September, 1900, p.178-86.
20 Ibid., p.186.

13.024. Robert Spencer. Wisconsin Farmhouse Design. 1900. Project. The Brickbuilder.

promoting the use of casements, "The Window Problem" in the May 1902 issue of *House Beautiful* and again in the eleventh installment of his series "Planning the House" for *House Beautiful* in 1905. In the "Window Problem" he wrote, "the two chief elements of exterior design are wall and opening ... In suburban and country homes, English casement windows are just beginning to be appreciated. Their picturesqueness made its first appeal to many Americans, otherwise ignorant of English houses, through Kate Greenaway's illustrations some years ago," and he admitted, "Possibly the reader has by this time begun to suspect that I am making an argument for casement windows as opposed to the ordinary type. I am."[21]

Casement windows were a prominent feature of the picturesque Shingle-style houses and of the English Arts and Crafts architecture that younger Chicago architects admired. The casement window had a number of important features. It offered better ventilation, and importantly for aesthetics, it could be ganged together horizontally offering larger expanses of glass, which Spencer referred to as "broad landscape windows." For adjacent double-hung windows, the spacing between windows had to be wide enough to accommodate two side by side pockets for the counterweights required for the window to remain open. With casements, the frames of the windows could be connected together. One problem with the use of casement windows was the expense of the European operating hardware available at the time. Casement window hardware was usually a push-out bar with notches or holes and pins to hold the window in different positions. Spencer, who was trained as a mechanical engineer, began devising improvements to casement hardware. In 1903 he was granted a patent for a casement latch, which he dubbed the "Hookfast." Next, he redesigned the push-out arm, designing it with an integral adjustable hold open feature, recessing the entire mechanism into the window sill. It was called the "Holdfast Casement Adjuster." This he had manufactured by the Federal Company in Chicago, while the latch was made by the Acorn Brass Manufacturing Company of Chicago. In 1906 Spencer, along with his architectural partner Horace Powers, and their lawyer William Ordway incorporated the Casement Hardware Company of Chicago. The

---

21 Spencer, "The Window Problem," *House Beautiful*, May, 1902, p.368-69.

following year Spencer received a third patent for a less expensive "hold open adjuster" that was surface mounted on the sill rather than recessed. This was marketed as the "Bulldog" adjuster.

Spencer and Powers were busy in 1911 and 1912 with over a dozen houses completed locally as well as in Wheaton and Galesburg, Illinois; Whitefish Bay, Wisconsin; Knoxville, Tennessee; and Seattle, Washington. In 1912, Spencer's son Charles took over as the manager of Spencer's Casement Hardware Company, a position he would hold for the next 40 years.

Spencer's partnership with Horace Powers lasted until 1923 and in 1928 Spencer joined the faculty of the Oklahoma A&M's school of architecture. He subsequently moved to the University of Florida in 1930. In 1934 during the Depression he left

13.025. Robert Spencer. The Holdfast Casement Adjustor

13.026. Robert Spencer. The Bulldog Casement Adjustor

teaching and worked for the United States Government painting murals. The Federal Arts Project, part of the WPA under the New Deal, employed artists who were salaried to produce art for school, hospitals, libraries, post offices, and other public buildings. Spencer retired in 1938, moving to Tucson, Arizona where he lived and painted until 1953 when he passed away.

Appendix 4

DWIGHT HEALD PERKINS

W hat Dwight Perkins shared with his fellow architects in the loft of Steinway Hall was his zeal as a reformer. Not just as a reformer of contemporary architecture, but also as a social reformer. He addressed first, the design of settlement houses, then he revolutionized the design of public schools, while taking on corruption in the awarding of public building contracts. Lastly, he reformed the state of Illinois's ideas about the importance of open public park land.

Dwight Perkins's parents Marion Heald and Marland Leslie Perkins were married at Tremont, Illinois where his grandfather was a country doctor. Perkins's father came to Chicago to complete his study of the law and decided to remain to open his own law practice. Marion's parents were early Chicago settlers, arriving when the city was still a swamp. Leslie Perkins, as he was known, enlisted as a captain in the 9th Illinois Cavalry during the Civil War. Afterwards President Lincoln appointed him judge advocate for Tennessee to represent its people before the Southern Claims Commission, a Federal Commission tasked with assessing southerners' claims for lost and damaged property as a part of Reconstruction. Memphis citizens felt that Captain Perkins would be fair to the people of the city.

14.001. Dwight Perkins

Leslie Perkins came out of the war in poor health. While still living in Memphis he had a stroke, leaving him partially paralyzed. Dwight was born there in March of 1867 and was named for Marion's brother. He was also given her family name, Heald. The family returned to Chicago when Dwight was 12 and Marion went to work as a clerk in the Chicago Internal Revenue office to support the family. After a year working full time she was unable to properly care for both her husband, who was dying, and for her son. Dwight's paternal grandfather came and took him to Tremont to take care of him.[1] Dwight's father died the following year and the family moved into the Heald's house on Indiana Avenue where he and his mother lived with his maternal grandparents. It was here that Dwight spent his boyhood. The family were all members of All Souls Church where Marion was known as "Lady Serenity," having stoically survived the death of her husband, and then, the deaths of her father and sister, all in a few short years.

When Dwight's maternal grandfather died, his family was unable to pay the mortgage on the house. Along with his mother and grandmother, they lived briefly in a boarding house. Feeling the need to help support his family Dwight took a job carrying weekly payrolls from the bank to one of the packing houses at the Chicago Stockyards and, like Frank Lloyd Wright, never completed high school. He later worked as an office boy for the firm of Wheelock and Clay Architects.[2] During this time he decided that he wanted to be an architect. Perkins wanted to attend the Massachusetts Institute of Technology, then one of only a few schools of architecture in the country. He began studying in the evening to prepare for the entrance exams, but failed French, one of the required subjects.

Perkins put off the idea of architecture school to continue helping his family financially. In April of 1884, in memory of Dwight's father, friends of the Perkins family paid the mortgage on the Heald's house on Indiana Boulevard. With his mother and grandmother assured of a place to live Dwight returned to his hope to study architecture. Annie Hitchcock, Marion's best friend and the widow of Charles Hitchcock, one of the framers of the Illinois state constitution, offered to give Dwight $40 a month for living expenses to attend MIT if he could qualify for a scholarship. At his mother's insistence the monthly stipend was

---

1 Marion Mahony wrote in *Magic in America*: Electronic Edition, Section IV, "The Individual Battle," p.256, "in our childhood there was really a sixth member of our family for our only first cousin Dwight, a few years older than Jerome [her brother] was with us much of the time. It was in his office that I had my first architectural experience." She includes a brief history of her mother's family in Tremont, Illinois.

2 Wheelock and Clay were a prominent Chicago firm. Harry Bergen Wheelock (1861-1934) took over his father's architectural practice and formed a partnership in 1876 with William Clay (1849-1926) who had worked with his father. They were the architects of the Methodist Book Concern, the Moody Bible Institute, the McVickers Theater, the Union Bank, and the Commercial Bank, all in Chicago, and of the Joilet State Penitentiary. They built a number of significant houses on Prairie Avenue and South Michigan Boulevard in the 1880s. Wheelock was one of the founders of the Chicago Architectural Club. He was largely responsible for the State of Illinois bill for licensing architects.

to be treated as a loan. His mother's friend Mary Hawes Wilmarth, who was fluent in French, tutored Dwight who passed the entry exams and was offered a two-year scholarship. She would also tutor Dwight's first cousin Marion Mahony[3] in French when she was preparing for the MIT entry exams. She also offered Mahony financial assistance. Marion was best friends with Mrs. Wilmarth's daughter Anna, who would marry Harold Ickes.[4] The Ickes hired Dwight in 1916 to design their house at Winnetka, Illinois.

At MIT Perkins met Lucy Fitch, who was to become his wife. She was an art student at the school of the Boston Museum of Fine Arts. On graduation, she was invited to teach art at the newly founded Pratt Institute in Brooklyn, while Perkins was offered a teaching instructorship at MIT. Their daughter Eleanor wrote of his MIT education that he had come to believe that the school's *Beaux-Arts* curriculum was antithetical to, "a genuine American Architecture expressing the forms and needs of American Life. ... [which] must be brought to birth."[5] In 1940, Dwight wrote to his daughter-in-law Margery Blair Perkins about his architectural education, "The Massachusetts Institute of Technology was the best school at the time ... At the institute we were taught to compose a plan and develop elevations to it as they would in any Italian Renaissance country. We were a branch of the School of Fine Arts in Paris [*Ecole des Beaux-Arts*]. Our problems were real enough but they were not real in the sense of being built in America at the present day ... The principal instructor was Eugene J. Letang. He was a graduate of the School of Fine Arts Paris. He was, according to the standards of the time, simply superb ... On the whole our work was only secondary to the library. There we got our clues."[6] One can wonder if Spencer, and Hunt, both MIT graduates, shared his feeling about the relevancy of their design education.

Perkins took a job with a Boston firm, and while Eleanor Perkins's biography doesn't identify his employer, we know from

3 Alice Friedman, "Girl Talk," in Van Zanten, ed., *Marion Mahony Reconsidered*.

4 Ickes was a social activist and reformer who would become secretary of the interior as well as director of the Public Works Administration under Franklin D. Roosevelt. Anna was elected and served from 1929 to 1934 as an Illinois State legislator.

5 Eleanor Perkins, op. cit., p.40.

6 Margery Perkins, *Evanstonia*, p.117-18.

a photograph of H.H. Richardson's office staff that he worked for a short time in Richardson's Brookline office. There is also a paycheck made out to Perkins signed by Richardson and dated April 20, 1886 that has survived in the collection of Wilbert Hasbrouck.

In 1888 Perkins returned to Chicago. He worked again for Wheelock and Clay Architects and then went to work for Burnham and Root as John Wellborn Root's principal assistant. Lucy spent that summer in Chicago living with her older Sister Nellie, whose husband was appointed superintendent of schools in Evanston, Illinois, a suburb just north of Chicago. Perkins later made his home there. Back in Chicago, Dwight went with his mother, a social activist to hear Jane Addams speak. She was talking to a group gathered at the home of Marion's friend Mrs. H.M. Wilmarth to raise funds for her and Ellen Gates Starr's plans for setting up an agency to assist immigrants in Chicago's slums. Addams intended to buy the old Hull Mansion on Halstead Street and adapt it to her purposes, creating what would become the nation's first social settlement house.

Perkins, who had become invaluable to Burnham and Root, decided in late 1892 that he was ready to open his own practice. He approached Burnham about leaving. Burnham had just been told that Chicago was selected as the site for the World's Columbian Exposition and that Burnham and Root were to be the architects in charge of the Fair. Burnham offered Perkins a large pay raise to stay and put him in charge of the entire office freeing himself to devote his full attention to the Fair. A further reason to stay with Burnham was financial. Perkins's mother had just been laid off from her job, making him their sole means of support. The pay raise that Burnham offered also allowed him to repay Mrs. Hitchcock the money she had given him during his three years at MIT. At the time of John Root's death, with Perkins in charge of the office, Burnham and Root had a number of major commissions in their office, including the Masonic Temple, the First Regiment Armory, the Ashland Block, and the Monadnock Building, projects for which Perkins was responsible.

In June of 1893 with the Fair open, Burnham returned to his office on the top floor of the Rookery Building. He had been running the temporary architectural office established for the World's Fair, referred to as the "Shack," which was located on the

fairgrounds. In 1893 the country was in the throes of a nationwide business depression. Burnham had very little work in his
office and began encouraging his employees to take on private
outside projects. Perkins got a commission for the design of a
Normal School at Stevens Point, Wisconsin,[7] which he worked
on with fellow Burnham employee George Selby in Burnham's
office. A drawing of the school was published in the *Stevens Point
Gazette* and then in the *Inland Architect* for November 1893.
Perkins also exhibited an exterior perspective of the school in
the 1894 Chicago Architectural Club exhibit.

Perkins left Burnham's office late in 1893 along with fellow
employee George Selby after receiving the commission for Steinway Hall, probably obtained through Burnham. Perkins's understanding was that Burnham would help him start his practice
and this had been a further incentive to remain with Burnham
during the construction of the Fair. Perkins and Selby set up an
office in the Marshall Field Annex Building, a Burnham project
that Perkins had worked on. In 1894, in spite of the depression, Perkins and Selby were busy. In addition to Steinway Hall,
they were working on a two-story house in Evanston.[8] In May
of 1895 Perkins moved into his new office in the recently completed Steinway Hall without Selby. His daughter Eleanor wrote,
"As a partner Selby failed him and did no work of any kind,
and Dwight was obliged to carry out the letter of the partnership agreement and pay him three thousand dollars to get rid
of him." She points out that buying out Selby used up the architectural fee for Steinway Hall and forced him to rent space to
Robert Spencer, Frank Lloyd Wright, and Jules Guerin in order
to meet his expenses.[9] Her recollection is probably incorrect as
Perkins was in Steinway Hall for nearly two years, from 1895–
1897 before inviting Wright, Spencer, Hunt, and Jules Guerin to
share expenses. Perkins's new office mates—Spencer, Hunt, and
Wright—were primarily designing residences while Perkins's
work was largely commercial and institutional.

During his time in Burnham's office Perkins was active in
the Chicago Architectural Club serving as an officer, on different

---

7 Normal schools were teacher training colleges.
8 The *Inland Architect*. 23, no.5., June 1894, carried an announcement but no illustration.
9 Eleanor Perkins, op. cit., p.89.

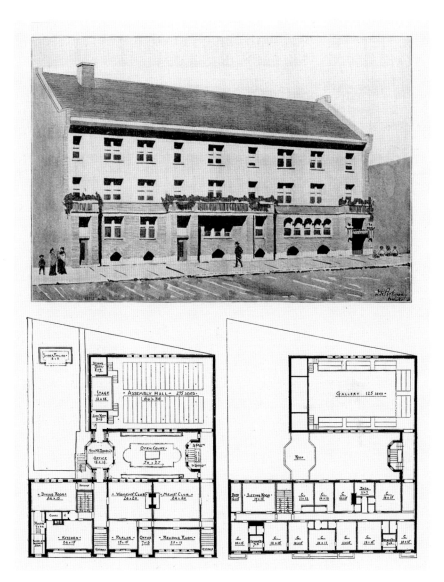

14.002. Dwight Perkins.University of Chicago Settlement. Chicago, Il. 1900.

committees, and as the editor of the club's publication. Perkins was also a prominent member of Chicago's architectural community. In September of 1895, Perkins who was also active in the American Institute of Architects (AIA) was elected to be secretary of the AIA's Illinois chapter. In 1897 the AIA helped form the Chicago Architects Business Association, of which Perkins was a

NORTHWESTERN UNIVERSITY SETTLEMENT.
Dwight Heald Perkins, Architect.

14.003.Dwight Perkins. Northwestern University Settlement. Evanston, Il. 1900.

founding member. The Association, along with the AIA, worked to get a state licensing law adopted and the Illinois licensing act was passed in June of that year.

As a child Perkins grew up with the idea of social service. This was probably the result of his mother's influence and the sermons at All Souls Church. In these the Reverend Jenkin Lloyd Jones presented the idea of service as one of the church's ideals. Perkins's mother, who was active in the church, organized and ran its kindergarten. In 1900 Perkins designed settlement houses for the University of Chicago and for Northwestern University. Both were published in the Chicago Architectural Club Annual, but only the Mary McDowell Settlement House and a gymnasium for the University of Chicago were built. The settlement movement became a cause that Perkins committed to as a practicing architect. He remained a proponent throughout his life.

By 1901 Perkins had built the Charles Hitchcock Residence Hall for the University of Chicago.[10] The commission came through Annie Hitchcock, the family friend, who had lent him money to

---

10 Enrico Fermi is said to have lived there in the 1940 while working on the Manhattan Project and in the 1950s it was home to astronomer and author Carl Sagan.

[IN DESIGNING HITCHCOCK HALL IT WAS NECESSARY TO GIVE DIS-
TINCTIVE CHARACTER TO THE BUILDING ITSELF, TO HARMONIZE
IN A GENERAL WAY WITH ALL OF THE OTHER BUILDINGS—TO JOIN
LITERALLY TO SNELL HALL, USING A PARTY WALL, AND TO MAIN-
TAIN PROPER RELATIONS BETWEEN THE MASSES OF HITCHCOCK
HALL AND THE HULL LABORATORIES. IT WAS ALSO NECESSARY TO
MAKE PROPER CORNER EMPHASIS AT THE CORNER OF ELLIS
AVENUE AND FIFTY-SEVENTH STREET, AND TERMINATE THE COM-
POSITION OF BOTH HITCHCOCK AND SNELL AS VIEWED FROM THE
NORTHWEST. THE STORY HEIGHTS OF SNELL AND HULL ARE
DIFFERENT. IT WAS IMPOSSIBLE TO PRESERVE THE LEVELS OF
BOTH—THEREFORE SNELL WAS COPIED AS REGARDS STORY HEIGHTS.

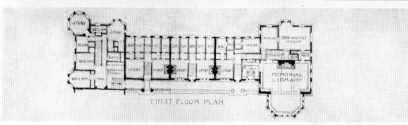

FIRST FLOOR PLAN

14.004. Dwight Perkins. Snell-Hitchcock Hall. University of Chicago. Chicago, Il. 1900.

attend MIT. She wanted to present the University with a dormitory
in memory of her husband. The commission came to Perkins with
the conditions that the building be designed to fit into the Gothic
style of the university. To that end, she sent Dwight (and Lucy)
to England for six weeks to study Gothic architecture. Describing Hitchcock Hall in the Chicago Architectural Club annual, Perkins's wrote, "In Designing Hitchcock Hall, it was necessary to
give distinctive character to the building itself. To harmonize in
a general way with all of the other buildings-to join literally to
Snell Hall, using a party wall and to maintain proper relations
between the masses of Hitchcock Hall and the Hull Laboratories."
Perkins's building fits nicely into the fabric of its surroundings and
the main interior spaces seem to show Louis Sullivan's influence
on the young designer.

14.005. Dwight Perkins. Perkins House. Evanston, Il. 1904.

That same year he designed the Machinery and Electrical Building at the Trans-Mississippi Exposition in Omaha, Nebraska. In 1903, Perkins built the Langdon Apartments and in 1905 the Abraham Lincoln Center Building was completed. The building was originally a commission he shared with Frank Lloyd Wright, the Reverend Jones's nephew.

Lucy continued to press Dwight to move to Evanston to be near Lucy's sister. In 1904 they sold the house on Indiana Avenue and the adjacent property, which they owned, and built a house in Evanston. It was adjacent to Lucy's sister and had a jointly owned tennis court connecting the two properties. The landscaping was done by Perkins's friend Jens Jensen. Perkins decided that he wanted to officially remain a citizen of Chicago. To that end he rented a room in Chicago from a friend where he slept a few nights a month. He had his mail sent there and installed a telephone, thus fulfilling Chicago's residency requirements, allowing him to continue to vote in Chicago elections.

Perkins was approached by friends from the City Club of Chicago who urged him to take the civil service exam so he could be considered for the position of chief architect for the Chicago School Board.[11] Eleanor Perkins wrote, "when the City

---

11 In 1905 the Chicago Board of Education began requiring applicants for the position of a supervising architect to take a civil service examination.

Club had put pressure on Dwight to serve as architect for the city's schools they were motivated by a general indignation over crime and graft in the school administration.[12] In 1905 Mayor Edward J. Dunne was elected as a reform candidate. His candidacy was supported by the Chicago Federation of Labor and the Chicago Federation of Teachers. Dunne appointed a number of social reformers, many of them women, to the Chicago Board of Education. Included were Jane Addams, a friend of Perkins's mother, and Cornella De Bey, also a family friend and a physician whose childhood was later portrayed in a children's book written by Lucy Perkins. There was a need for new schools as the city rapidly expanded and reformers on the board wanted a chief architect who, in addition to bringing good design to Chicago's new school buildings, would fight graft in the cities' building contracts and payrolls.

Perkins, as chief architect for the Chicago School Board, led the design and building of some of the finest and most innovative schools in the country. Further, the entire bidding and construction process was reformed. Perkins abolished the practice of letting general contracts and let contracts separately to each building trade, assuring competitive pricing rather than bids that had been prearranged by collusion with members of the Building Committee, as had been the practice. He used terra cotta trim rather than limestone on his schools to save cost. This angered several members of the School Board who had previously been suppliers of cut stone for Chicago's school buildings. The architect's office supervised the construction of each job verifying not only the cost of materials and labor, but assuring that the materials supplied were the materials that had been specified.

When Fred Busse replaced Edward Dunne as mayor in 1909, he appointed new Board of Education members with ties to Chicago business interests. The new Board set out to stop Perkins. The president, Alfred Urion, chief counsel for Armour and Company, accused Perkins of extravagance, claiming that the schools cost too much, were too "artistic"; "were built of fancy materials"; and "were full of useless ornamentation." Eleanore Perkins wrote, "He [Dwight] was required to justify why he didn't use one plan for every school instead of drawing different

---

12 Eleanor Perkins, op. cit., p.123.

ones. He explained that he was ordered to build different types of schools, i.e., high schools, elementary schools, technical schools, etc., which required different plans. There were six basic plans, but the exteriors were different enough to give each building some identity and distinction."[13] Urion also claimed that the work being done under Perkins was inefficient. Perkins explained to Urion that making additions to existing schools was more time consuming than the design of new buildings and was causing the hours spent by his office to look inefficient.

On February 4th, 1910, Urion requested Perkins's resignation. He had been authorized by the board to take any measures necessary to remove him. Perkins refused to resign. Urion advised him that if he would not resign, he would be suspended, in which case there would be a trial. Perkins demanded that specific charges be brought against him and that he be given a public trial—allowed to answer the charges—and that he be given access to School Board records to prepare his defense. Urion, as president, would preside over the trial and the Building and Grounds Committee would sit in judgement. Urion released a statement to the Chicago newspapers that Perkins had refused to resign and that charges would be brought against him at a trial relative to his dismissal. The pending trial made the front pages with *The American* reporting, "Mr. Perkins is accused of failing to distinguish between foreign and domestic compositions in asphalt work. Mr. Urion is general counsel for Armour and Company which controls the Standard Rubber and Asphalt Company for which he is also counsel. The asphalt of this company was rejected by Mr. Perkins."[14] The charges finally brought against Perkins were incompetence, insubordination, and extravagance.

With support from the Chicago newspapers and a number of public groups, the School Board was forced to open the trial to the public and allow Perkins to retain counsel. The American Institute of Architects, the Municipal Art League, the City Club, and a number of building contractors—including the Carpenter's Union—all wrote in support of Perkins. Urion, known to have a drinking problem, was drunk at the trial and was lambasted

13 Eleanor Perkins, op. cit., p.127.
14 Quoted in Eleanor Perkins, op. cit., p.131.

by the newspapers, one of which ran a front-page cartoon of him questioning Perkins from inside a bottle of rum. After the first day of the trail, the Board stated that there would be no more testimony and that the Board would vote in closed session. On March 31st they voted thirteen to two to dismiss Perkins on grounds of extravagance. They dropped the charges of incompetence and insubordination.

According to Perkins's son Lawrence, the Board of Education then approached Carbys Zimmerman, who had offices in Steinway Hall, about taking the position as Dwight Perkins's successor. His reply was "What do you want me for? I'm honest too."[15]

The 40 schools built or remodeled in Dwight Perkins's five-year tenure set new standards for public school buildings. In addition to fireproof construction and wider corridors and stairways, he pioneered the inclusion of auditorium spaces in each school, a feature that could also serve the local community. Perkins wanted each classroom to have running water, coat closets, storage, and better natural lighting. Previously, toilets were often located in the basement, he advocated for boys' and girls' toilets on each floor of multi-story school buildings. He also made sure that each new school designed had ample open space for school playgrounds. Two of his schools, Grover Cleveland Elementary School and Carl Schurz High School have been designated as Chicago Landmarks. Other important schools he designed during this period were Lyman Trumbull, Tilden, Bowen High School, and Lane Technical School.

When Perkins left his position with the Board of Education, he sent out notices that he was returning to private practice in the firm of Perkins and Hamilton. In 1905 Perkins had formed a partnership with John L. Hamilton who had resigned from the Board of Education. Although at that time they had very little work, the publicity surrounding Perkins's trial brought notoriety to his school designs and soon Perkins and Hamilton had commissions for school and college buildings throughout the United States. In 1911 the firm became Perkins, Fellows and Hamilton.

---

15 "Oral History of Lawrence Bradford Perkins," interviewed by Betty Blum, Chicago Architects Oral History Project, Department of Architecture, The Art Institute of Chicago, 1986 (revised 2000).

They would become one of the leading school design firms in the country.

In addition to his contributions to the design of schools, Perkins was a lifelong proponent of open space and parks. When he was a young man he loved exploring the wooded areas that bordered on the villages of Kenwood, Hyde Park, and Englewood, walking the trails beside the Calumet River. Along with public service, environmentalism, was to become a defining element in his life. His daughter Eleanor wrote, "As a man, later on, he was able to formulate his conviction that human beings do not remain fully human if they are entirely cut off from the natural beauty of the world."[16]

The Chicago Park District had been formed in 1869, and Chicago built Garfield, Humbolt, Douglas, Jackson, and Washington Parks, making it second only to Boston in space devoted to public parks. By the time of the 1893 World's Fair, Chicago had expanded annexing adjacent Lakeview, Edgewater, and Hyde Park, however, no new parks had been built in the city. In the late 1890s Perkins had begun meeting for dinner on a regular basis with a group of men, mostly from the City Club, including Charles Zueblin from the University of Chicago and landscape architect Jens Jensen. This was a group that Perkins would later refer to as the "Committee on the Universe." In 1898 they sent a report to the City Council on Chicago's parks and open spaces noting that most of Chicago's citizens lived over a mile away from any park and that only six public schools had yards big enough to be used as playgrounds. As a result of the report mayor Carter Harrison IV appropriated funds for school playgrounds and appointed Zueblin, Jensen, and Perkins, along with eight Chicago aldermen to a Special Park Commission as a part of his administration. The Commissions' first report was submitted in 1901. In May of 1905, after four years of work, the Commission submitted a report on the Metropolitan Park System proposing a comprehensive plan for parks and open land within and just outside the city limits. The report also contained recommended language for enabling legislation allowing for the acquisition of land. Perkins wrote, "Instead of acquiring space only, the opportunity exists for preserving country naturally

---

16 Eleanor Perkins, *Perkins of Chicago*, p.26.

beautiful ... Another reason for acquiring these outer areas is the necessity for providing for the future population which will extend to the boundaries of Cook County and occupy the intervening sections as well."[17] The report called for the existing city park system to be knit together by boulevards, coordinated with highways, all ideas that were later incorporated into the 1909 Burnham and Bennet plan for Chicago. In the publication *Amps* (Architecture Media Politics Society), Jennifer Gray wrote of the Perkins's report, "He collaborated with social scientists affiliated with the University of Chicago, and with local, grass-roots activists to leverage design as a vehicle for social change. He argued that strategically placed, small-scale interventions would ameliorate the devastating impact that unplanned growth had on the urban poor ... He abandoned illusionistic rendering techniques and illustrated the city as a series of sociological data-maps that combined statistical facts on population density, disease transmission, mortality rates, and criminal activity with geographic projections of Chicago. This new cartographic strategy helped him to identify and create public spaces and social services that benefited underprivileged communities."[18]

In 1905 when the Metropolitan Park Report was approved by the City Council, enabling legislation was drawn up to establish a Forest Preserve District in Cook County with the power to issue bonds to raise funds to buy land that the report recommended. An altered version of the bill was passed and presented to the governor for his signature. Eleanor Perkins writes, "The Special Park Commission hurriedly denounced it," explaining, "that the bill did not include the comprehensive and coordinated park system of the report, but only authorized the purchase of certain areas outside the city, in which presumably the proponents of the bill were interested."[19] It wasn't until two years later that the Special Park Commissions' own bill was submitted to the state legislature, where it was voted down. The bill was rewritten and was finally passed by the legislature in November of 1910 as the Forest Preserve Act. Political infighting occurred over the

17 Quoted in Eleanor Perkins, *Perkins of Chicago*, p.115. Dwight H. Perkins, *The Metropolitan Park System, Report of the Special Commission to the City of Chicago*-1904, p.63.

18 Jennifer Grey, "Social Practice and the Laissez-faire Metropolis: Dwight Perkins in Chicago, 1895-1915," *Amps* (Architecture Media Politics Society), May 2014, vol. 5, no.1, p.1-2.

19 Eleanor Perkins, op. cit., p.117.

bill, which was challenged and declared unconstitutional by the Illinois Supreme Court in April of 1911. Members of the original commission paid for the cost of re-submitting the bill that again passed the legislature and was ratified by voters. To make sure that the Forest Preserve Act wouldn't be struck down again Dwight Perkins, as a test, brought suit against the Act, which, this time, was upheld by the court. A Forest Preserve Commission was formed and authorized to begin the acquisition of land. Dwight Perkins and Charles Wacker, one of the forces behind the Burnham and Bennett Plan, were appointed members. By 1918, 13,000 acres of land identified in Perkins and Jensen's report had been purchased for $5,000,000. This land created the nucleus of Chicago's present-day Forest Preserve System, which eventually grew to 68,000 acres.

As an Evanston resident, Perkins designed a number of houses in that Suburb. These incorporated features similar to the model houses designed by Spencer and Wright for the *Ladies' Home Journal* a few years earlier. Perkins's most significant residential commission was the Harold Ickes House in Winnetka. It was built in 1916 for Ickes, a family friend, who would serve as the Secretary of the Interior under Franklin D. Roosevelt. That same year a house he designed for Mrs. Cyrus McCormick was completed in Lake Forest. The McCormick House could best be described as Prairie Tudor in style. The design is of formal interest because of its continuous horizontal sill at the second floor at the rear façade. It weaves behind the corner piers of the windows in the wing that extends into the back yard. This sill also appears to weave behind the narrow corner piers between the windows in the bay, but it does not continue across the service wing. The banding of the second-floor windows gives the main portion of the house a subtle emphasis. Along with the half timbering on the third-floor gables and the overall massing, the design probably owes something to the contemporaneous work of Spencer and Powers.

In 1908 Perkins designed the Lincoln Park South Pond Refectory, often considered, along with his schools, to be a masterpiece. With low hipped roofs and covered porches, it is distinctively Prairie style. It is all brick and its decorative glazed tile interior with exposed steel trusses and sky-lit central hall make

14.007. Perkins, Fellows and Hamilton. Mrs. Cyrus McCormick Residence. Lake Forest, Ill. 1916.

14.008. Perkins, Fellows and Hamilton. Harold Ickes House. Winnetka, Il. 1916.

14.009. Perkins and Hamilton. Lincoln Park South Pond Refectory. Chicago, Il. 1908.

it a unique and dramatic space. In 1912 Perkins designed the Lion House another building for the Lincoln Park Zoo.

Suffering from poor health and going deaf, Perkins retired from Perkins, Fellows & Hamilton in 1927 and formed a new partnership with Melville, Clarke, Chatten, and Charles Herrick Hammond, architects with offices in Steinway Hall. He served this firm in an advisory capacity until 1933.

Perkins had been instrumental in establishing the West Park System for Chicago and later the Cook County Forest Preserve System. He served as chairman of the City Planning Commission of Chicago, the Municipal Commission, was honorary president of Chicago's Regional Planning Commission, and served on the Planning Commission of the Cook County Forest Preserve. He was also the president of the Northwest Park District of Evanston, Illinois. When he finally retired, he built a house for himself in Pasadena and spent his final years drawing and painting. He died in 1941 while traveling in New Mexico. In a 1915 biographical sketch of Perkins, the author and architect Thomas Tallmadge, a friend and fellow Evanston resident, wrote: "Mr. Perkins injected into the designing of the schools of Cook County, science of a high order and a certain amount of idealism and originality ... In Chicago when we think of Dwight Perkins ... we think of him as a citizen and patriot almost before we think of him as an architect."[20]

---

20 Thomas Tallmadge, *Brickbuilder* July, 1915, p.146.

Appendix 5

MYRON
HUBBARD
HUNT

Myron Hunt was a friend of Robert Spencer's and a kindred spirit. His early Evanston, Illinois houses, explored the same progressive ideas of programmatic, spatial, and material simplification as his Steinway Hall colleagues.

Although Myron Hunt was born in Sunderland, Massachusetts in 1886, a year before Frank Lloyd Wright, he grew up,

15.001. Myron Hunt

from the age of two, just outside of Chicago. The Hunt family lived in Lakeview, a community immediately north of Chicago's city limits. Hunt's father ran a horticultural business and in 1885 had co-founded the Society of American Florists and Ornamental Horticulturalists. In 1893 the senior Hunt wrote *How to Grow Cut Flowers: A Practical Treatise*. Interestingly, the book included architectural drawings and detailed information on how to build greenhouses. Although the Hunt family moved from Chicago to Terra Haute, Indiana, Hunt chose to attend Northwestern University located in Evanston, the first municipality north of Lakeview along Lake Michigan. There Hunt attended the University from 1888 to 1890.

At Northwestern Hunt studied liberal arts and joined the Sigma Chi fraternity. He was elected chapter president in his sophomore year and was described by his friends as a "social gadfly." His fraternity and university social circles would later be the source of many of his commissions for the residences and apartment houses he designed in Evanston between 1896 and 1903, when he left Chicago for California.

Evanston, where Hunt would make his home, had been established in 1854 by Methodists who founded the Garrett Theological Institute and later Northwestern University. The town had a law prohibiting the sale of alcohol and would later become the center of the temperance movement. Its most important proponent, Francis Willard would serve as the first dean of women students at Northwestern University. The picturesque town connected to the city by rail was a center of intellectual and artistic pursuits. Architects William Holabird, Daniel Burnham, Dwight Perkins,[1] and Thomas Tallmadge all lived in Evanston—as did the sculptor Lorado Taft. Addressing the Evanston Woman's Club, Daniel Burnham remarked, "Evanston is the most beautiful city in the world ... There are cities that surpass Evanston in natural beauty ... But take the city as a whole, as a place of residence, there is none equal to it ... many of its residences are incomparable examples of high-class architecture ... Besides these points of beauty there are the lake shore and the bordering sands."

When Hunt decided to study architecture, he transferred from Northwestern to the Massachusetts Institute of Technology. He attended MIT beginning in 1890 and graduated in 1893. While the University of Illinois had established a school of architecture in 1867, at the time, MIT was the preeminent American School of Architecture. For Americans it was second only to attending the *Ecole des Beaux-Arts* in Paris. At MIT Hunt joined the local chapter of the Sigma Chi fraternity. Here he would meet fellow member Robert Spencer. Hunt could also have met Howard Van Doren Shaw, who graduated in 1892 and would be active in the Chicago Architectural Club and a member of the Eighteen. After his graduation in 1893, Hunt remained In Boston and worked for the firm of Hartwell and Richardson (no relation to H.H. Richardson) who were residential architects. They were described as, "basically suburban architects ... most effective in the opening up of interior space ... Hartwell and Richardson's best shingled houses ... achieve a pleasing simplicity and sensitivity in the handling of shingles."[2]

Hunt married Harriette H. Boardman in 1893 and that year, like Robert Spencer, departed for Europe for two years travel to enrich his study of architecture. Hunt traveled through England and Scotland and finally on to Italy. In February of that year Hunt

---

1 Hunt built his house in 1896, Perkins didn't build his Evanston house until 1904.

2 Susan Maycock Vogel, "Hartwell and Richardson: An Introduction to Their Work." *Journal of the Society of Architectural Historians*, vol. 32, no. 2, May 1973, p.132-46.

and his new bride arrived in Florence where they lived for a year making trips to surrounding areas to study the architecture of the Italian Renaissance.[3] He returned to the United States upon the death of his parents, moving back to Boston where he took a job with Shepley, Rutan & Coolidge. In 1891 the firm won the competition for a new building for the Chicago Public Library. The following year Shepley, Rutan & Coolidge were chosen to design the Chicago Art Institute, and in 1893 Coolidge went to Chicago to open an office. Robert Spencer was sent to Chicago to work on the interiors of the library, which were under construction starting in November of that year. Hunt would join the Chicago office in 1895.

Hunt returned to Evanston, renting a house from Charles Wightman, a Northwestern fraternity brother who would give Hunt his first independent commission, the design of a speculative house in Evanston. Wightman would also commission Robert Spencer, that same year to design speculative houses to be built in Evanston. In 1896 Hunt left Shepley, Rutan & Coolidge to open his own practice with an office listed as room 1309 in the Venetian Building. That year he built his own house in Evanston, subsequently building two speculative houses on adjacent lots that he subdivided from his property. Hunt built three double houses for speculation for Harvey Hurd, who in 1893 was the first president of the town of Evanston. He also built three speculative houses for Harlow Higinbotham, Marshall Field's partner and president of the 1893 World's Columbian Exposition. Hunt went on to build 30 houses in Evanston before he left for California.

In 1895, while still working for Shepley, Rutan & Coolidge, Hunt joined the Chicago Architectural Club. For the year 1895–96 he was elected the club's second vice president and served on both the executive committee and the catalog committee along with George Dean, Hugh Garden, and Richard Schmidt. Robert Spencer and Irving Pond, one of the club's founders, served on the jury of admission for the club's annual exhibition. In the 1896 exhibit, held at the Art Institute, Hunt had 16 items exhibited including architectural drawings and some of his European

---

3 Block, Jean, "Myron Hunt in the Midwest," David Gebhard, ed., Myron Hunt, 1868–1952. The Search for A Regional Architecture, 1984, p.9.

travel sketches. The following year he moved into the loft space in Steinway Hall. Active in Club activities, in 1897 he and his wife hosted a "Ladies Night" for members and their wives. It was organized by Myron and Harriet Hunt along with the Robert and Ernestine Spencer and Dwight and Lucy Perkins. While the club listed no female members that year, Lucy Perkins, Dwight's wife, a talented illustrator, was one of the few women who had work included in the club's annual exhibit.

Hunt—along with his wife Harriet—Dwight and Lucy Perkins, Robert Spencer, Frank Wright, and Marion Mahony were among the founding members of the Chicago Arts and Crafts Society. Established at Jane Addams's Hull House in October of 1897, the purpose of the society was, "to call attention to those engaged in the production of articles of everyday use to the possibility of developing in these articles the highest beauty through a vital harmony with the conditions of production."[4] In 1898, the society jointly exhibited work at the Art Institute along with the Chicago Architectural Club.

By 1897, ensconced in Steinway Hall, Hunt's practice was flourishing. In the first full year of his practice he built eight houses in Evanston, one in Chicago, and one in Wilmette—the suburb just north of Evanston. He would also build a two-story commercial building and a small school building, both in Evanston. The school building that he designed was for one of his residential clients to lease to the Evanston School Board. Hunt's early houses show the influence of Richardson's Shingle-style residential work, as well as the influence of the English Arts and Crafts movement. Most of Hunt's houses were either shingled or covered in unpainted clapboards with shingled roofs and open interior floor plans.

Hunt's own house, built in 1896, was sheathed in cedar shingles. Its wood-shingled hipped roof had a wide overhang with exposed rafter tails. It had a distinctive stringcourse at the sills of both the first- and second-floor windows. Although the house was mono-material, the lower stringcourse had the effect of creating a base that the house appears to sit on. The second floor's stringcourse, like many of the houses of the day, created

---

4 Constitution of the Chicago Arts and Crafts Society adopted October 31, 1897 and reprinted in the 11th Annual CAC Journal, 1898, p.11.

a distinct reading for the second floor by tying together all the second-floor windows. The multiple stringcourses, as well as the coursing of the shingles, had the effect of giving the house a horizontal appearance. This was an intentional feature of the houses that Hunt, and a number of like-minded younger architects were designing. The use of stringcourses to create horizontality has been noted as a feature of the work of H.H. Richardson and his followers. All of these elements would be characteristic not only of Hunt's Midwestern work, but of the residential work of Spencer, Wright, Perkins, and many of the other Steinway Hall architects.

Hunt's house is entered through a covered porch at its side, but it is the sequence of entry spaces and their vertical development that is worth noting. Beginning at the arched entry door the sequence proceeds to the living room through a series of arched openings in the entry and stair hall. The stair ascends around a vertical space that is open to the second floor through arches infilled with square spindled railings. Hunt published the plans for his house and for the house he designed for John T. Pirie Jr. of Carson, Pirie, Scott & Company (1898) in his 1903 article in Gustav Stickley's *Craftsman* magazine entitled, "Thumbnail Sketches from an Architect's Notebook."

15.002. Myron Hunt. Myron Hunt house. Evanston, Il. 1896.

15.003. Myron Hunt. Myron Hunt Residence.
Evanston, Il. 1896. Entry Hall.

15.004. Myron Hunt. Myron Hunt Residence. Evanston, Il. 1896.
Second Floor looking toward first floor Library.

15.005. Myron Hunt. Van Deusen house. Evanston, Il. 1897.

Drawings of the double house that Hunt designed in Evanston for Mrs. Catherine White in 1897 were featured in the Chicago Architectural Club annual exhibit and catalog for 1899. This was arguably Hunt's most significant house from the years of his practice in Chicago.

15.006. Myron Hunt. John Pirie Jr. house, Evanston, Il. 1898.

15.007. Myron Hunt. Double House for Harlow Higinbotham.
Evanston, Il. 1898.

15.008. Myron Hunt. Speculative House for Harlow Higinbotham.
Evanston, Il. 1898.

Catherine White was the wife of Hugh A. White, a lawyer. Catherine lived in a large Italianate house built in Evanston in 1867. Alice Zook, Catherine's niece, had lost her parents and her husband, David L. Zook, a Chicago attorney. Catherine, who had no children and whose husband had also passed away, decided to build a double house for herself and her niece. Catherine probably hired Hunt to design her double house at the recommendation of Hunt's client Harvey Hurd who was married to her sister Susanna. In January of 1897 the "Real Estate Notes" in the

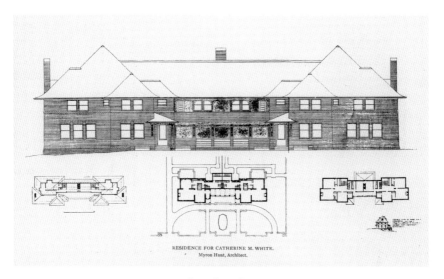

RESIDENCE FOR CATHERINE M. WHITE.
Myron Hunt, Architect.

15.009. Myron Hunt. Catherine White Double House. Evanston, Il. 1898.

Evanston Index carried the following notice: "Mrs. Catherine M. White's new residence has begun ... The building will be of red brick and stone and will be 140 feet long on its Ridge Avenue frontage. The plans were made by Myron Hunt and the first-floor plan of Mrs. White's house, which is to be a double house, one half being occupied by her niece, Mrs. Zook, now of Winnetka, is patterned after the first floor plan of Mr. Hunt's own residence on Wesley Avenue. The great two-story loggias between the north and south wing will be the only unusual feature. The scheme of the exterior is otherwise broad and simple, depending for its effect upon its proportions." The house was completed in February of 1898. Catherine White died in 1899, although her niece continued to live there.

The White House's simple massing, the roof forms and the second-floor stringcourse are all somewhat similar to Hunt's own house, if one imagines it joined to its mirror image. The house's two-story loggia has been compared to H.H. Richardson's Stoughton House in Cambridge, Massachusetts. Rather than shingles the house was clad in brick like Hunt's Emerson Street School built that same year in Evanston. The house was Hunt's largest and most expensive commission to date, with a cost of $15,000 listed on the building permit. Like his shingled houses, Hunt employed a stringcourse under the second-story windows, but here it is of limestone. The stringcourse is continued and becomes the sill of the brick railing at the open second-floor loggia. The overhanging eaves flare out providing wide soffits at the second floor. The loggia and the roofs on the covered entryways rest on heavy timber beams supported in turn by arched timbers. On the first floor these spring from square brick piers. The interiors have spacious living rooms that are connected to the dining room through large cased openings. The handsome main stair of each house ascends between walls like the stair

15.010. Myron Hunt. Catherine White Double House. Evanston, Il. 1898.

15.011. Frank L. Wright. Wright's George Smith house. Oak Park, Il. 1898.

15.012. Myron Hunt. John Sweet house. Evanston, Il. 1898.

in Hunt's house. The stair's side walls are paneled with wide polished quarter sawn-wood boards with beading between the boards that corresponds in size to the nosing of each stair tread.

While the design of the house is clearly Hunt's work, two of his Steinway Hall colleagues later claimed credit. It is entirely possible that Wright may have aided Hunt in preparing the drawings and offering design suggestions. Further, Barry Byrne, who worked in Wright's Oak Park Studio, tells us that Marion Mahony claimed she designed the White House.[5] At this time Mahony was doing work for her cousin Perkins as well as helping both Hunt and Wright in the Steinway Hall loft. In "The Early Work of Marion Mahony Griffin," David Van Zanten writes, "Barry Byrne remembers Marion once telling him that she designed the Catherine White double house at 1302–1307 Ridge in Evanston for Myron Hunt,"[6] and commenting on Hunt's White House in *The Prairie School,* H. Allen Brooks wrote, "Interesting as a collaborative design from Steinway Hall is the duplex house for Catherine M. White at 1313, 1319 (the street number is 1307–13) Ridge Avenue in Evanston. Hunt was the architect, but he was apparently assisted by Wright. Parallels to the work of both architects exist in the design, as well as to the work of H.H. Richardson. Wright's George W. Smith house at 303 Home Avenue, Oak Park (1898) has a similar double-pitched roof, three two-window arrangement[s] and string course merging with the second story sills, while the crisp angular quality of the White house, the bold voids for windows and the ridged symmetry are characteristic of Hunt."[7] Brooks notes that on October 27, 1956 Wright told him "that Myron Hunt came to him to for help in designing this house and that he, Wright, had assisted in preparing the design."[8]

Built in the same year, Hunt's John W. Sweet House in Evanston and Wright's George Smith House in Oak Park both have high peaked roofs with a double pitch.[9] This is the only similarity

5 Barry Byrne in a letter to David Van Zanten, August 23, 1965.

6 Van Zanten, David "The Early Work of Marion Mahony Griffin," *The Prairie School Review* 3, no.2, 1966, p.10.

7 Brook, H. Allen, *The Prairie School*, Toronto: University of Toronto Press, 1972, p.32.

8 Ibid., p.32.

9 William Storrer in his 1974 *The Architecture of Frank Lloyd Wright: A Complete Catalogue* suggests a relationship between the White House and Wright's George Smith House of 1898: "The roof is very steeply pitched ... The similarity between the roofline of this house and that of the 1889 [this should read 1898, the correct date], Catherine M. White house in Evanston, Illinois, suggest that Wright may have assisted Myron Hunt in the design of the White house." This assertion was eliminated in the 1978 edition of Storrer's book.

and it is equally possible that Wright's house was derived from Hunt's high peaked roof design a feature Wright never repeated. The massing of the White and Smith houses is entirely different. The Smith House is far more picturesque, and its roof gives the house a distinct verticality in contrast with the horizontality of the White House. The house's distinctive timber work may have been influenced by the heavy timbering of the first-floor porch of Spencer's Grepe House of 1894—also in Evanston. Unique to the White House is the complex terracing in front of the entrance porch, a geometric structure of steps, balustrades, and benches creating horizontals that relate the house to the ground. Perhaps Mahony did some of the detailing for this house while Hunt was responsible for the general design. Historian Jean Block points out that, "The window boxes in the loggia with their trailing vines would become almost a hallmark of the Prairie School and were an appealing feature of many of Marion Mahony's renderings."[10]

It is an acknowledgment of the importance of the Catherine White House that both Mahony and Wright wanted to claim a hand in its design. Hunt was proud of the house and in addition

---

10 Block, Jean, op.cit., p.16.

15.013. Myron Hunt. Livingston Jenks house. San Francisco, Ca. 1903-1904.

to exhibiting it at the Chicago Architectural Club and its inclusion in their catalog, he arranged for its publication in both the *Inland Architect* and the *House Beautiful.* Mahony's claim of authorship and Wright's claim of assistance were both likely based on design suggestions they offered in the preparation of Hunt's drawings, the kind of contributions often found in collaborative circles.

Hunt spent only three years in the loft space in Steinway Hall.[11] His wife Harriet had contracted tuberculosis and her doctors recommended that she relocate to a warmer climate. In 1901 Harriet spent the winter in California and by 1903 Hunt had moved most of his family to Pasadena, while his sister Fannie remained in Evanston until 1909. At that time Pasadena was a winter resort popular with Chicagoans. In fact, among Hunts first California houses was a commission from Livingston Jenks, a friend and Northwestern University classmate. Jenks had married a woman from San Francisco and moved there in 1896. Located on the edge of a cliff on Russian Hill, Hunt's house for Jenks was published in the *Architectural Review* in 1906, receiving 12 pages of coverage.

---

11 In 1900 Hunt moved from Steinway Hall to 123 La Salle Street.

15.014. Myron Hunt. Myron Hunt Residence. Pasadena, Ca. 1905.

The house that Hunt built for his family in Pasadena had a stucco first floor and was reminiscent of his house in Evanston. It had a shingled second floor and a shingled roof with wide overhangs and exposed rafter tails. Although his own house was similar to his Evanston residence, Hunt's residential work would soon begin to respond to the local vernacular, California's milder climate, and its landscape. Hunt's work would look to both Spanish and Mediterranean models and his interest in small vernacular buildings is documented in his 1925 book *Farmhouses and Small Provincial Buildings in Southern Italy*, which he co-authored with Katherine Hooker.

Hunt's practice was soon thriving, and in 1904 Hunt took on Elmer Grey as a partner—another transplanted Midwesterner from Milwaukee. While published sources suggest that Hunt and Grey first met in California, Grey, who had worked in Milwaukee, had family—Josephine Clarke Grey—in Evanston. He was active in the Chicago Architectural Club and exhibited work in the 1895 member's annual exhibition. In June of 1900 when the club acted as a host to the Architectural League of America's conference in Chicago, Grey gave a major speech. It was reprinted in the *Inland Architect* for June 1900 and his talk was complemented publicly by Louis Sullivan who was at the conference. Grey must have known Spencer, Hunt, and the Steinway Hall group as he did a model house for the September 1901 issue of *Ladies' Home Journal*. This was the same year that Spencer's Farmhouse designs appeared. Grey exhibited his *Ladies' Home Journal* house design in 1902 in the fifteenth annual Architectural Club exhibition. In 1903 Grey moved to California for his health. He was recovering from a nervous breakdown.

Hunt and Grey practiced together until 1910[12] by which time, in addition to residential work, churches, and hotels, Hunt was receiving large institutional commissions including buildings and campus planning work for Pomona College in Claremont and Occidental College in Los Angeles. During this period railroad magnate Henry Huntington commissioned Hunt and Grey to design a 55,000-square-foot house for the 600-acre

---

12 Grey continued to practice in California after he and Hunt dissolved their partnership. In 1941 he moved his practice to Florida. Grey also painted and did a 35-foot mural for the U.S. Naval Air Station in Jacksonville, Florida. The Chicago Art Institute has several of his watercolors in their collection. He died in Pasadena in 1963 at the age of 91.

15.015. Hunt and Grey. Henry Huntington house.
San Marino, Ca. 1911.

15.016. Hunt and Grey. Henry Huntington house. San
Marino, Ca. 1911. Entry Terrace

ranch he had purchased in the San Gabriel Valley. The house was done in a *Beaux-Art* classical style with French interiors designed in collaboration with Huntington's wife Arabella. The house was designed to house Huntington's enormous collection of art, which included Gainsborough's *Blue Boy*. It was completed in 1911 and that year Hunt designed a freestanding classical library building, just north of the house, to contain Huntington's growing collection of books, which included a Gutenberg Bible. For the design of "Huntington's Palace," as the press dubbed it, Hunt acknowledged the formality required for the commission, which he said would have been unattainable using a vernacular style and open plan.

In the early 1920s, Hunt received the commission for the Rose Bowl stadium in Pasadena as well as the Pasadena Public Library. The library was done with a new partner, Harold C. Chamber, with whom he practiced from 1920 until 1947 when he retired to Port Hueneme, California. He died there in 1952.

Appendix 6

FRANK LINCOLN WRIGHT IN CHICAGO

Wright's life and long architectural career has been chronicled over the years. His early life is described in *An Autobiography*, then *sotto voce* in book collaborations with Grant Manson and Henry Russell Hitchcock. Both had personal access to Wright as well as depending on his early writings. Later biographers such as Robert Twombly began to chip away at the mythology Wright created about his life culminating in Thomas Hines's research that established Wright's actual birth date, the extent of his education, and the facts of his parents' divorce, all of which Wright misrepresented.[1] Donald Johnson in *Frank Lloyd Wright: Early Years* established a chronology, ascertained and documented the actual authorship of early work by Silsbee that Wright represented as his own, and analyzed the development of Wright's formal ideas. What follows is a description of Wright's first years in Chicago and a reassessment of the influence of his various mentors. It is an attempt to understand who Wright was as an architect when he moved his practice to Steinway Hall in 1897, 10 years after he arrived in Chicago.

In January of 1887 after only two semesters as a special student in engineering[2] at the University of Wisconsin, Madison, Wright decided to move to Chicago to pursue his chosen profession. He had entered the University as a special student because, according to records, he never completed high school. In Madison he worked briefly for Allan D. Conover, a professor of engineering at the University and it is possible that Conover arranged for Wright's enrollment. There, records show he took classes in descriptive geometry, engineering, drawing, and French, which he never completed. In *An Autobiography* Wright tells us that he studied civil engineering even though he was never actually enrolled in the school of engineering. Further, he tells us that he left the university one semester before completing his education and receiving an engineering degree. This is not in accordance with the University's records. Wright was anxious to begin his architectural apprenticeship and according to *An Autobiography* his uncle, the Reverend Jenkin Lloyd Jones, when consulted

---

1 Hines, "Frank Lloyd Wright—The Madison Years: Records versus Recollections," JSAH, December, 1967

2 This is the way Wright was listed in the 1886–1887 University Catalog. Hines, op. cit., p.231.

16.001. Frank Wright and Cecil Corwin circa 1888.

about his proposed move to Chicago, wrote to Wright's mother, "On no account let the young man come to Chicago. He should stay in Madison and finish his education."[3]

Once Wright arrived in Chicago, he was probably counting on the assistance of his uncle Jenkin Lloyd Jones, the pastor of All Souls Unitarian Church. Having been rebuffed by him, Wright decided he would not utilize any of his uncle's contacts. He wrote, "I was sure of one thing, never would I go near Uncle Jenkin Lloyd Jones nor ask his help nor use his name."[4] Wright says he applied for work unsuccessfully at a number of architectural offices including those of S.S. Beman and Jenney &

3 Wright, An Autobiography, New York: Longmans, Green and Company, 1938, p.59.
4 Ibid., p.63.

Mundie, where he claims to have met with Mundie. He finally went to the office of Joseph Lyman Silsbee, and he tells us that after meeting first with Cecil Corwin, who was to become his close friend, Silsbee offered him a job as a "tracer" for $8.00 per week. Wright soon attached himself to Corwin and his early professional education was by his own admission provided by his colleagues. He wrote, "I could not get along without somebody. No, never."[5] In Silsbee's office he noted that, "I began to go to school to Cecil."[6]

Wright suggests that when he met Silsbee, Silsbee had no idea who he was. This is highly unlikely as Silsbee had completed a new building for All Souls Church for Wright's Uncle in Chicago in June of 1885 and the following year designed a Unity Chapel for Wright's family that was built in Helena, Wisconsin and completed in August of 1886. In January of 1887 a rendering of the chapel signed by "F.L. Wright Delineator" was first published in the annual of All Souls Church for June 6, 1887. It is a copy of an earlier drawing by Silsbee. We also know of Wright's involvement with the chapel through an article in *Unity* 17, August 28, 1886, "Christening a Country Church," written by the Reverend William C. Gannett. Silsbee, who was the son of a Unitarian minister, was related to Gannett by marriage. Earlier, Gannett had written to Jones suggesting Silsbee as an architect. In his article in *Unity* Gannett suggests that the chapel's interior was looked after "by a boy architect belonging to the family." We now know that Wright's involvement with the chapel was minimal. He claimed to have designed the ceiling, but he probably just painted the interior walls. In the 1943 edition of *An Autobiography* he wrote of, "The old chapel walls under the high wooden ceiling of the interior which I had put there when a boy."[7] We know that Wright, who was in Madison at the time working for Conover, had wanted to design the chapel. He sent his uncle a letter containing sketches, "I have simply made them in pencil on a piece [sic] of old paper but the idea is my own

---

5 Wright, op. cit., p.99.

6 Wright, op. cit., p.70.

7 Wright, op. cit., p.436 in "Book Five" added to the 1943 edition. He also wrote on p.380, "Every word I have written is fact, at least." By "had put there," Wright is suggesting that he helped with the carpentry

and I have copied from nothing."[8] It would have made no sense for Jones to let his 18-year-old nephew with no training and no experience design the structure, but Wright no doubt would have been upset by the refusal.

Silsbee would have known the young Wright through his close ties to the Jones family and as Robert Twombly points out, "there is every reason to believe that Wright went directly to Silsbee who knew him from work on Unity Chapel the year before."[9] Silsbee, no doubt, would have considered hiring Wright a favor to his friend and client, the Reverend Jones. We know[10] that Wright joined Jones's All Souls Church in January of 1887 upon his arrival in Chicago. He was listed in the Church's Annual published January 6, 1887 and Silsbee arranged lodging for him with the Waterman family who lived a block away from the church. The Waterman's son had begun the year before as a draftsman in Silsbee's office. Further, on March 9th Wright's Aunt Nell wrote, "I hope you are well, happy and satisfying Mr. Silsbee."[11]

In "The Early Drawings of Frank Lloyd Wright Reconsidered"[12] Eileen Michels, investigating Wright's early published drawings of both work he claimed as independent commissions and his work for Silsbee, offers an alternate scenario for the period between 1887 and 1888. Wright tells us that Silsbee, unlike his later employer Louis Sullivan, permitted him to do outside work taking on independent commissions, while in his employ. This apparently was a very common practice at the time with so many draftsmen taking outside work to supplement their wages that the Illinois State Association of Architects considered expelling any members who permitted this practice. In the period between June of 1887 and May of 1888 Wright published five of his drawings in the *Inland Architect*. The first is the rendering of Unity Chapel in Wisconsin, which is a copy of Silsbee's original drawing. There are then two drawings claimed as independent

8 Secrest, *Frank Lloyd Wright, A Biography*, p.7. Wright to Jenkin Lloyd Jones, August 22, 1885, in Pfeiffer, *Frank Lloyd Wright Letters to Clients*, 1986, p.1.

9 Twombly, *Frank Lloyd Wright, His Life and His Architecture*, p.17.

10 Johnson, *Frank Lloyd Wright. Early Years*, p.74.

11 Ibid., p.75.

12 Michels, "The Early Drawings of Frank Lloyd Wright Reconsidered," JSAH, vol. 30, no.4., December 1971, p.294--303.

commissions. The first of the two is for a "Country Residence, Helena Valley." It is a drawing for the "Home Building" (the first Hillside Home School), which was Silsbee's commission and arguably Silsbee's design. The school building opened on September 10, 1887 and Wright left for Chicago in February of that same year. So, it is possible that he may have had something to do with this design. The second drawing, which was Wright's work, was published as a proposal for a "Unitarian Chapel for Sioux City, Iowa." Wright had heard, through his uncle, that the church founded in March of 1985 was expanding and in need of a new church building. He prepared this unsolicited scheme, which he sent to his uncle on August 22, 1885. He must have hoped that the Reverend Jones would submit it to the Sioux City congregation. Lastly, there were two other projects from Silsbee's office that Wright published. Michels writes about them, concluding, "Perhaps another interpretation of Wright's first Chicago year may be offered here. It is possible that Wright, newly arrived in Chicago sometime after the late spring of 1887 and ambitious to succeed attempted for a brief period to establish himself as an independent architect, and only after becoming disenchanted with that endeavor applied to Silsbee."[13] She may have been right about Wright's eagerness to be on his own, hoping to find independent commissions through his Uncle's connections, even while employed by Silsbee. He would have soon realized that this was impossible, and this would help explain the animosity for his uncle expressed in his *An Autobiography* (1932). Robert Twombly in his 1979 biography of Wright seems to concur with Michels, offering three possible explanations for Wright's "somewhat independent status in 1887." Among these are the "possibility … that Wright actually tried to establish himself as an independent architect or delineator in his own employ."[14] In further support of this Twombly points out that the Lakeside City Directory for 1887 doesn't list Wright at Silsbee's address but at Room 88, 175 Dearborn Street. This was the office of architect, William W. Clay. However Wright tells us that, unhappy about his low salary, he left Silsbee's office briefly to work for Clay

---

13 Ibid., p.298.
14 Twombly, op. cit., p.18.

before returning to Silsbee's employ. It is possible that he was simply there at the time the directory was compiled.

Historians have written about Wright's debt to Louis Sullivan based on Wright's own descriptions of his early apprenticeship. Only recently has it been suggested that Wright might have been equally influenced by Silsbee and by Dankmar Adler, Sullivan's partner. In Silsbee's office, Wright worked with Cecil Corwin, Silsbee's chief draftsman, and with George Grant Elmslie and George Maher, colleagues who could have also had a formative influence on the neophyte architect.

Joseph Lyman Silsbee, Wright's first employer, had built important commercial buildings while practicing in Syracuse New York. Silsbee came to Chicago in 1882 and established a distinguished residential practice. At one time, he had partners and offices in Syracuse, Buffalo, and Chicago.

Silsbee began in Syracuse building high Victorian Gothic structures as well as Romanesque and Second Empire styles popular at the time. Sometime around 1877 be began building what the local press noted as Queen Anne-style houses, attributing to Silsbee the introduction of this style to the Syracuse area. After 1885 his work was in the Shingle style. Both Henry Russell Hitchcock[15] and then Vincent Scully credit Silsbee with the Midwest introduction of this style. Scully wrote, "he [Silsbee] may be considered as the architect who brought the mature Shingle style to Chicago."[16]

Silsbee was born in Salem, Massachusetts in 1848. He graduated from Harvard University in 1869 and then studied architecture at the Massachusetts Institute of Technology. William Ware founded the first college curriculum in architecture at MIT in 1868. Silsbee would have studied with Ware who directed the design courses and then went to work for Ware and Van Brunt in Boston in 1870. Ware and Van Brunt's work was High Victorian Gothic and Silsbee would have been introduced to the precepts of both Viollet-le Duc and Ruskin in their office. These were the ideas of: truth of materials; honesty of architectural

---

15 Henry Russell Hitchcock, author of In the Nature of Materials, first mentions both Silsbee's Unity Chapel and his houses in Edgewater in an article in the Journal of the Warburg and Courtauld Institutes, January-June 1944, p.57-58. He credits Silsbee with bringing the Shingle style to Chicago; Donald Robert Pulfer, "The Early Work of Joseph Lyman Silsbee," thesis for Syracuse University, 1978.

16 Scully, The Shingle and Stick Style, Yale University Press, 1971, p.158.

expression; and the importance of a rational approach to prob-lem-solving in architectural design. Wright would have been exposed to these ideas in Silsbee's office before he worked for Sullivan. These would have been reinforced by Wright's reading of Ruskin and Owen Jones. The year that Silsbee spent in Boston working for William Ralph Emerson was important to Silsbee's development and his later residential practice in Chicago. Emer-son's work was highly picturesque, and he would later become an important architect in the development of the Shingle style. Vincent Scully identified Emerson's 1879 house at Mount Desert, Maine as, "the first house in the whole development to be com-pletely shingled." Discussing the development of this style Scully wrote, "One architect in the late 70s probably contributed more to the development of the new architecture than any designer discussed so far, William Ralph Emerson of Boston."[17]

In Emerson's office Silsbee would have been exposed to Queen Anne architecture and to the ideas of picturesque plan-ning underlying the Shingle style. The latter was a new form of residential architecture; flexible in plan in its relationship to both site and internal planning requirements; simplified in both its massing and architectural elements; and a completely free geo-metric composition of parts including classical elements disposed without compositional or stylistic dependence on previous his-torical styles. The spaces in Shingle-style houses were also more open to one another and to their exterior porches and verandas than in previous American residential architecture. In his dis-cussion of the development of Wright's early work in relation to the Shingle style, Werner Seligmann observes of Shingle-style houses, "In addition, horizontal layering constitutes one of the most potent architectural compositional devices in organizing such a profusion of different masses ... The elements of the house are woven together by continuous horizontal bands, gath-ering eaves, ridges, windows, gables, fronts, and balconies ... It would be too much to expect that such a compositional massing strategy would produce well-ordered plans."[18] Well-order plans were frequently missing in the published Shingle-style work of

---

17 Ibid., p.84.
18 Werner Seligmann, "Evolution of the Prairie House," in McCarter, *Frank Lloyd Wright: A Primer on Architectural Principles*, p.60-61. Seligmann's architectural theory course at Cornell in the late 1960s was my first introduction to Wright's spatial and planning ideas.

Bruce Price; McKim, Mead & White; and Emerson. It was the regularization and geometric ordering of the plan that Wright, Spencer, and Hunt worked to develop. Although Emerson's Shingle-style work dates from the time after Silsbee's employment, Silsbee could have followed Emerson's later work through its publication, and he would employ many of the same architectural motifs. Oak Park, Illinois historian Christopher Payne has pointed out parallels between Silsbee's Edgewater houses and Emerson's work on Mount Dessert Island.[19]

Emerson was noted for his distinctive soft pencil sketching technique, which quickly posited the overall form of his designs. This was a technique Silsbee clearly modeled in his own work. Wright would comment on it in his description of Silsbee: "Silsbee could draw with amazing ease. He drew with soft deep black lead pencil strokes and he would make remarkable freehand sketches of that type of dwelling peculiarly his own at the time. His superior talent in design had made him respected in Chicago. ... Silsbee's way was magnificent; his strokes were like standing corn in the field waving in the breeze ... God the man could draw." Wright would also say of his time in the office, "I learned a good deal about a house from Silsbee."[20]

Silsbee had been a teacher. In 1873, after returning from a tour of Europe, he relocated from Boston to Syracuse, New York taking a partnership with Horatio White and filling White's position as a professor of Architecture at Syracuse University. In the mid-1870s Silsbee was offered the position of dean of Cornell University's new school of architecture, which he turned down. He resigned his Syracuse professorship in 1878 to practice full time. In 1882 Silsbee consolidated his practice from Syracuse to Chicago. In Chicago, he lectured at the Art Institute of Chicago's school of architecture on "Color in Architecture."[21] He also lectured at the Chicago Literary Club as part of a series that

---

19 Payne writes, "another notable local example is in the McNally Row Houses [1885] on Clark Street. The corner turret and adjacent gabled townhomes strongly resemble Emerson's Boston Arts Club Building [1882]." Correspondence with the author on October 28, 2018.

20 Wright, A Testament, p.113. This was added to the Horizon Press reprint, 3rd edition, 1977, p.92-93. Wright is describing a technique in which all the lines representing tone and shadow were drawn parallel to one another and at an angle, rather than employing conventional cross hatching.

21 The architecture school at the Art Institute of Chicago was known as the Chicago School of Architecture before the title was applied to Jenney and the other firms building steel-frame buildings.

included Louis Sullivan and Peter B. Wight on the subject, "Can Architecture Become Again a Living Art?"

Silsbee's Chicago office was considered a good place for young apprentices to learn the profession.[22] H. Allen Brooks wrote that Silsbee, "Simultaneously had [George Washington] Maher, Frank Lloyd Wright and George Grant Elmslie as his draftsmen, a fact which testifies to his status as a teacher, and to his influence on the Midwest scene."[23] Brooks suggests a comparison to Peter Behren's Berlin office around 1910 when Mies van der Rohe, Walter Gropius, and Le Corbusier all worked there at the same time. Unlike Behren's apprentices who went on to shape 20th-century architecture, Maher and Elmslie, both talented architects, would go on to have distinguished practices, but, were known primarily in the American Midwest. In addition to Wright, Maher, and Elmslie, Irving Gill worked for Silsbee from 1890 to 1891. At this point Wright, who left in 1887, was working for Sullivan. However, Wright and Gill did work together in Sullivan's office, as did Elmslie. They overlapped from 1891–1893, at which time they were both let go. Gill then moved to San Diego.

Wright spent only one year in Silsbee's office. The published renderings from this period, which he signed, suggest that he had worked primarily on the houses Silsbee did for the real estate developer John L. Cochran. These were built in Edgewater, a development of houses along the lakefront about seven miles north of the center of the city, just beyond what were then the city limits. The following description was published as part of a profile of Cochran in *A Biographical History with Portraits of Prominent Men of the Great West*. "From the inception of the undertaking the object in view was to make Edgewater a model and ideal place of residences within the reach of families of moderate income, and to establish a suburb to which Chicagoans could point with pride."[24] The first Edgewater houses started construction in the spring of 1886. As Wright has suggested,

22 Perhaps the most significant office that trained Chicago architects was that of William LeBaron Jenney. Among his significant employees were Daniel Burnham, John Root, William Holabird, Martin Roche, Alfred Granger, Normand S. Patton, W.A. Otis, James Gamble Rogers, and Howard Van Doren Shaw.

23 Brooks, *The Prairie School*, 1972, p.34.

24 *A Biographical History with Portraits of Prominent Men of the Great West*, Chicago: Manhattan Publishing Company, 1894, p.439.

16.002. J. L. Silsbee, Shingle Style House. Edgewater, Chicago, Il. 1888.

the design for these houses probably originated as sketches by Silsbee with his staff working out the details of each house. The exterior of the houses drawn by Wright and signed with his name should be compared not only to Silsbee's houses and the house George Maher built for himself, but to a drawing of an Edgewater House signed by Henry G. Fiddelke, an Oak Park architect who worked for Silsbee in 1887–88 and who, like Wright, also went from Silsbee's office to Sullivan's.[25]

If we examine the first of Wright's 1888 renderings for Silsbee, published as a house for J.L. Cochran in Edgewater, and compare it to Wright's rendering published as a "House in Edgewater," these can offer an insight into what Wright worked on and what he learned in Silsbee's office. The Cochran House published in the *Inland Architect* from May 1988 shows a house whose plan has a central stair-hall with rooms that pinwheel around it including the entry vestibule. Only one of the ground-floor rooms, which ends in a round bay, extends beyond the compact volume of the house.

---

25 Fiddelke's drawing was published in *Building Budget*, March 31, 1888. Fiddelke opened an office in Oak Park in 1893.

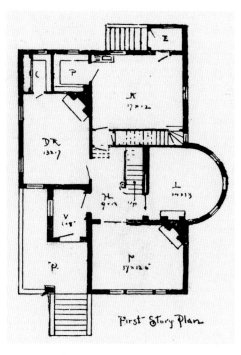

16.003. J. L. Silsbee. Cochran house. Edgewater, Chicago, Il. 1888. Plan Drawing, Frank L. Wright.

The overall massing of the two Edgewater houses and their roof forms are similar and should also be compared to the form of Silsbee's earlier All Souls Church as well as the published drawing of the Hillside Home School where the wing forming a cross gable is elongated.

It is impossible to know if the plan of the first of the Edgewater houses was Silsbee's or Wright's. In *An Autobiography*, Wright suggests that Silsbee made only loose sketches of a house's massing and plan leaving his draftsmen to work out a house that reflected his sketches. He wrote of Silsbee, "His work was a picturesque combination of gable, turret and hip with broad

16.004. J. L. Silsbee. Cochran house. Edgewater, Chicago, Il. 1888. Rendering, Frank L. Wright.

16.005. J. L. Silsbee. "House in Edgewater." Chicago, Il. 1888. Drawing, Frank L. Wright.

porches quietly domestic and gracefully picturesque. A contrast to the awkward stupidities and brutalities of the period elsewhere … Silsbee got a ground-plan and made his pretty sketch, getting some charming picturesque effect he had in mind. Then the sketch would come out into the draughting room to be fixed up into a building, keeping the floor-plan near the sketch if possible."[26]

The idea of a house with the spaces organized around a central element, either a stair or a fireplace, would become a motif in Wright's early independent work. The house he built for himself in Oak Park in 1889 is a Shingle-style house with the entry, stair hall, and the three principal ground floor rooms assembled in a pinwheel around a central fireplace inglenook.

---

26 Wright, An Autobiography, op. cit., p.70. Wright criticizes Silsbee's working method as beginning with a preconceived image of the exterior, a method Wright would also employ. Charles E. White Jr., who worked in Wright's Oak Park Studio, wrote of Wright that he, "develops his unit first, then fits his design to the requirements as much as possible, or rather, fits the requirements to the design … and never allows the petty wants of his client to interfere with the architectural expression of his design." Quoted in the Journal of Architectural Education, vol. 25, no.4 (autumn 1971). Also see Nancy K. Morris Smith, ed, "Letters 1903-1906 by Charles E. White Jr. from the Studio of Frank Lloyd Wright," p.104-12.

The pinwheel form being reiterated in the plan of the front terrace. The exterior, showing Silsbee's influence, is completely shingled with a large front-facing gable and a Palladian window atop two polygonal bays that sit on a masonry base. The house is frequently compared to Bruce Price's 1886 William Kent house in Tuxedo Park, New York. More importantly, the way in which

16.006. J.L. Silsbee. "House in Edgewater." Chicago, Il. 1888. Drawing by Henry G. Fiddelke.

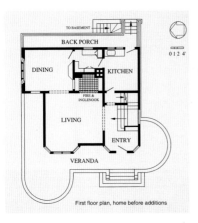

16.007. Frank Lloyd Wright. Wright house. Oak Park, Il.1889. Plan

16.008. Frank Lloyd Wright. Wright house. Oak Park, Il. 1889. Exterior

16.009. George W. Maher. Maher Residence, Woodlawn Park, Il. 1889. Showing the influence of Silsbee.

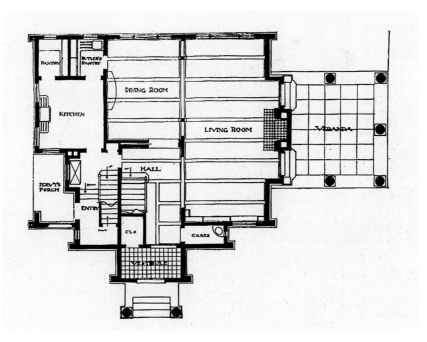

16.010. George W. Maher. Rudolph House, Highland Park, IL. 1907, Plan. Showing an extraordinary open plan.

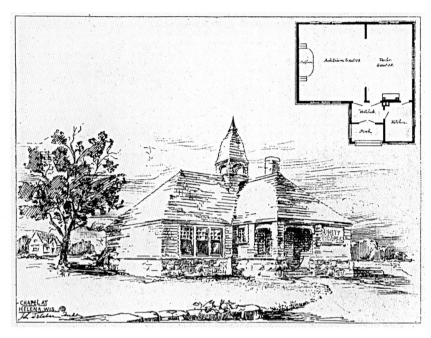

16.011. J. L. Silsbee. Unity Chapel. Helena, Wi. 1885. Drawing by Silsbee.

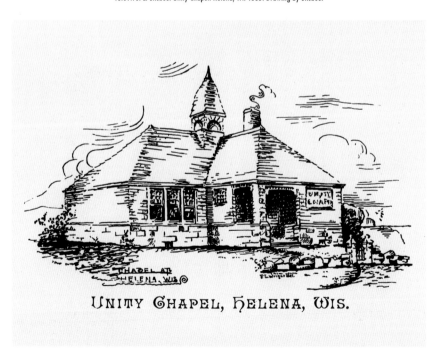

16.012. J. L. Silsbee. Unity Chapel. Helena, Wi. 1887. Drawing by Frank L. Wright.

16.013. J. L. Silsbee. All Souls Church, Chicago, Il. 1885. Drawing by Wright based on Silsbee's drawing.

16.014. J. L. Silsbee. All Souls Church. Chicago, Il. 1885.

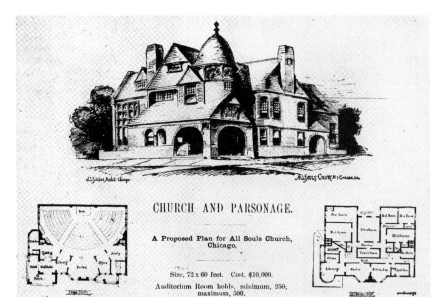

16.015. J. L. Silsbee. All Souls Church. Chicago Il. Plans and Rendering published in Unity 15. June 20, 1885.

the rooms on the ground floor of Wright's house open to one another offered spatial interconnections which were a prominent feature of Shingle-style houses.

The Unity Chapel for Wright's family and the shingled All Souls Church must have been strong early influences on Wright. Drawings by Silsbee for the Unity Chapel in Wisconsin and his All Souls Church in Chicago were published in *Unity*[27] and Wright published nearly identical sketches based on these. His sketch of All Souls is based on a sketch by Silsbee published in the All Souls Church Annual in 1886, which was slightly different from the version shown here from 1885.

All Souls Church was a unique interpretation of the liberalism of the Unitarian Church, of Jones's non-creedal stance, his disavowal of the doctrine of the trinity and the divinity of Jesus, and his call for a universal religion. This can be seen expressed in the freedom of the building's massing, in its almost complete lack of exterior architectural or religious ornament, in its lack of

---

27 *Unity* was a publication of the Western Conference of Unitarian ministers. It reported news from various Midwest congregations and contained invited essays on religion. The publication began in March of 1878 as the *Pamphlet Mission* for "Freedom, Fellowship, and Character in Religion" with Jenkin Lloyd Jones as a member of the original publishing committee. Renamed *Unity* in September of 1878, it was to be printed "semi-monthly" at a price of $1.50 per year.

16.016. J. L. Silsbee. All Souls Church "Auditorium Room" set up for a social event.

identifiable church precedents, and in its residential rather than ecclesiastical character. These expressed Jones's ideas about church buildings and were reflected in a sermon he gave in May of 1885 titled "The New Problems in Church Architecture" in which Jones wrote, "the larger family and its building must be made the larger home." In this vein Jones asked rhetorically, "Would you build us a house of worship? Oh architect, build it low with humility, and make it warm with human tenderness." Jones urged, "let architects give us buildings so simple, earnest and ethical that they will present no external excrescence."[28] It is worth noting that Silsbee, the son of a Unitarian minister, was a member of All Souls Church. Along with Wright, Dwight Perkins, and his family were also member of All Souls and Perkins's mother Marion, sister Myra, and cousin Marion Mahony were all active at the Helen Heath Neighborhood Settlement House in Chicago, which was founded in 1894 by the Reverend Jones.

Wright's friend Cecil Corwin had worked on All Souls and according to Wright asked him if he would, "like to see 'The Church' … with curious emphasis on 'Church.' … We'll go down

---

28 Quoted in Joseph Siry, *Unity Temple: Frank Lloyd Wright and Architecture for Liberal Religion*, Cambridge University Press, 1996, p.14.

to Oakwood Boulevard and Langley Avenue after dinner and have a look at it." We went. Why the curious emphasis? "I knew now. It was in no way like a Church, more like a 'Queen Anne' dwelling."[29]

Historian Joseph Siry, wrote about the interior, "The room was like an expansive parlor, as if to express the motto carved on its foyer's mantel: 'Here Let No Man Be a Stranger.'"[30] The carving of ethical and literary sayings in the mantels of All Soul's fireplaces may have inspired Wright's similar practice in his own home in Oak Park and in many subsequent houses."[31]

In 1886, Wright published, under his name and while still working for Silsbee, a drawing of a "Country Residence for Helena Valley."[32] This was probably an early version of the "Home Building"—the Hillside Home School built on family property. It was done for his aunts Nell and Jane Lloyd Jones. In March of 1887 Wright received a letter from his Aunt Nell (Ellen Lloyd Jones) and according to Wright biographer Meryle Secrest, "The letter contained detailed instructions about floor plans ... His resulting designs were evidently derived from those of Silsbee ... this architect played the largest role."[33] Historian Donald Johnson subsequently credits the design of the shingled building entirely to Silsbee and identifies an early photograph of it as having "additions organized and constructed post 1887, likely by Wright's carpenter uncle, Thomas Jones in 1889."[34]

Wright's aunts' private school was noted for its progressive educational ideas and was the first coeducational boarding school in the country with boys and girls attending the same classes. The school took children ages five to eighteen. Wright's published sketch for the project, which appeared in the August 1887 issue of the *Inland Architect* is remarkably similar in its massing, roof forms, and arched entry porch to Silsbee's R.A. Waller House in Buena Park published in 1889. It also recalls the

---

29 Wright, *An Autobiography*, op. cit., 1938, p.69.

30 Siry, *Unity Temple*, p.15.

31 Ibid., p.258 (footnote 19 for p.15-16).

32 The similarity of Wright's Country Residence and the Waller House was first suggested by Patrick Pinnell in Robert McCarter's, *Frank Lloyd Wright: A Primer on Architectural Principles*, p.23.

33 Seacrest, op. cit., p.95

34 Johnson, op. cit., p.54. Thomas Jones was Wright's uncle, a carpenter with whom Wright worked summers repairing Jones's farm buildings.

16.017. Country Residence, Helena Valley, 1886. Drawn by Frank L. Wright.

16.018. J. L. Silsbee. R. A. Waller House. Buena Park, Il. 1889.

16.019. J. L. Silsbee. Helena Valley House. Drawn by Frank. L. Wright.1888.

16.020. J. L. Silsbee. Hillside Home School. Helena Valley, Wi. 1887.

gable forms to either side of the entry porch at Silsbee's All Souls Church further suggesting Silsbee's authorship. Silsbee received the commission in March of 1887 from Wrights aunts, and it was built by a local builder with the construction supervised by their brother Thomas. In *An Autobiography* Wright claims he designed the school, however, it is more likely that he worked on the project in Silsbee's office. Maginel Barney, his sister, in her 1965 description of her aunts' school writes, "They began in 1887, by summoning Frank, then a very young architect, to design a new building."[35] Barney would have been a young child at the time, and is probably just repeating her brother's claim in *An Autobiography*.

A further possible influence from Silsbee may have been Wright's interest in Japanese prints. William Allin Storrer tells us that, "The Japanese prints that decorated the office walls were provided by Silsbee's cousin, the noted orientalist Ernest Francisco Fenollosa, who was in the United States from 1890 to 1897 between stints in Japan. Thus, it was that Wright became acquainted with Japanese art in his formative years."[36] While it is possible that there were Japanese prints in the office, the dates 1890 to 1897 do not correspond to Wright's time with Silsbee.[37] It is also possible that Wright could have known of Arthur Wesley Dow's interest in Japanese prints. In 1891 Dow wrote, "one evening with Hokusai gave me more light on composition and decorative effect than years of study of pictures."[38] Wright would be an early collector of Japanese prints in Chicago, although he would later vehemently deny that they had any influence on his work.

Wright's time with Silsbee exposed him to a progressive style of American house design. It is easy to see Wright absorbing these lessons not only from Silsbee but from architectural

---

35 Barney, *The Valley of the God-Almighty Jones*, p.114.

36 Storrer, *The Frank Lloyd Wright Companion*, University of Chicago Press, 1993, p.3.

37 Fenollosa, whose mother was Mary Silsbee, Silsbee's aunt, attended Harvard and studied at the school of the Boston Museum of Fine Arts. He first traveled to Japan in 1878 and taught philosophy at the Imperial University at Tokyo for eight years. He amassed a substantial collection of Japanese art, which he sold to a Boston physician in 1886 to be given as a gift to the Boston Museum of Fine Arts—where, beginning in 1890 he served as the curator of the department of Oriental Art. In 1893 he was asked to curate an exhibit of Japanese art at the World Columbian Exposition in Chicago. He returned to Japan in 1897 as a professor of English Literature, returning to the U.S. in 1900 to write and lecture. Arthur Wesley Dow, a proponent of the "Pure Design Movement," became friendly with Fenollosa through his interest in Japanese Art.

38 Arthur Johnson, *Arthur Wesley Dow, Historian, Artist, Teacher,* Ipswich, 1934, p.54.

publications. Silsbee was in Wright's view, educated, cultured, and stylish in his dress and manners. He was someone Wright sought to emulate in his demeanor and architecturally—particularly in his houses, which Wright perceived as done in a popular and stylish manner. He wrote, "I adored Silsbee ... He had style. His work had it too."[39] It is interesting that while Wright found fault with Silsbee's working process, in all the various additions and revisions of *An Autobiography* his admiration for Silsbee remained unchanged.

Wright claims to have left Silsbee over a salary dispute and gone to work briefly for another architect, William W. Clay, then returning to Silsbee's office. Impatient to advance his career, Wright heard from a fellow employee that Adler and Sullivan were looking for people to work on the Auditorium Theater. In *An Autobiography* he wrote, "My heart jumped. I had already formed a high idea of Adler and Sullivan. They were foremost in Chicago. Radical-going strong on independent lines. Burnham and Root their only rivals."[40] Walter Wilcox, who worked part time for Silsbee, was the "fellow employee" who heard that Adler and Sullivan were looking for draftsmen. He applied but was not hired and then told Wright, who applied. This was probably around February of 1888. Louis Sullivan, who was outspoken in his criticism of the architectural status quo, was an important figure to Chicago's young architects. Ever impatient, Wright determined that he wanted to work for him.

Sullivan had attended Massachusetts Institute of Technology for less than a year. He then worked briefly for Frank Furness in Philadelphia before moving to Chicago where his family was located. There he worked for William Le Baron Jenney. In July of 1874 he left for Paris to attend the *Ecole Des Beaux-Arts*. Returning to Chicago in 1876, he worked for John H. Edelmann who was to influence his architectural philosophy. Edelmann, who became Sullivan's friend and supporter, wrote an essay entitled "Pessimism of Modern Architecture" (1892), in which he states, "Emotional expression is the very essence of architecture." This was to be the principal underlying idea of Sullivan's work. Edelmann continued, "To the present writer it seems that a new

---

39 Wright. op. cit., *An Autobiography*, p.70.
40 Ibid., p.89.

master has arisen, not popular as yet ... Mr. Louis H. Sullivan. I select the Wainwright Building in St. Louis as the most complete expression of American commercial architecture."[41]

After working for Edelmann, Sullivan then worked as a consultant to a number of architects including Dankmar Adler. He went to work for Adler full time in 1881 and was soon made a junior partner, then a full partner in 1883. He remained in partnership with Adler until 1895 at which time Adler, who was older, retired from practice, having no work due to the continuing nationwide depression.

Sullivan, who drank and was difficult to get along with, must have found a sympathetic ear in the young Wright, an autodidact, who was happy to discuss philosophy with him. Sullivan's ideas about the relationship of function to form, about the organic nature of design and society, and about the need for architecture to embody a transcendental essence were vague in their relationship to any actual process of design. While Wright would reiterate Sullivan's architectural pronouncements, it is questionable what he learned about the design of buildings. In his book *Genius and the Mobocracy,* Wright recognizing this, tells us, "He taught me nothing nor did he ever pretend to do so except as he was himself."[42]

The nature of what Sullivan taught Wright is well agreed on. Grant Manson wrote that Sullivan "had much to do with the materialization of Wright's vision of architecture; but he could have offered little of a specific nature."[43] H. Allen Brooks wrote, "Sullivan was the philosopher, the teacher who offered a manner of thinking rather than specific means to achieve an end."[44] Even more insightful with respect to the actual process of design, Donald Johnson wrote, "ideas of a hypothetical vitalism [*elan vital* or life force or energy] could not induce an architectural planning or design methodology. Because it is about arranging matter, architectural theory does not easily accept an invisible essence or life force that in itself is not causative. The idea of a life force as something with organic potential came to Sullivan via

---

41 Quoted in Johnson, op. cit., p.16. Also see, Gregersen, *Louis Sullivan and His Mentor, John Herman Edelmann, Architect.*

42 Wright, *Genius and the Mobocracy,* p.55.

43 Manson, *Frank Lloyd Wright to 1910,* 1958, p.30.

44 Brooks, *Prairie School,* 1972, p.7. Johnson makes this point quoting both Manson and Brooks.

talks with Edelmann, as well as by reading Whitman, Emerson, Thoreau, and Greenough ... as with Sullivan, Wright's verbalized doctrine was not sustained in architectural productivity."[45]

For Wright, an important design lesson taken from both Sullivan and from Adler was the use of the planning module for the subdivision of space. Adler, who was influenced by the writings of Viollet-le-Duc, tells us that, "The unit of subdivision will also be the unit of construction and the unit of design."[46] The lessons of spatial organization that Wright would extrapolate from Sullivan were contained in the two-dimensional organization of Sullivan's ornament, which derived from *Beaux-Arts* design principles.[47] These were: axial organization, repetition, translation, reflection, and the inversion of design motifs. It was through Wright's development of the ornament for the Auditorium Building that he came to grasp this way of working. Perhaps the best answer to the question, what did Wright learn from Sullivan is suggested by Robert Spencer in his 1900 article on Wright's work, "in all his ornament, there is evidence of ... the same synthetic method which successfully develops the ground plan of a great building."[48]

Wright claimed that he was let go by Sullivan because he had breached his contract by taking outside commissions, now known as the "the bootleg houses." Wright's story of his dismissal is probably an exaggeration. As a result of the national recession and financial panic in May of 1893 many of Chicago's architectural offices had no work. Wright, Irving J. Gill, and other employees were laid off that spring by Adler. In a letter dated June of 1893, Adler & Sullivan's superintendent of construction,

---

45 Johnson, op. cit., p.92.

46 Adler, Dankmar, "The Tall business Building," *Cassoer's Magazine* 12 (November 1897), p.197. Quoted in Siry, op. cit., 1996, p.121 (also see footnote 116 on p.299).

47 In *The Autobiography of an Idea Sullivan* wrote about his education at the Ecole des Beaux-Arts, "He [Sullivan] familiarized himself thoroughly with the theory of the school, which in his mind settled down to a theory of plan, yielding results of extraordinary brilliancy," p.240. As discussed by David Van Zanten in *Sullivan's City*, p. 95-119, "It is not that the house plans reach out to become ornamental, but rather the opposite: his ornament reformulated spatially produces such planning compositions," p.119. "The foundation of the conventional misreading of Sullivan's work has been the refusal to see it spatially, as the architectural enframement of an experience of movement to a goal, in spite of the theme of movement proclaimed in his ornament," p.113. Also see Thomas Beeby, *The Grammar of Ornament/Grammar as Ornament.*

48 Spencer, "The Work of Frank Lloyd Wright," the *Architectural Review*, June 1900, p.70. In *Sullivan's City*, David Van Zanten argues that the graphic order of Sullivan's ornament is the key to understanding the spatial development in his noncommercial work.

16.021. J.L. Silsbee. Hillside Home School. Helena Valley, Wi. 1887.

Charles Bebb,[49] wrote, "Adler & Sullivan are doing nothing and Mr. Adler told me he could not even make collections of money's due him, and consequently has had to reduce the office force to three men, and these have nothing to do ... Adler having reduced the office to 3 men, as a matter of fact, is borrowing from friends each week to pay his payrolls."[50] Why George Grant Elmslie was kept and Wright was not may well have had to do with Wright's taking outside work as he has so often suggested. Elmslie worked for Sullivan for another 10 years after Adler left the practice and helped produce Sullivan's midwestern bank buildings.

The authorship of one of the so called "bootleg houses," the Clark House, was later disowned by Wright even though plans for the house were found at Taliesin in 1966. It clearly shows Silsbee's influence on Wright's work even when he was still employed by Sullivan. It is easy to see why Wright disowned it.

---

49 English-born Charles Beeb was hired by Adler & Sullivan as the Auditorium Building was nearing completion. He became their chief supervising architect. Beeb was sent to Seattle to work on the Seattle Opera House, which was never built. Beeb moved to Seattle in 1893 and opened an architectural practice.

50 Charles Beeb, letter to Thomas Burke, June 14, 1893, as quoted in Ochner and Andersen, "Adler and Sullivan's Seattle Opera House Project," JSAH 48, no.3, September 1989, p.288.

The slightly projecting second-floor window bays topped by pediments with elongated reverse Chicago Windows were original but truly ill proportioned. In spite of the emotional bond Wright formed with Sullivan as a mentor and father figure, the "bootlegged houses" owed nothing to Sullivan architecturally. Never having learned the ideas of plan making and spatial organization taught by the *Beaux-Art* firsthand, Wright extrapolated Sullivan's ornament into his architectural planning strategies. However, the spatial breakthroughs to be seen in Wright's houses for the *Ladies' Home Journal* and the Willits House came while he was working in Steinway Hall. Here he would develop new ideas about residential architecture along with Robert Spencer and the other members of his collaborative circle.

BIBLIOGRAPHY
BOOKS AND ARTICLES

Books by Frank Lloyd Wright that are quoted or referenced in the text are listed, articles by Wright and publications of his work from the period covered by this study are cited in the footnotes and are to be found in Sweeney's *An Annotated Bibliography*. A list of Robert Spencer's numerous articles for *The House Beautiful Magazine* on "Planning the House" are to be found in Paul Kruty's "Planning the Suburban House, Robert Spencer's Advice to Clients." These plus Spencer's series of articles on "Building a House of Moderate Cost" for *The Architectural Record* ; his articles on Farmhouse design for *The Ladies Home Journal* and for the Chicago Architectural Club Annual; and publications of his work and the work of Spencer and Powers are to be found in the bibliography and in Lestra Litchfield's 1994 Tufts University Master's Thesis.

The following abbreviations are used in the footnotes and bibliography. JSAH for the Journal of the Society of Architectural Historians. JAE for the Journal of Architectural Education.

Allen, Hannah, *Perkins: Off the Prairie*. Chicago: Thesis, School of the Art Institute of Chicago, 2016.

Alofsin, Anthony, *Frank Lloyd Wright: The Lost Years, 1910–1922: A Study of Influence*. Chicago: University of Chicago Press, 1993.

_____ ed., *Frank Lloyd Wright: An Index to the Taliesin Correspondence*, vol 4. New York: Garland Publishing, 1988.

_____*Wright and New York. The Making of America's Architect*. New Haven: Yale University Press, 2019.

Barney, Maginel Wright, *The Valley of the God-Almighty Joneses*. New York: Appleton-Century, 1965.

Beeby, Thomas, "The Grammar of Ornament/Ornament as Grammar." *Via III*, Journal of the Graduate School of Fine Arts, University of Pennsylvania, 1977, p.10–29.

Blum, Betty, interviewer. *Oral History of Lawrence Bradford Perkins*. Chicago Architects Oral History Project, Department of Architecture, The Art Institute of Chicago, 1986 (revised 2000).

Bock, Richard W., Dorathi Bock Pierre, ed., *Memoirs of an American Artist, sculptor Richard W. Bock*. Los Angeles: C.C. Publishing Co., 1991.

Bok, Edward, *The Americanization of Edward Bok, An Autobiography*. New York: Charles Scribner's Sons, 1924.

Bragdon, Claude, *Architecture and Democracy*. New York: Alfred A. Knoff Publisher, 1918.

Brooks, H. Allen, *The Prairie School, Frank Lloyd Wright and His Midwest Contemporaries*. Toronto: University of Toronto Press, 1972.

_____ ed., *Prairie School Architecture, Studies from the "Western Architect."* Toronto: University of Toronto Press, 1975.

_____"Steinway Hall, Architects and Dreams." JSAH, vol. 22, no.3, October 1963, p.171–75.

_____"Frank Lloyd Wright and the Destruction of the Box." JSAH, vol. 38, no.1, March 1979, p.7–14.

Clarke, Vanessa Balbach, *Henry Webster Tomlinson*. Chicago: The Coventry Group, 2018.

Condit, Carl W., *The Chicago School of Architecture*. Chicago: University of Chicago Press, 1952.

Crew, Henry and Basquin, Olin H., *Pocket Hand-Book of Electro-Glazed Luxfer Prisms*. Chicago: W.B. Conkey Company, 1898. M-Library Google Books Reprint from the University of Michigan Library.

Davis, Eric Emmett, *Dwight Heald Perkins: Social Consciousness and Prairie School Architecture*. Exhibition catalog. Chicago: Gallery 400, University of Illinois Chicago, 1989.

Drexler, Arthur, *The Drawings of Frank Lloyd Wright*. New York: Horizon Press, 1962.

Eaton, Leonard, *Two Chicago Architects and Their Clients: Frank Lloyd Wright and Howard Van Doren Shaw*. Cambridge: MIT Press, 1969.

Eidlitz, Leopold, *The Nature And Function Of Art, More Especially of Architecture*. New York: Sampson Low, Marston, Searle & Rivington, 1881.

Farrell, Michael P., *Collaborative Circles, Friendship Dynamics & Creative Work*. Chicago: The University of Chicago Press, 2001.

Frank, Marie, "The Theory of Pure Design and American Architectural Education in the Early Twentieth Century," JSAH. vol. 67, no.2, June 2008, p.249–73.

_____"Emil Lorch: Pure Design and American Architectural Education." *JAE* , vol. 57, no.4, 2004, p.28–40.

Gebhard, David, ed.,, *Myron Hunt, 1886–1952. The Search for a Regional Architecture*. California Architecture and Architects IV. Santa Monica: Hennessey & Ingalls, 1984.

Gregersen, Charles E., *Louis Sullivan and His Mentor, John Herman Edelmann, Architect*. Bloomington: Author House LLC, 2013.

Griffin, Marion Mahony, *The Magic of America: Electronic Edition*. August 2007. The Art Institute of Chicago and the New York Historical Society, October 29, 2008.

Gutheim, Frederick, *Frank Lloyd Wright on Architecture: Selected Writings, 1894–1940*. New York: Duell, Sloan and Pearce, 1941.

Handlin, David P., *The American Home*. Boston: Little Brown and Company, 1979.

Hartzell, Kris, *Myron Hubbard Hunt: The Creation of the Prairie School and the Architecture of the Suburban Midwest*. Chicago: Master's Thesis, Department of Historic Preservation, The School of the Art Institute of Chicago, 2013.

Hasbrouck, Wilbert, *The Chicago Architectural Club, Prelude to the Modern*. New York: The Monacelli Press, 2005.

Hines, Thomas, "Frank Lloyd Wright—The Madison Years: Records vs. Recollections." JSAH 26, December 1967.

Hitchcock, Henry Russell, *In the Nature of Materials 1887–1941: The Buildings of Frank Lloyd Wright*. New York: Duell, Sloan, and Pearce, 1942.

Hoffman, Donald, *Frank Lloyd Wright, Louis Sullivan and the Skyscraper*. Mineola, New York: Dover, 1998.

_____*The Architecture of John Wellborn Root*. Baltimore: The Johns Hopkins University Press, 1973.

_____ed., *The meaning of Architecture, Buildings and Writings by John Wellborn Root*. New York: Horizon Press, 1967.

James, Henry, *The American Scene*. Las Vegas: Lits., reprint, 2010.

Johnson, Donald Leslie, *Frank Lloyd Wright: Early Years: Progressivism: Aesthetics: Cities*. New York: Routledge, 2017.

Kaufmann, Edgar and Raeburn, Ben t, ed. *Frank Lloyd Wright: Writings and Buildings*. New York: Meridian Books, 1960.

Kruty, Paul, "A Prairie-School House in Coastal Maine." *Nineteenth Century*, vol. 27, no.2, fall 2007, Victorian Society in America.

_____*Prelude to the Prairie Style*. Urbana: School of Architecture University of Illinois, 2005.

_____ "Wright, Spencer, and the Casement Window." Winterthur Portfolio, vol. 30, no 2/3 summer–autumn, 1995, p.103–27.

_____ "Planning the Suburban House, Robert Spencer's Advice to Clients." *Nineteenth Century*, vol. 36, no.1, Victorian Society in America, p.14–23.

_____ "At Work in the Oak Park Studio." ARRIS (Southeast Chapter of the Society of Architectural Historians), vol. 14, 2003, p.17–31.

Levine, Neil, *The Architecture of Frank Lloyd Wright*. Princeton: Princeton University Press, 1996.

_____*Modern Architecture. Representation & Reality.* New Haven: Yale University Press, 2009, p.180–212.

_____*The Urbanism of Frank Lloyd Wright.* Princeton: Princeton University Press, 2016.

Lipman, Johathan, *Frank Lloyd Wright and the Johnson Wax Buildings*. New York: Rizzoli International Publication, Inc., 1986.

Litchfield, Lestra M., *Robert C. Spencer, Jr., Contributions to the Formation of The Prairie School*. Medford, Mass.: Thesis Master of Arts in Art History, Tufts University, 1994.

Longstreth, Richard, ed., *The Charnley House, Louis Sullivan, Frank Lloyd Wright, and the making of Chicago's Gold Coast*. Chicago: The University of Chicago Press, 2004.

Martone, Fran, *In Wright's Shadow*. Oak Park: The Frank Lloyd Wright Home and Studio Foundation, 1998.

Marty, Myron A., *Communities of Frank Lloyd Wright*. DeKalb: Northern Illinois University Press, 2009.

Michels, Eileen, "The Early Drawings of Frank Lloyd Wright Reconsidered." JSAH, vol. 30, no.4, December 1974, p.294–303.

Manson, Grant Carpenter, *Frank Lloyd Wright to 1910, The First Golden Age*. New York: Van Nostrand Reinhold Company, 1958.

McCarter, Robert, ed. *Frank Lloyd Wright, A Primer on Architectural Principles*. New York: Princeton Architectural Press, 1991.

Nelson, Donna R., "School Architecture in Chicago during the progressive Era: The Career of Dwight Perkins." 1988, PhD Dissertation, Loyola University of Chicago.

Neumann, Dietrich, "Triumph in Lighting: The Luxfer Prism Companies and Their Contribution to Early Modern Architecture." Journal of the Society of Architectural Historians, vol. 54, no.1, March 1995, p.24–53.

Nielsen, David, *Bruno Taut's Design Inspiration for the Glashaus*. New York: Routledge, 2016.

Peisch, Mark L., *The Chicago School of Architecture, Early Followers of Sullivan and Wright*. New York: Random House, 1964.

Pfeiffer, Bruce Brooks, *Letters to Clients, Frank Lloyd Wright*. Fresno: The Press at California State University, 1986.

Pond, Irving K., David Swan and Tatum, Terry ed., *The Autobiography of Irving K. Pond, The Sons of Mary and Elihu*. Oak Park: The Hyoogen Press Inc., 2009.

Prestiano, Robert, *The Inland Architect: Chicago's Major Architectural Journal, 1883-1908*. Ann Arbor: UMI Research Press, 1985.

Price, William L., *Model Houses for Little Money*. New York: Doubleday, Page & Company, 1904.

Perkins, Eleanor Ellis Perkins, *Perkins of Chicago*. Evanston, unpublished manuscript. 1966. Copies at The Evanston History Center and The Art Institute of Chicago.

Perkins, Margery Blair, *Evanstonia*. Chicago: Chicago Review Press. 1984.

Pulfer, Donald Robert, *The Early Work of Joseph Lyman Silsbee*. Thesis. Syracuse University. 1978.

Quinan, Jack, *Frank Lloyd Wright's Larkin Building, Myth and Fact*. Cambridge: The MIT Press, 1987.

Roth, Lehland M., "Getting the Houses to the People. Edward Bok, The Ladies' Home Journal, and the Ideal House." Perspectives in Vernacular Architecture, vo. 4,1991, pp. 187-196.

Scully, Vincent J. Jr., *The Shingle Style, Architectural Theory and Design from Richardson to the origins of Wright*. New Haven: Yale University Press, 1955.

_____ *Frank Lloyd Wright. Master of World Architecture Series*. New York: George Braziller, 1960.

Secrest, Meryle, *Frank Lloyd Wright. A Biography*. New York: Harper Collins Publishers, 1993.

Siry, Joseph, "The Abraham Lincoln Center in Chicago." JSAH, September 1991, p.235–65.

Siry, Joseph M., *Unity Temple, Frank Lloyd Wright and Architecture for Liberal Religion*. Cambridge: The Press Syndicate of the University of Cambridge, 1996.

Smith, Kathryn, *Wright on Exhibit, Frank Lloyd Wright's Architectural Exhibitions*. Princeton: Princeton University Press, 2017.

Smith, Norris Kelley, *Frank Lloyd Wright: A Study in Architectural Content*. Englewood Cliffs: Prentice-Hall, 1966.

Sorell, Susan Karr, "Silsbee: The Evolution of a Personal Architectural Style." *Prairie School Review* 7, no. 4, 1970.

Spencer, Robert C. Jr., "The Work of Frank Lloyd Wright." The *Architectural Review*, June 1900, pp.61–72.

Storrer, William Allin, *The Architecture of Frank Lloyd Wright, A Complete Catalog*. Cambridge: The MIT Press, 1974.

_____*The Frank Lloyd Wright Companion*. Chicago: The University of Chicago Press, 1993.

Sullivan, Louis H., *Kindergarten Chats* [revised 1918] *and other Writings*. New York, George Wittenborn, Inc., 1947.

_____*The Autobiography of an Idea*. New York: Press of the American Institute of Architects, 1924.

Sweeney, Robert L., *Frank Lloyd Wright, An Annotated Bibliography*. Los Angeles: Hennessey & Ingalls, Inc., 1978.

Tallmadge, Thomas Eddy, *The Story of Architecture in America*. New York: Norton, 1927.

_____*Architecture in Old Chicago*. Chicago: University of Chicago Press, 1941.

Thomas, George E., *Arts and Crafts to Modern Design, William L. Price*. New York: Princeton Architectural Press, 2000.

Twombly, Robert C., *Frank Lloyd Wright, His life and His Architecture*. New York: John Wiley & Sons, 1979.

_____ed., *Frank Lloyd Wright, Essential Texts*. New York: W. W. Norton & Company, 2009.

Van Zanten, David, *Sullivan's City, The Meaning of Ornament for Louis Sullivan*. New York: W. W. Norton & Company, 2000.

_____ed., *Marion Mahony Reconsidered*. Chicago: University of Chicago Press, 2011.

Wright, Frank Lloyd, *An Autobiography*. New York: Longmans, Green and Company, 1938.

_____*Genius and the Mobocracy*. New York: Horizon Press, 1949.

_____*The Natural House*. New York: Horizon Press, 1954.

_____*A Testament*. New York: Horizon Press, 1957.

_____*The Future of Architecture*. New York: Horizon Press, 1953.

Wright, John Lloyd, *My Father Who Is on Earth*. New York: G.P. Putnam's Sons, 1946.

Zaitzevsky, Cynthia, *The Architecture of William Ralph Emerson*. Boston: Fogg Art Museum, 1969.

List of Steinway Hall Illustration Credits

The illustrations in this book are primarily from the *Inland Architect* and the yearly catalogs of the Chicago Architectural Club. These images are in the public domain as are plans taken from the Wasmuth Portfolio. Issues of the *Ladies' Home Journal* were not copyrighted until 1925. Most of the images from the *Inland Architect* and the Chicago Architectural Club catalogs were supplied by the Art Institute of Chicago's Ryerson and Burnham Library's Digital Archives or downloaded from the hathitrust.com (HT). For archival photographs reproduced from these publications, photographer's names were rarely listed. Photographers are listed for contemporary building images.

Due to the worldwide pandemic, which closed archives and institutional libraries, only previously digitized materials were available. Some of the images not available were scanned from secondary sources. These are listed with both the owner of the original image and the secondary source (see bibliography). For images from Avery Library's Frank Lloyd Wright Archive and from the Meadville-Lombard Theological School's Jenkin Lloyd Jones Collection that were scanned from secondary sources, permission to publish them was obtained from these respective institutions. For many of the images from early twentieth-century periodicals detailed citations of month and year are in the text and omitted here. Images from digital collections are cited with the publication first followed by the collection. In the case of the Art Institute of Chicago, complete citations for images can be found online in their digital archives.

Credits

Courtesy of the **American Academy of Arts and Letters:** 5.011 Pond/Swan, Tatum.

Collection of the Art Institute of Chicago. **Ryerson and Burnham Digital Archive 1.001** Photo: Fuerman; **5.003, 5.005; 5.0012** Pond/Swan, Tatum; **7.002, 7.003, 7.018; 8.003** Photo: Fuerman; **8.014, 9.001, 9.002, 9.003, 9.005, 13.017; 15.002** Gebhard; **15.011** Photo: Lane; **15.015, 15.016, 16.008, 16.012.** *Architectural Review.* **13.008, 15.013** Gebhard.

Avery Library, Frank Lloyd Wright Archive, Columbia University. Frank Lloyd Wright Foundation. **4.009**. K. Smith, photo: Fuerman; **4.003**; **6.005**. Hoffman. Skyscraper; **6.010, 7.009; 7.016**. Hoffman. Skyscraper; **7.017**. Hoffman Skyscraper; **13.013, 16.001** Marty. Communities.

Brickbuilder: **13.001, 14.001.**

Chicago Architectural Club (Catalog) Chicago Architectural Sketch Club (catalog). Collection of the Art Institute of Chicago. **Ryerson and Burnham Digital Archive: 4.001, 4.002, 4.007HT, 4.008HT, 7.004, 7.005, 7.019, 7.020, 8.001, 8.009, 8.010, 12.001, 12.002, 12.003, 12.004, 12.005, 12.006, 12.008, 12.009, 12.018, 13.015, 13.019, 13.020, 14.002, 14.003, 14.004, 14,009, 15.009, 15.010, 16.010.** Columbia College Chicago Archive (online): **5.006.**

Chicago History Museum: 5.002. Hasbrouck, **7.006.** Davis, **12.014.**

Courtesy of the **Glessner House Museum: 12.011, 12.012.**

Courtesy of Charles Hasbrouck. **Collection of Wilbert Hasbrouck: 5.007** drawn by David Waldo. **13.004** Hasbrouck

House Beautiful: **13.006** HT, **13.007** HT, **13.011HT, 13.012HT, 13.025** HT (advertisement), **13.026** HT (advertisement).

Inland Architect, (*Inland Architect and Building News*, 1883–87. *Inland Architect and New Record,*1887–1908), Collection of the Art Institute of Chicago. **Ryerson and Burnham Digital Archive 4.006, 5.001, 5.005, 5.008, 5.009, 5.014, 5.015, 6.006, 6.007, 6.008, 6.009, 6.011, 7.011, 7.014, 7.015, 9.004, 10.002, 10.005, 10.006, 10.007, 12.007, 12.010, 12.013a, 12.013b, 12.017, 12.019, 12.020, 12.021, 12.022, 13.009** Brooks PS; **13,010, 13.016, 13.021, 13.022, 13.024, 14.007, 14.008, 15.002** Gebhard; **15.005, 15.012, 16.003, 16.004, 16.005, 16.009, 16.017, 16.018, 16.019, 16.021.**

Ladies' Home Journal: **8.002** HT, **8.004** HT, **8.005** HT, **8.006** HT, **8.008** Hitchcock, **8.011HT.**

Lake Bluff History Museum: 12.023.

Meadville-Lombard Theological School. Jenkin Lloyd Jones Collection: 7.001 Siry.UT, **7.007** Siry.UT, **7.008, 7.010** Siry.UT , **16.011** Siry.UT, **16.012** Siry.UT, **16.013** Siry.UT **16.014** Siry.UT. **16.015** Siry.UT. **16.016** Siry.UT.

Courtesy of the **Luxfer Gas Cylinder Company**: **6.001, 6.004a & 6.004b** Crew, Basquin.

Courtesy of **William Allin Storrer,** *The Frank Lloyd Wright Companion:* **4.004. 4.005, 8.007, 16.007.**

Wasmuth Portfolio. *Ausgefuehrte Bauten und Entwuerfe von Frank Lloyd Wright:* **5.013, 8.012, 8.013.**

Western Architect: **10.001.** Brooks. **5.010** photo: John Vasilion; **6.002 & 6.003** U.S. Design Patents No. 27977 and 27989, 1897; **7.012** Condit, Chicago Board of Education; **7.013** Chicago Board of Education Annual Report 1908-09; **10.003** author; **10.004** cardcow.com. pinterest.com/pin/235453886743182733/ on 8-2020; **11.001.** Chicago Central Business and Office Directory, 1903; **12.015.** Betsky, Aaron, *James Gamble Rogers and the Architecture of Pragmatism;* **12.016.** Saylor, Distinctive Homes of Moderate Cost, 1911; **12.024** Google Maps-/place/304+Nicholson+St.+Joliet+IL+6043ten; **13.002** MIT Archive, Litchfield; **13.023** flicker.com/photos/chicagogeek/7117691645 on 8-2020; **14.005** photo: @ properties; **14.006** courtesy of Bill Latoza; **15.001** Wikipedia; **15.003 & 15.004** photos: James Brannigan; **15.006** photo: Hans Friedman; **15.007 & 15.008** photos: Kris Hartzell; **16.020** Wikipedia.

INDEX

Page numbers in italics denote illustrations. References to Frank Wright and Frank L. Wright are indexed under Frank Lloyd Wright. Not all architects mentioned in the text are indexed and names of historians and scholars mentioned and quoted are not indexed except for Michael Farrell.

River Forest House (Wright), 65, 84n
Robert Lamp House (Wright), 138, *139*, 140
Robinson House (Spencer), 218
Rogers, James Gamble, 184, 185, 196–97
Root, John Wellborn, 26, 84, 117–18, 119, 144, 233, 274
Ross, Denman Waldo, 32–33, 152
Ross House (Wright), 138
Rotch Traveling Scholarship, 208
Rudolph House (Maher), *279*

Schmidt, Richard, 47, 51, 52, 55, 57, 184, 188, 198
School of Education, University of Chicago (Rogers), *197*
Selby, George W., 65, 234
settlement movement, 50, 236
Shaw, Howard Van Doren, 32, 51, 52, 53, 54, 58, 184, 185,
    199–201, 251
Shaw Residence (Shaw), *199*
Shepley, Rutan & Coolidge, 26–27, 31, 41, 42, 187, 189, 210,
    211, 252
"A Shingled Farmhouse for $2700" (Spencer), 141–43
Shingle style, 24, 225, 253, 271, 272, 273, *275*, 277, 282
Silsbee, Joseph L., 24, 91, 266, 268–88, 291
Sisley, Alfred, 38
skyscrapers, 27, 84, 96, 119, 124
"A Small Farmhouse That Can Be Enlarged" (Spencer), 141
"A Southern Farmhouse" (Spencer), 135–37
Spencer and Powers, 74, *144*, 213, *214, 220, 223,* 226, 244
Spencer Memorial Library (Spencer), 218, *220*
Spencer Residence (Spencer), *222*
Spencer, Robert Closson, 9, 26, 41, 42, 171, 252
    architectural principles of, 150–61
    biography, 206–26
    farmhouses, 130, 135–43, 223–24
    fellow architects and, 20, 39, 150, 153, 234
    Ladies' Home Journal and, 130–46, 218
    Luxfer competition entry, 94–96, 99
    on Pure Design, 33, 152
    residential architecture, 48, 134, 222
    at Steinway Hall, 71, 74, 165, 184, 218
    Wright and, 10, 39, 134, 143, 150–54, 158, 161, 222